WIVES, HARLOTS AND
CONCUBINES

Alice L. Laffey

WIVES, HARLOTS AND CONCUBINES

THE OLD TESTAMENT
IN FEMINIST PERSPECTIVE

First published in the USA in 1988
by Fortress Press, Philadelphia, as
An Introduction to the Old Testament: A Feminist Perspective

This edition first published in Great Britain in 1990 by SPCK
Holy Trinity Church, Marylebone Road, London NW1 4DU

British Library Cataloguing in Publication Data

Laffey, Alice L.
   Wives, Harlots and concubines : the old Testament in
Feminist perspective.
   1. Bible. O.T. (Critical Studies)
   I. Title   II. [Introduction to the old Testament in
feminist perspective]
   221.6

   ISBN 0-281-04492-9

Printed and bound in Great Britain by
Biddles Ltd, Guildford and King's Lynn

CONTENTS

PART II
THE DEUTERONOMISTIC HISTORY

PART III
THE MAJOR AND MINOR PROPHETS

PART IV
THE WRITINGS

PREFACE

This book represents, in some ways, the development of my own feminist critical consciousness. For more than seven years I studied the Bible in an almost exclusively male institution (the Pontifical Biblical Institute in Rome, Italy). The professors were men, mostly priests; the students were almost all men, mostly priests; the bibliographies contained, with few or no exceptions, the scholarship of men; the content of the scholarship was almost totally about men. I was the first woman to receive a doctorate from the Biblicum and, though I was awarded the degree in 1981, less than a handful of women, and none American, have since been awarded the doctorate there.

Some would say my experience radicalized me; some would say I am not radical enough. I came away from that experience knowing in the depths of my being that something was wrong, that I personally had been trivialized, and that the entire female sex had effectively been minimalized both within the Old Testament itself and especially in its interpretation. No wonder women are second-class citizens in the churches and in society!

When I returned to the States I discovered that others had already come to similar conclusions. I also discovered that increasing numbers of people—both men and women—had begun to act on these insights, that critical feminist scholarship on the Bible was beginning to appear. I had begun to read work by Phyllis Trible, Phyllis Bird, Katherine Doob Sakenfield, Paul Hanson, Rosemary Radford

Ruether, and Elisabeth Schüssler Fiorenza. It was time to move beyond the lessons of my Biblicum education. This book represents my efforts to share with a new generation of students, both men and women, what was lacking in my own and many other people's formal education. Ultimately, its purpose is not to add to the body of information which students must master. Rather, it is my hope that *those who read this book will themselves develop a feminist critical consciousness.*

It is impossible for me to dedicate this book to one person or even to a few. The influence of very many people lies within its pages. To my family, especially to my mother, who is fully a feminist, to the members of the Pittsburgh Sisters of Mercy, to the many women and men feminists of my Roman experience, especially Sandra M. Schneiders and Dennis McCarthy, S.J., and to my community at Holy Cross, I am deeply grateful. I am also grateful to my editors at Fortress Press, Davis Perkins, Stephanie Egnotovich, and Mimi McGinnis, whose initiative, good judgment, and patience have made the completion of this book possible.

INTRODUCTION

This book is intended to complement those books which have traditionally been used to introduce students to the study of the Old Testament. Most introductions currently on the market employ historical-critical methodologies (i.e., tradition criticism, source criticism, form criticism, and redaction criticism); these methods endeavor to establish the cultural, political, and religious background of the ancient Near East to determine the precise purpose for which particular segments of the biblical record were produced. Some introductions also incorporate canonical criticism; few include sociological criticism; none, to my knowledge, systematically applies feminist interpretation. In spite of the excellent scholarly research accomplished in the last decades that exposes the patriarchal character of the biblical texts, the results of this scholarship have not yet been incorporated into an Old Testament introduction.

This state of affairs makes teaching the Old Testament a very difficult task if the students are women with raised consciousnesses about the effect of patriarchy on church and society. It makes teaching the Old Testament an irresponsible and hypocritical task if no mention is made of the extent to which patriarchy has shaped the texts (their content as well as their omissions). It makes Old Testament scholars who write such textbooks and continue to legitimate the marginalization of women oppressors, though they do not like to see themselves in that role. Finally, for many it makes the Bible an obstacle to faith rather than a source of inspiration.

I

PATRIARCHY AND FEMINIST
INTERPRETATION

Patriarchy, closely associated with hierarchy, is a way of ordering reality whereby one group, in this case the male sex, is understood to be superior to the other, the female sex. Men are stronger than women, more intelligent, more competent, more responsible, braver, more adapted to the marketplace, more aggressive, more rational, better suited for positions of management and leadership—the list goes on. Usually oppression is subtle in a patriarchal culture. Role delineation makes certain attitudes, types of behavior, and occupations stereotypically acceptable for females (e.g., motherhood and the rearing of children) and extols these roles while at the same time denying to women other forms of behavior considered appropriate "for men only." Sexual-role stereotyping has been legitimated by many religions and by Western society for thousands of years. Women who break out of "their place" and assume positions normally reserved to men are "exceptions." The exceptions may even be lauded by men—as long as they remain exceptions. But whenever there is danger that the exception will become the norm, men rebel. Accordingly, patriarchy functions best when the oppressed sex, the women, support the status quo and choose for themselves the security their role provides.

Since the Old Testament was produced between the tenth and the second century B.C., and its oral traditions even earlier, and since that period in ancient Israelite history was undoubtedly patriarchal (one need only survey the texts to recognize that it is men's history which is recorded; women are relegated to ancillary roles), any historical critique of the texts needs to make explicit their patriarchal bias. This is a function of feminist interpretation.

The underlying presupposition of feminist interpretation is that women are equal to men. It insists that all texts be interpreted by this principle. Since the biblical texts are historically conditioned and were produced by a patriarchal society, they are patriarchal in character. They must, therefore, be approached with suspicion. Whenever, and in whatever ways, the biblical texts undermine the full humanity and equality of women—by their allusions, their assertions, or their omissions—interpreters have the obligation of unmasking their patriarchal bias. Those aspects of the texts that reinforce the church's and society's relegation of women to an inferior status (i.e., everything from polygamy to the equation of Israel's sinfulness with harlotry) must be uncovered, and if possible, reinterpreted.

Reinterpretation is necessary because most of the biblical interpreters have been men. Patriarchy did not end when the Old Testament was completed. On the contrary, when one studies how the Old Testament texts have been interpreted during the last two thousand years, one is continually confronted with patriarchal biases. Any contemporary student of the Old Testament, particularly one who would revere the Bible as the fount of faith and inspiration, must come to understand the patriarchal prejudices of its authors as well as the patriarchal prejudices of its interpreters.

And when one discovers just how permeated with patriarchal bias the Old Testament is, one may be tempted to reject it totally. Such a direction, however, is not the one this author has taken, nor is it the one recommended by this kind of study. Rather, one learns from history as well as from experience. Because more and more women are coming to recognize that they have been, as women, objects of discrimination and injustice in both the church and society for millennia—the church reinforcing the culture and the culture reinforcing the church—women are now called upon to discover their history and create a new future.

Who are the heroines who emerge in the biblical texts *in spite of* . . . ? Who are the women one glimpses whose images are distorted? Who are the nameless ones who live in the texts only through their husbands and their sons? Who are the exceptions who survived, those even who are lauded?

Moreover, what are the themes in the biblical texts which, if interpreted by twentieth-century believing communities, can help to liberate women? The Israelite conviction of God's presence to the oppressed and God's power working on their behalf is a thread running through the texts, despite the multiplicity of authorship and the expanse of time over which the texts were composed. Similarly, attention to the "exceptions" which emerge in spite of the pervasive patriarchal bias testifies to a struggle for women's liberation even within the ancient culture. The fact that several of those passages point toward the future is a source of profound hope for our present. Feminists can create together a different future—one in which there is peace, mutuality, interdependence, and true equality between the sexes. Interpreting the biblical texts with a view toward this end is here offered.

PLAN OF THE BOOK

Because this book may accompany, rather than replace, any one of many Old Testament introductions now available, it presupposes a general historical background. Because the organization of introductions differs, every effort has been made to make the organization of this book compatible with as many as possible and adaptable to each. The biblical material is situated within larger literary units (i.e., the Pentateuch, the Deuteronomistic History, the Prophetic Writings, the Writings). Where possible, every effort has been made to order the biblical books chronologically (e.g., Amos before Isaiah), though not at the expense of literary integrity. Each pertinent section and/or female character will be studied with that methodology most appropriate to feminist interpretation (i.e., the historical context, a literary interpretation, hints of exegetical history).

A NOTE ABOUT TRANSLATION

Because the Old Testament texts were produced in a patriarchal culture, the Hebrew text very often uses male terms "by preference" when the generic is intended. (Often many persons speaking and writing in English do the same thing; that is, they use "he" when the referent is either "he" or "she"; they use "man" when the statement refers equally to a "woman.") Because this tendency so permeates the Old Testament, it is impossible to indicate its every occurrence. Effort will be made, however, to indicate the most egregious violations of women in this regard.

"She is more righteous than I . . ."
(Genesis 38:26)

✢ PART I ✢

THE PENTATEUCH

INTRODUCTION

Historical Considerations

The literature now contained in the Pentateuch is thought to have been written anywhere from the twelfth century B.C. (e.g., Num 22—24) through the exile (e.g., Deut 30:1–10), and much of it is believed to have had an even earlier oral history. Scholars distinguish among four sources in the Pentateuch: the Yahwist (composed about the tenth century B.C., a product of the south, whose writer called God "Yahweh"), the Elohist (composed about 850 B.C., thought to have been produced in the north by an author who called God "Elohim"; either produced only as segments or only segments of which were incorporated into the Pentateuch), the Deuteronomic source (dated to Josiah's reform, about 621 B.C. with postexilic additions), and the Priestly writing (a product of the exile, mid-sixth century B.C.). Scholars believe that the Yahwist and the Elohist were combined into a JE source, to which the Deuteronomic source was added; finally, the Priestly writers both combined the sources and added their own materials.

Literary Considerations

Modern scholars have analyzed the variety of literary genres contained in the Pentateuch, pointing to myths (e.g., Gen 2—3), sagas (e.g., Gen 12), narratives which explain the origin of things (e.g.,

Gen 22), law codes (e.g., Exod 20; Deut 5), rites for cultic cere-
monies (e.g., Exod 12), genealogies, (e.g., Gen 5), treaty formulae
(e.g., Deut 5), and so on. Others have focused their attention on
literary techniques such as foreshadowings, key words, repetitions,
character development, conflicts, climaxes, retardations of action,
resolutions, and the like. From a literary perspective, some scholars
have argued for a Hexateuch rather than a Pentateuch. After all,
Genesis 12 promises the land and only in the Book of Joshua is the
land attained. Closing the "story" at Moses' death leaves a key literary (and theological) theme unresolved. Others, noting the role
which the Book of Deuteronomy plays in directing the structure of
Joshua through 2 Kings, speak of a Tetrateuch, aligning Deuteronomy with the so-called Deuteronomistic History.

THEMES FROM A FEMINIST
PERSPECTIVE

Patriarchy and Hierarchy

Etymologically the word "patriarchy" derives from two Greek
words—*pater* meaning "father" and *archē* meaning "beginning" or
"first"—and refers to that form of social organization in which the
father has first place. The word "hierarchy" also derives from the
Greek, from *archē* meaning "first" and from *hieros* meaning
"priest." The word, though it has come to mean "ranking" or
"ordering" of any kind, referred originally to the priests' having
first place in a community. In ancient Israel, during those centuries in which the Pentateuch was compiled, the culture was patriarchal and then hierarchical. The Pentateuch verifies this by (1)
the paucity of its references to women; (2) the way in which women
are portrayed, and this in contrast to the way men are portrayed;
and (3) the ordering of persons.

Paucity of References to Women

The Primeval History (Gen 1—11) has few references to women:
the "female" whom God created (Gen 1:27); Eve (Gen 2—3) and
Adam's daughters (5:4); the daughters of humans who are taken by

the sons of God (Gen 6:2); and Noah's wives and daughters-in-law (Gen 6:18; 8:18). The other women, all unnamed, are cited as men's daughters within the genealogy of Gen 11. The fact that Sarai is Abram's wife and Milcah is Nahor's (v 29) introduces Gen 12.

Scholars have called Gen 12—50 "the Patriarchal History"—and rightly so, unless we are able to write women back into that history. The major events in those chapters involve God's self-revelation to men in the form of a promise and a covenant (to Abraham in Gen 12; 15; 17; renewed through Isaac in Gen 26; renewed to Jacob in Gen 28:35; and through Joseph in Gen 37—50). Though women are named in Gen 12—50—that is, Eve (chaps. 2—3); Milcah (chaps. 11; 22); Sarai renamed Sarah (chaps. 11; 12; 16; 18; 21; 23); Hagar (chap. 16); Reumah (chap. 22); Keturah (chap. 25; cf. 1 Chr 1:32); Rebecca (chaps. 25—27); Judith and Basemath (chap. 26); Maha-lath (chap. 28); Leah (chaps. 29—30; cf. 1 Chr 7:13); Rachel (chaps. 29—30; cf. 1 Chr 7:13); Zilpah (chaps. 29; 46; cf. 1 Chr 7:13); Bilhah (chaps. 29; 35; cf. 1 Chr 7:13; 4:29); Dinah (chaps. 30; 32; 34); Debo-rah (chaps. 35; 38); Timna, Oholibamah, Mehetabel, and Matred (chap. 36); Tamar (chap. 38; cf. 1 Chr 2:4); Asenath (chap. 41); and Serah (chap. 46)—their roles, with very few exceptions, are minor and stereotypical.

Only fourteen other women are named in the entire Pentateuch:

   in the Book of Exodus, Shiphrah and Puah (chap. 1), Zipporah (chaps. 2; 4; 18), Elisheba (chap. 6), and Miriam (chap. 15; cf. Num 20; 26; Deut 24);

   in the Book of Leviticus, Shelomith (chap. 24);

   in the Book of Numbers, Cozbi (chap. 25), Mahlah, Noah, Hoglah, Milcah, Tirzah, Serah, and Jochebed (chap. 26).

Most of these women are identified as wives and mothers of promi-nent men, though occasionally, as we shall see, a few emerge as actors in their own right.

The Portrayal of Women

How women are identified in the texts is the key to our under-standing of their role in society as well as what value society placed on them. In contrast to what one might expect, the patriarchal centuries during which the Pentateuch was produced did value women. Women's value, however, was associated with certain roles or functions. A woman justified her existence as daughter by her future role as son-bearer for her husband. Women who failed to achieve the responsibilities of this role (sterile women); those who were unfaithful to the role (harlots, adulterers); or those who endangered Israel's self-understanding by idolatry (foreign women)—all these the society rejected.

DAUGHTERS, WIVES, AND MOTHERS

Women are almost always identified in terms of the men who are their fathers, their husbands, or their sons, and occasionally vis-à-vis their brothers (e.g., Lev 21:3). For example,

> three of Abraham's women (Sarah, Hagar, and Keturah; Gen 16; 25) and the sons whom they bear;
>
> two of Nahor's wives (Milcah and Reumah; Gen 22) and the children whom they bear;
>
> Isaac's wife, Rebecca, and her twin sons (Gen 25);
>
> three of Esau's wives (Judith, Basemath, and Mahalath; Gen 26; 28);
>
> four of Jacob's women (Leah, Rachel, Zilpah, and Bilhah; Gen 29) and their children—twelve sons and one daughter, Dinah (Gen 30);
>
> Judah's daughter-in-law, Tamar (Gen 38), and the son whom she bore;
>
> Joseph's wife, Asenath (Gen 41);
>
> Jacob's granddaughter, Serah (Gen 46);
>
> Moses' wife, Zipporah (Exod 2; 18);
>
> Aaron's wife, Elisheba (Exod 6);
>
> Aaron's sister, Miriam (Exod 15);
>
> Dibri's daughter, Shelomith (Lev 24), and the blasphemer whom she bore;
>
> Zelophehad's daughters, Mahlah, Noah, Hoglah, Milcah, and Tirzah (Num 26);
>
> Asher's daughter, Serah (Num 26);
>
> Moses' mother, Jochebed (Num 26);
>
> Lot's unnamed daughters and their two named sons (Gen 19).

Fathers' daughters will be given to future husbands, and the function of these women as wives is clearly to bear children for their
husbands. Their activities are, almost without exception, limited
to the domestic realm.

As a consequence, then, the woman who is barren is clearly a
disgrace, a victim of God's displeasure. Because the Israelites did
not believe in life after death, continuation of one's life took place
through one's children. When the barren woman did finally give
birth, the child or children whom she delivered were understood to
be a special favor from God and particularly blessed. Because
women could not be physically circumcised—the sign of covenant
partnership with Yahweh (see Gen 17)—their participation in the
community of Israel took place through their fathers and their
husbands.

Such a societal structure made the woman who was a widow as
well as the child who was fatherless especially to be pitied. The
widow was no longer under the protection of her father and had
lost her husband; the child had no father—nor yet a husband if the
child was female—by whom to be protected. These had no way of
"connecting" to the community, since connection was made possible by the men with whom the female was identified.

HARLOTS, ADULTERERS, AND SEDUCERS

Women, though inferior to men, were honorable when they were
identified with their appropriate men—as daughters, wives, and
mothers. On the other hand, women became dishonorable if they
had sexual relations with men other than their husbands (e.g., Gen
39). A woman who had had sexual relations before marriage was
considered defiled (e.g., Lev 21:14; cf. Deut 22:23–24). In biblical
texts outside the Pentateuch this theme will take on greater strength.

FOREIGN WOMEN

The Pentateuch does not employ this category often and when it
does its usage is anachronistic (e.g., Gen 28; Exod 34). Because
foreign women posed a major threat to monotheism—they
brought to their relationships with Israelite males their worship of
foreign gods (e.g., Deut 7:4)—they were frequently rejected by the
religious establishment.

The Ordering of Persons

In addition to the ordering of women as inferior to men (patri-archy) and the ordering of lay men as inferior to priests (hier-archy), Israelite society legitimated other orderings of people, most obviously the ordering of the free person over the slave (e.g., Exod 11:5; Lev 19:20; 25:44–46) and the Israelite over the alien (e.g., Exod 12:43, 45).

Israel's History as Men's History

The theological history recorded in the Pentateuch is written from the perspective of men. God is like a man, a father (Deut 1:31; 8:5; 32:6); men are the narrative's major characters. For ex-ample, it is the birth of males which is celebrated (e.g., Exod 13); they are the ones who recount the exodus to their sons (e.g., Exod 13), the ones to whom God promised Canaan (e.g., Exod 13), the ones who went down to Egypt (e.g., Num 20). They are the ones who become covenant partners with Yahweh (e.g., Gen 17; Lev 26; Num 32), the ones to whom God belongs (e.g., Deut 1; 6; 12; 26; 29), and the ones who receive Israel's laws (e.g., Exod 20; Deut 13:6; 21:10–14). Males are the rightful worshipers (e.g., Exod 23:17; 34:23; 36:2) and the potential priests (e.g., Exod 35:19; Lev 21). The male animal, even, was the appropriate offering (e.g., Lev 1:10; 3:1; 9:3). Men were the sexual initiators (e.g., Lev 18), the warriors (e.g., Num 1; 26:2; Deut 20), the leaders (e.g., Num 10:14–16; 11:16; 32:1–3; Deut 1). Time itself is recorded in gener-ations: from father to son. Furthermore, when a census was taken (e.g., Num 1—4; 26; cf. 32) it numbered the men—the heads of tribes, clans, and families.

There are many indications that the men who lived during the centuries in which the Pentateuch was produced were considered more important to the society than their female counterparts. There are more episodes recorded about the men, and there are more laws provided to protect them. For example, provision is made to guarantee that the first-born son of a man who has two wives is specially blessed, even if he is not the son of the preferred wife (Deut 21:15–17). Obviously there is no such provision for the first-born daughter, regardless of which wife was her mother.

Provision was made for parents who were unable to discipline a stubborn, rebellious, extravagant, alcoholic son: to bring that son before the city elders who would stone him (Deut 21:18-21). No similar provision is made for a rebellious daughter; presumably no stubborn, rebellious, extravagant, alcoholic daughter whom her parents could not discipline could even have been imagined in the patriarchal centuries during which the Pentateuch was being produced. Provision is made that men who have a dispute take their dispute to court so that the judge may decide between them (Deut 25:2). This presupposes that each is head of a family or they are of different families. One suspects that women were not expected to have disputes outside the family, and those women who did have disputes would have their disputes judged and decided within the family by its male head.

Language: Masculine by Preference and a Male God

In the Hebrew language, unlike English, gender is either masculine or feminine. Nouns that the English language would consider neuter—things as distinguished from persons—are subsumed in Hebrew by either the masculine or feminine gender. For example, the word for "table" (*slḥn*) is feminine while the Hebrew word meaning "name" (*šm*) is masculine. Similarly, biblical Hebrew lacks a neuter personal pronoun. The gender of the noun to which a pronoun refers determines its gender, masculine or feminine.

Sometimes even when Hebrew has the words to describe accurately those persons being spoken to or spoken about, it fails to do so; that is, it fails to name females with feminine vocabulary, subsuming them under masculine terminology. For example, several times in the Pentateuch the word "sons" is used to refer to both the men and the women of Israel. The situation would be more accurately described had the author added the words "and daughters" (e.g., Gen 32:11; Exod 34:7; Lev 19:18; Num 36:1). In Num 25:1 the word which literally means "daughters" is used generically, but ironically, the people are bad! The term "fathers" is intended to subsume the "mothers" and refer to Israel's ancestors when in fact the word "fathers" is insufficient and inaccurate when used alone.

In like manner "forefathers" is used when the word is intended also to subsume the "foremothers" (i.e., Deut 19:14). The word "brother" is frequently used when the terms "relative" or "neighbor" would have been more accurate (e.g., Deut 1:16; 15:7). The Hebrew word for "man" (*'îsh*) occurs where the more generic "human" (*'ādām*) would have been more accurate (e.g., Deut 4:3; 24:16). In Exod 16, "no man" would more appropriately be expressed as "no one."

Moreover, when it cannot be determined from the context what the appropriate form of a pronoun should be—that is, when a person is being referred to but he or she has not been named and therefore his or her sex has not been determined—Hebrew, like traditional English, uses the masculine form of the pronoun. This phenomenon is often called "masculine by preference." There are countless examples of this in the Pentateuch (e.g., Lev 35; Deut 27).

In addition to the fact that the Hebrew language employs masculine forms for undetermined gender, English translators have consistently, though unnecessarily, followed their lead, and often even to the point of mistranslation. An introduction such as this cannot analyze the history of the translation of the Pentateuch into English, nor even the many translations currently on the market; it can, however, alert the astute student to suspect that some inaccuracies in translation still exist today. For example, in spite of the fact that the Revised Standard Version (RSV) is considered to be a very literal translation, it often renders the word *nĕphĕsh,* a "living being" or "person," as "he" (e.g., Lev 17:15–16).

In contrast, when the RSV uses the words "herdsman" (e.g., Lev 27:32) and "manslayer" (e.g., Num 35; Deut 19), the terms are most likely accurate translations. We might presume that more often than not the men took care of the herds, and the gravity of killing a man—even unintentionally—was certainly greater than killing a woman. In fact, it is logical to presume—though the Pentateuch does not explicitly document this—that killing a female would have been understood not as an offense against the victim but as an offense against the man or men whose woman she had been (cf. Gen 34).

Masculine by preference may often refer to the way readers interpret a text, even proper names. For example, the reader is familiar with the character Noah, who takes his family and the animals into the ark during the flood (Gen 6:9—9:17). But, one might ask, is the reader aware that "Noah" is also a woman's name? Noah is the daughter of Zelophehad (Num 26:33; 27:1; 36:11). The reader may be less familiar with the name "Puah," but the name clearly identifies a midwife in Exod 1 (see pp. 46–48 below). The name "Puah" also occurs elsewhere (Gen 46:13; Judg 10:1; 1 Chr 7:1), in each case referring to a male descendant of Issachar. Miriam is the sister of Moses (e.g., Exod 15:20; Num 26:59; see pp. 51–55 below). The proper name "Miriam" also appears, referring to a different character, in a genealogy (1 Chr 4:17). Must one read there a son of Mered or is it more likely, in fact, that the name there refers to a female, a daughter? How often have biblical interpreters presumed proper names to refer to men when, in fact, they may just as well refer to women? The fact that Israel's culture was a patriarchal one renders a masculine translation in the face of uncertainty more reasonable, but it is important to note that such an attribution is only calculated conjecture, and not certainty. Anyone familiar with Hebrew knows that the ending *āh* suggests a feminine noun, one reason for being suspicious about all the proper names ending in *āh* that have been attributed to men.

I have already suggested that the patriarchal culture of the Bible produced a patriarchal God. Deuteronomy 32 refers to God as "Father." At a time when the Israelites were struggling to affirm monotheism in the midst of the many male and female gods of the surrounding peoples, one should not be surprised to learn that Yahweh came to be understood in male terms and to be described with masculine language. Such is the logical consequence of the fact that the Pentateuch was most probably written entirely by men and directed only to men. Men were warriors and God was the warrior who would fight for them (Exod 14; Deut 1—4; 20:4). God is portrayed as One who destroys his enemies (e.g., Deut 7:10; 9:14, 19–20; 28:48) and Israel's (e.g., Deut 9:3; 11:4; 31:3–4). God is compared to a "man" carrying his "son" (Deut 1:31) and to a "man" who disciplines his "son" (Deut 8:5).

Women as Men's
Possessions

When we speak of patriarchy we may have any one of several models in mind. A father may rank first in prestige or power or both. He may assume the primary role—or the only role—in family or tribe decision making. In extreme cases the father as head of the family (and therefore head of the wife) may also have the final say between life and death.

Israel's patriarchal society during those centuries in which the Pentateuch was produced understood the father—that is, the adult male head of the family—as possessing both power and prestige. He could, for example, sell his daughter as a servant (Exod 21:7). A young woman living in her father's house could make a vow to the Lord which would stand only if her father, when he learned about it, did not contest it (Num 30:3-5). A married woman could only make such a vow if her husband, when he heard about it, did not protest (vv 10-14). Similarly, the young woman who had made such a vow before she married would only be bound to that vow if, after she had married and her husband heard about it, he did not contest it (vv 6-8). Women could be taken as spoils of war (e.g., Num 31:9; Deut 21:11-13).

Sexual transgression was not understood as violation of the woman in question, but violation of the man whose woman she was. Many examples from the Pentateuch, dated across the centuries, illustrate this. When the Decalogue reads that "you shall not covet your neighbor's wife" (Exod 20; Deut 5), it is addressed to men and based on the fact that the woman belongs to another man. The man who does violate another man's wife should be stoned, precisely because he has violated the other man by violating that man's wife (Deut 22:22, 24). A son is commanded not to dishonor his father by entering into an incestuous relationship, that is, by having sexual relations with his father's wife (Lev 18:7; cf. Deut 22:30; 27:20), or with the daughter of his father's wife who is born to his father (v 11). Approaching the wife of one's father's brother to have sexual relations with her would dishonor one's father's brother (v 14). A man may not remarry a wife whom he had once divorced if she had married another, because such a second marriage would have defiled her (Deut 24:1–4). It is only the husband who may initiate divorce (e.g., Deut 21:14; 24:1–4); women could not—or would not because of their dependence on men—divorce their husbands.

No woman was allowed to be promiscuous while still living in her father's house. If she was found to have been so, she would be stoned (Deut 22:13–21). Provision is made also in behalf of a husband who suspects his wife of being unfaithful; he is to bring her to the priest, and if she is found to be unfaithful, she will be stoned (Deut 22:21) or at least she will be accursed among her people (e.g., Num 5:11–31). *There are no similar laws recorded which apply to either the unmarried or the married man.*

The penalty for a man who rapes an unengaged young woman is only that he pay her father a bridal price, and that, if her father is willing, he marry her, in which case he may not divorce her (Deut 22:28–29; cf. Gen 34; Exod 22:16–17). Though our century might lament her double victimization—first the rape and then having to marry the rapist—in the culture of which she was a part, lack of a husband (and she would not have had opportunity for another under the circumstances) would have been considered the greater evil.

The Levirate law is further evidence of the fact that women were men's possessions and that their value lay in producing children for their husbands. Deuteronomy 25:5–10 details what is to happen if a husband dies without having begotten a son. In such a situation, the deceased's widow is not allowed to remarry outside the family. Rather, her brother-in-law is to marry her. The first son born of that union is to carry on the name of the woman's dead husband. Genesis 38 records the story of a daughter-in-law of Judah whom he praises as "more righteous than he" precisely because of her concern to have sexual relations with a member of her dead husband's family in order to provide a son, a name, for him—that is, to fulfill the obligations of Levirate marriage.

Women who have had sex—either prostitutes or divorced women or even widows—are inappropriate as wives for the priests. A priest is holy, and the woman whom he marries is to be a virgin—that is, sexually pure (Lev 21:7, 13–14). Such a law indicates that a woman's having had sexual relations made her impure.

Though the divorcée may have had no voice in her expulsion—
and the widow certainly had no choice in the loss of her husband!—still, the woman who had had sexual relations was
somehow tainted and inappropriate. A priest (remember the
derivation of the term "hierarchy"!) deserves an unspoiled object,
undamaged goods, so to speak.

Elsewhere also in the Pentateuch the "untouched virgin" is given
special consideration. The Israelites are to destroy all of the Midianites including every woman who has slept with a man (Num
31:17). The Israelites, however, may save for themselves every
young woman who has never slept with a man (31:18, 35). This
implies the superiority of the unused female sexual partner. Related to this is the law which asserts that a man, once married and
divorced, may not take back his former wife if she has been with
another man. Her having had sex with another has defiled her
(Deut 24:4).

Other phenomena such as surrogate mothers (e.g., Gen 16),
polygamy (e.g., Gen 26; 29; Deut 21:15), the powerless widow (e.g.,
Deut 14:29; 24:17, 19–21; 26:12), and the many, many unnamed
women of the Pentateuch (e.g., Gen 19—20; Exod 6) testify to
women's inferior role as unequal partners in a patriarchal society.

Role Stereotyping and Sexual Discrimination

Discrimination against women was signaled already at their
birth. The length of time prescribed for the infant's mother's pu-
rification differed, depending on which sex she had borne (e.g.,
Lev 12:1–5). The recognition of certain biological differences between men and women (e.g., menstruation) led also to certain
forms of discrimination. The Israelites considered life to be in the
blood (e.g., Lev 17:13–14; Deut 12:16; when one bleeds extensively
one dies!), and therefore regarded blood with awe and fear. We
have no idea of the extent to which they understood the relationship between menstruation and conception, but this was another
indication of blood's close connection with life. The menstruous
woman, her bed, her chairs, as well as those who touched her, her
bed, or her chairs during her menstrual period, were considered

unclean (e.g., Lev 15:19–23, 32). A husband should not have sexual relations with his wife during her period (Lev 18:19; cf. 20:18). Any flow of blood a woman had outside her menstrual cycle would have the same effect, also making her, her bed, and her chairs unclean for whatever length of time she was bleeding (15:25–26). Those who touched her at that time would be unclean until the evening (v 27). Moreover, for seven days after the ceasing of the flow of blood, the woman would remain ceremonially unclean (v 28), and atonement would have to be made for the uncleanness of her discharge (vv 30, 33). Moreover, when persons were to be dedicated to the Lord by an offering of money as the equivalent of the person dedicated, the values set by law were dependent on the person's age and sex. Consistently the female was less valued (e.g., Lev 27:1–7).

Another indication of role stereotyping came with the separation of clothing and of work. Deuteronomy 22:5 forbids a woman from wearing men's clothing, or a man from wearing women's clothing. Distinction between the sexes—not only biological distinction but social distinction—is to be expressed by a strict regulation of what clothing is appropriate for whom. Women are, most commonly, the bakers of bread (Lev 26:26; but cf. Gen 40). I have already pointed out that women were relegated to the domestic sphere. One should not be surprised to learn therefore that "woman's work is in the home."

Deuteronomy 25:11–12 presents us with an obscure case law. The situation described is two men fighting with each other. One of the men's wives, to help her husband defend himself, gets involved in the fighting. She reaches out and seizes her husband's opponent's genitalia. Under such circumstances the law provides that the woman's hand is to be cut off. The text as it reads gives us no precise explanation for the penalty. Is it because women should not be fighting at all? Is it because, though women may in certain circumstances fight, they may not, under any circumstances, touch with their hand the genitals of a man not their husband? Is it because women may not, under any circumstances, touch any man's genitals? In any case, the penalty underlines inappropriate activities for wives!

Exceptions within a
Patriarchal Culture

The fact that a culture is patriarchal does not imply that all relationships—individual and social—are always hierarchical. There are exceptions. Sometimes those exceptions come in the form of equal condemnation of the same crime—regardless of which sex commits it. For example, both male and female cult prostitutes are forbidden (Deut 23:17). Both sexes may be the object of curses (e.g., Deut 28:32, 41, 53, 56, 68). Both sexes are forbidden to practice idolatry (Deut 17:2–5; 29:18) though both sexes may become victims of idolatry (Deut 18:10). Women as well as men may eat of the tithes of the grain, the wine, the oil, of the firstlings of the flock and the herd, of the votive offerings and the freewill offerings (Deut 12:17–18). The women, the children, and the aliens, as well as the men, are to assemble to hear the law so that they all may follow it (Deut 31:12). Both Hebrew males and Hebrew females may become slaves of other Hebrews (Deut 15:12–18).

A priest may make himself ceremonially unclean to mourn the death of either his father or mother, his son or daughter, or his brother or unmarried sister (Lev 21:2–3; cf. v 11). The first two pairs suggest a kind of equality, while the last speaks again of the inferiority of woman. He may only mourn an unmarried sister; a married sister now belongs to her husband. A captured woman is permitted to mourn both her father and mother (Deut 21:13). This text, too, betrays a dubious equality. It is only the female who is captured, taken alive, to become the sexual partner of the battle's victor.

In an unusual usage, both Israel's "sons and daughters" have sinned and become the objects of God's anger (Deut 32:19). One suspects, however, that the addition of the "daughters" has more to do with poetic parallelism than it does with equality between the sexes! In the same segment (Deut 32), the poet wishes to emphasize the universality of Israel's future destruction and therefore lists in detail all those to be destroyed—the fathers and the homes (the mothers!), the young men and young women, infants and gray-haired men (v 25). While the first and third lines of the verse contain "male by preference" forms, the young men and young women balance each other perfectly. Again, however, one suspects that the verse is more concerned with poetic parallelism than with sexual equality.

Mothers are often paralleled with fathers in statements to or about their children. One is to honor one's father and mother, for example (Exod 20:12; Deut 5:16; cf. Lev 19:3; Deut 21:18–19; 22:15; 27:16; 33:9). One is not to have sexual relations with either one's father's daughter or sister or one's mother's daughter or sister (Lev 18:9, 12–13; Deut 27:22). The offspring who curses his father or his mother is to be put to death (Lev 20:9).

One text which emerges from the Pentateuch and which is of peculiar interest because it truly suggests the equality of women and men is Num 11:12. The verse compares Moses' protective leadership of Israel to "a nurse carrying a sucking child." The simile does place the women in the stereotypical domestic role, but it honors that role by placing Moses, Israel's mediator with Yahweh and the leader of their deliverance, within that same ambit. Critics of this interpretation, however, point out that Yahweh is compared to a father with his son (Deut 1:31; 8:5) and Moses to the woman. Since Yahweh is superior to Moses, the same hierarchy—God over human, male over female—is here preserved.

A text which historical critics date to the exilic period because of its warnings about the behavior of Israel's kings is Deut 17:14–20. Our interest in the text has to do with its assertion that the king is not to consider himself better than his brothers. Such an attitude might allow him to become a law unto himself and forsake his covenant obligations. Such behavior could only lead to the end of the monarchy. The author's hindsight here evaluates the dangers of hierarchy and speaks against it.

TEXTS FROM A FEMINIST PERSPECTIVE

The Badly Maligned Eve
(Genesis 2—3)

The Story

Typical introductions to the Old Testament point to two accounts of creation. Genesis 1:1—2:4a tells the story in an orderly fashion and is considered to be the work of the Priestly author. In this story,

God created the human species (ʾādām) on the sixth day, male and female he created them (1:28). There is no dialogue in this account of creation; a narrator simply records what happened.

In contrast to the Priestly account of creation is the Yahwist's account (Gen 2:4b—3:24), an earlier source whose narrative takes place in two scenes, each interwoven with dialogue. There are altogether four characters, in addition to the narrator, who speak— God, ʾādām, a serpent, and Eve. God and ʾādām speak in scene 1. The serpent, the woman, Yahweh, and the man speak in scene 2.

Genesis 2:4b–15 narrates the creation of heaven and earth, of ʾādām, of a lush garden. Yahweh speaks first, to ʾādām, designating for him appropriate food (v 16). ʾādām may eat from almost every tree in the garden, all except one, that is—the tree of the knowledge of good and evil. (In this account no animals and nothing else human has yet been created.) Yahweh continues his word to ʾādām. It is not good for ʾādām to be alone and so Yahweh will make a helpmate for him (v 17).

At this point the narrator again picks up the story, reporting that God created all the birds and the beasts but that since none was an appropriate helpmate for ʾādām, Yahweh, having put ʾādām into a deep sleep, took one of his ribs from ʾādām's side and made a woman (vv 18–22). When ʾādām is presented with the woman, he speaks for the first time in the narrative (v 23). ʾādām's words testify that this creation is the appropriate helpmate: they are now ʾîsh and ʾîshāh, man and woman, intimately related. The narrator picks up the story to emphasize the unity of the two persons. To become one with a woman (ʾîshāh) is just cause for a man (ʾîsh) to leave his parents; they are not embarrassed to be exposed to one another. These verses (vv 24–25) would seem to signify that the "helpmate" for ʾādām is ʾādām's equal.

"The man" of scene 2 (chap. 3) is both the ʾādām and the ʾîsh of scene 1. He is ʾādām as person in relation to God and ʾîsh as man in relation to woman. Scene 2 also takes place in the garden but the dialogue partners have changed. The narrator suggests that the woman is in the presence of a serpent. The serpent asks the woman a question. Did God really forbid you to eat from any of the trees in the garden (v 1)? The woman's answer suggests that the man had told her God's directive, for she replies to the serpent that they may eat of any of the trees except one. The forbidden tree she describes as "the tree in the middle of the garden" and she adds what the text has not yet told us: Not only may they not eat from it; they may not touch it. If they do either, they will die (vv 2–3).

The serpent's response to the woman is to contradict her (and God), making the reader certain that the "tree in the middle of the garden" is, in fact, the "tree of the knowledge of good and evil." They will not die. Rather, says the serpent, they will be like God, knowing good and evil (vv 4–5).

The woman does not answer the serpent in words. The narrator reports what happened, how she thought, what she did, what her man (*'îsh*) did, what happened as a result of what they did. She looked at the tree, and desired its fruit. She took it, and ate it, and gave some of it to her man (*'îsh*) who also ate it. The consequence of their eating was knowledge: they knew they were naked. They hid from God (vv 6–8).

God now speaks. Calling to the man (*'ādām*), God, like the serpent, also asks a question: Where are you (v 9)? The man answers God with the truth: I heard you. I feared because I was naked (he knew he had changed from how he had been created!). I hid (v 10).

God replies, not with immediate condemnation, but with two more questions: Who told you you were naked? Have you eaten from the forbidden tree (v 11)? The man (*'ādām*) equivocates now in rendering God answers to the questions. He sidesteps altogether how he knows he is naked. Though he admits that he has eaten from the tree, he blames God (you gave me the woman!) and the woman (she gave me some fruit from the tree) for his act (v 12).

God then turns his attention from the man and addresses the woman: What have you done (v 13a)? She answers God, also admitting that she ate, but she protests that the serpent deceived her (v 13b). Lurking behind her explanation is the confession that she believed the serpent rather than trusting God!

God then directs attention from the woman to the serpent. God does not ask the serpent a question, however. Rather, God curses the serpent for what "she" (serpent is feminine in Hebrew) has done: she will crawl on her belly and she will always be regarded by humans as their enemy (vv 14–15).

Then God turns back to the woman with words of punishment: she will have increased pain in childbirth and she will be the victim of patriarchal structures (vv 16–17).

Finally, God turns back to the man (*'ādām*) with words of punishment: because he obeyed the woman and disobeyed God, he will have to work very hard to make a living, and he will die (vv 17–19).

The narrator inserts a report that the *'ādām* named her "woman" (*'ishāh*) who would become the mother of all the living (cf. 2:19) and God made clothes for both the man (*'ādām*) and his woman (*'ishāh*) (vv 20–21). God then speaks for the last time in the scene (v 22). The addressee is indefinite. God acknowledges that the *'ādām* is now like God, knowing good and evil (what the serpent had promised the woman! cf. 3:5). God now seems to give them another "forbidden tree" in place of the violated tree. For Yahweh's curse on the *'ādām*—that he die—to be fulfilled (cf. v 19), the *'ādām* must not touch and eat from the tree of life (v 22). To guarantee that the *'ādām* not have access to the tree of life, and to fulfill the curse on the *'ādām* that he work hard for a living, God banishes them from the garden and places cherubim at its entrance to guard the tree (vv 23–24).

Interpretation

Key Words

There are words that appear and are repeated in these two chapters that are considered key to the narrative's interpretation. The first, already indicated above, is "helpmate." Is *'ādām*'s helpmate intended to be his equal or his adjunct? The noun is limited to chapter 2 (vv 18, 20), but too often it is interpreted in light of the action recounted in chapter 3, and this through prejudiced eyes. There is no linguistic evidence whatsoever that the term is meant to designate an inferior. Quite the contrary.

Another significant use of language occurs with a play on the letters *'rm* in the word for "cunning" (*'ārûm*), an adjective used to describe the serpent, and "naked" (*'êrŭmmĭm*), an adjective used to describe both the man and the woman both before and after they eat the fruit. Such plays on words are common in biblical Hebrew. The words do not have to relate in meaning and, very often in biblical Hebrew, they do not. In other words, if "cunning" is used in a pejorative sense (which it may or may not be), the nakedness of the human persons—both before and after they have eaten the fruit—is not necessarily pejorative (2:25; 3:1, 10). The choice of the word "cunning" to describe the serpent may simply have been the author-artist's way of connecting the two scenes. The choice of a feminine creature—the serpent—to deceive the female may be purely coincidental but it is nevertheless linguistically suggestive.

Another key word which interpreters have expounded on is "curse." Because of the technical meaning usually attributed to curses and blessings in the Pentateuch (e.g., Deut 28) and the Old Testament generally, many commentators have taken pains to point out that only the serpent is cursed (Gen 3:14). The author may have been distinguishing hierarchically here between the fates of the animal and of the humans, but the text has no other indicators to verify this.

Another play on words involves the names of the human (*'ādām*) and the earth (*'ădāmāh*). *'ādām* is created from the earth (2:7) and will return to the earth (3:19) at death. The name *'ādām* gives to the woman, "Eve" (*hăwwāh*), is etymologically derived from the Hebrew word for "life" (*hâ*). The woman's role—as this patriarchal culture understood it—is to bear life. She is to be the mother of all the living (3:20).

Aetiologies

The term "aetiology" describes a narrative whose primary purpose is to explain the present situation, why things are the way they are. Many contemporary interpreters suggest that the punishments provided in Gen 3:14–19 serve to explain human experiences which were not considered desirable, the causes of which were not understood, and the realities of which were not, at that time, subject to human control. Snakes do crawl on the ground, and often a human bitten by a snake becomes very sick and dies. Clearly this is an evil.

Whereas other animals could provide good things for humans—for example, food and clothing—the snake made no known contribution to human well-being. Why was the snake such an undesirable creature? Because it had lured humans into disobeying the command of God.

In contrast to snakes, there were many good things about women. But women, too, had their problems. It was a patriarchal society and men ruled over women. Moreover, women's value lay in their giving birth to sons. But this was neither an easy nor a safe task. Childbirth was very painful (no anesthetic) and many women died giving birth. That was an unhappy reality, and there was no known way to alter it. Why did men control women and why was childbirth so painful? Because woman had eaten the forbidden fruit and shared it with the man.

In contrast to snakes and similar to women, there were many good things about men. Yet they too, like women, had their problems. "No work, no eat," as they say. Farming was necessary and it was not an easy occupation. Moreover, humans die. Both work and death were experienced realities and neither could be prevented. Why did men have to work and why did humans have to die? Because man had eaten the forbidden fruit which the woman had shared with him.

Summary

Those who study this narrative from the perspective of literary genre designate it a myth of origins. The story explains how things came into existence in the first place. Our reading has shown that the character Eve has a minor role in the story as a result of the patriarchal culture in which the text was produced. She speaks very little; the dialogue which takes place between Yahweh and the man is both more copious and more significant. Moreover, the woman's punishments are limited to those which the patriarchal culture had assigned her, inferiority to men and her primary role as mother. That she is the first to eat of the forbidden fruit has no literary emphasis. On the contrary, it is the narrator who details what happened, not with an emphasis on process, the woman and then the man, but with an emphasis on result: both ate. And God's words to her about the act, and then later about its punishment, are sandwiched between Yahweh's words to the serpent and Yahweh's words to the man.

Yet the fact does remain that she is depicted as the first to eat. Male chauvinists interpreting this text have blamed her for all the sin in the world. Feminists are now lauding her as a true initiator, the significant decision maker in the story. Acknowledging that it was a patriarchal culture which produced the story, one must conclude that it was not the author's intention to laud her. She—and the serpent and the man—each had a role is disobeying God. Each bore a punishment; most likely, the author intended to explain the present reality of female submission—a situation contrary to the man's equal helpmate (chap. 2) and a situation worthy of lament—as well as the lamentable situation that women gave birth to their babies with great pain, as the price paid for woman's part in the disobedience. Nothing more and nothing less. The man's act was the greater wrong, because the culture that produced the story considered him the superior person. His offense led to tilling the soil—a man's work—but also to human death. Death was understood as the greater tragedy by far, the punishment of the more significant offender. His punishment extended not to a situation peculiar to his state—like the serpent's and the woman's—but to one which affects all the living.

One must conclude then that to malign Eve as the cause of sin in the world and to defend such a depiction on the basis of Gen 2—3 is to do a grave injustice to textual interpretation and to women. It is to do interpretation out of a gross patriarchal bias.

Sarah, Abimelech's Wives, and Rebecca: Victims of Deceit (Genesis 12; 20; 26)

The Story

Genesis 12 is usually celebrated as the call of Abraham, the promise to him of land and progeny, and the beginning of the Patriarchal History. Most introductions spend little time explaining the contents of vv 10–20, and if they do, it is to use the episode, along with Gen 20 and 26:1–11, to illustrate the presence of sources in the Pentateuch. Few commentators either deny the historical basis of the story altogether or admit and condemn its patriarchal overtones. Because the texts involve several women whom the story makes victims of male deceit—indeed victims of deceit by Israel's patriarchs, Abraham and Isaac—let us examine these texts in greater detail.

The setting of Gen 12:10–20 is Egypt. Abram and Sarai are en route there to avoid a famine. Abram speaks, instructing Sarai to lie to the Egyptians, to tell them that she is Abram's sister. That way they will treat him well—after all, she is a beautiful woman and who would not wish to cater to the brother-protector of a beautiful woman? That way, also, he will be safe. Abram fears that if the Egyptians realize that Sarai is his wife, they will kill him in order to have her.

When Abram and Sarai arrived in Egypt, the narrator reports, everything happened as Abram had predicted. The Egyptians took the beautiful Sarai for the Pharaoh and because of Sarai, they treated Abram well. He prospered—with sheep, cattle, donkeys, and servants.

The narrator then adds a new character, Yahweh, to the story. The narrator reports that, whereas Abram fared well because of Sarai, the Pharaoh and his household fared poorly. The Lord inflicted them with diseases. Pharaoh must have somehow concluded the reason for his suffering, for he summoned Abram and asked him why he had lied, why he had not told Pharaoh that Sarai was his wife, why he had said that she was his sister. Pharaoh gave Sarai back to Abram and told him to depart, which he did.

Interpretation

A close look at the story reveals its totally patriarchal character. Sarai never speaks. In addition to the narrator, only Abram and the Pharaoh speak. Sarai tacitly obeys her husband's command. And what is that command? To become another man's bed partner. A contemporary evaluation might say that her husband ordered her to become an adulteress. Yet when we recall the century in which this text was composed, we recall that the woman belonged to her husband. He was the decision maker and she was to be submissive to him. Though, with the exception of these three texts, there are no others in the Old Testament where a husband orders his wife to become another's, there are texts in which the male makes crucial decisions about a woman's situation (e.g., that she will marry, whom she will marry, etc.).

The Story

When one compares Gen 12:10–20 with Gen 20, one finds both similarities and differences. The setting has changed from Egypt to Gerar. The Pharaoh has been replaced by the king of Gerar, Abimelech. The characters Sarai and Abram remain constant, though their names have been changed to Sarah and Abraham. There is no famine which occasions Abraham's moving to Gerar, but he is living there in a foreign land (v 1). The narrator records what words Abraham used to describe Sarah: she was his sister. The narrator then goes on to say that Abimelech sent for Sarah and took her (v 2). One notes that it is the narrator who reports all the events, except to quote Abraham's words about Sarah. The narrator seems to be laying directly at Abraham's feet what then transpired.

Similar to the passage in Gen 12, it is God who sets the ruler straight. In Gen 12 God uses affliction, in Gen 20 God reveals to Abimelech that he has taken another man's wife (v 3; a man has taken another man's property; how the property feels about the situation is not the issue). The revelation takes place in a dream, Abimelech responding to God that he was duped, that both Abraham and Sarah had lied. Here, in contrast to the account in Gen 20, Abimelech quotes Sarah's words which confirmed Abraham's, that she and Abraham were siblings (vv 4–5). God then assures Abimelech that "he" knows Abimelech was deceived, that it was "he" who prevented Abimelech from violating the woman, and that if Abimelech will only return the woman, all will be well (vv 6–7).

The narrator tells us how Abimelech reacted to this new information. He called Abraham in and asked: What have you done? Why did you do it (vv 8–10)? Abraham answers Abimelech in two ways. The first the reader is familiar with from Gen 12: he feared that they would kill him to have her. The second is new, a legalistic insertion that vindicates Abraham. She actually is my sister, that is, we have the same father. She is, however, also my wife (vv 11–13).

We learn Abimelech's response to Abraham's revelation through the narrator. Abimelech returned Sarah to Abraham, and—in contrast to Gen 12—both gave him many gifts and allowed him to continue to live in his land (vv 14–15). The text gives Abimelech's precise words to Sarah. Abimelech gave Sarah money in exchange for any awkwardness the situation had caused her and he announced her vindication (v 16).

The story ends with an artist's stroke. Abimelech's wives had apparently been infertile during the time that Sarah had been in Abimelech's household. The reader had not known this. The characters had not associated the infertility with Sarah—why would anyone suspect Sarah's presence to be the cause of the misfortune until they learned that Sarah was Abraham's wife? But the women had been unable to conceive during that time. God had punished them for what Abraham and Abimelech had done.

Interpretation

Commentators use this text to illustrate either two sources (J in Gen 12 and E in Gen 20) or to stress this text as an essential rewriting of the earlier account, pointing out the crucial ways in which this telling differs from Gen 12. For one thing, though Sarah does not actually speak in this version, her words are quoted by Abimelech so she is portrayed as a more active character. Second, God tells Abimelech that Abraham is a prophet (v 7). As one reads the story, one may wonder how it will work out. Can it be that the prophet Abraham has lied? One's concern is quieted when Abraham tells Abimelech that Sarah is, in fact, his sister. Abraham may not have told the whole truth—in fact, he may even have intended to deceive!—but he did not lie. The patriarch is thus vindicated here in a way that he was not so vindicated by the resolution of the story in Gen 12.

From a feminist perspective, however, this story has even more patriarchal overtones than its Gen 12 counterpart, for not only is Sarah victimized but all of Abimelech's wives are also victimized. They bear the brunt of men's decisions. What Abraham and

Abimelech decide to do determines their lives, whether or not they can become pregnant, their children or the absence thereof. And lest we not notice, the story portrays a culture which, though it condemns taking a woman who is another man's wife, fully accepts a man's taking many wives!

The Story

The account in Gen 26:1–12 resembles the story in Gen 12:10–20 in that a famine occasions their presence in the land. The land itself, however, is Gerar, the setting for Gen 20. The character of the king of Gerar, Abimelech, remains constant, though here he is identified as the king of the Philistines in Gerar (v 1). The other characters—Abraham and Sarah—are replaced by Isaac and Rebecca so one concludes that this narrative is supposed to have occurred a generation later.

Most scholars would suggest that 26:2–6 (cf. v 24) is an insertion into the story. If one reads carefully the episodes associated with Abraham and the episodes connected with Jacob in Gen, and then reads the episodes associated with Isaac, one will notice that Isaac gets shortchanged. There are very few narratives about him, per se, as a patriarch. His story seems closely interwoven with Abraham's and Jacob's in such a way that scholars suggest that he functions more as a "connector" between Abraham and Jacob than as a significant patriarch in his own right. Yet, as connector between Abraham and Jacob, he too is a patriarch who receives the covenant promise. And the insertion is precisely that: he is told what land to be in, and promised God's blessing. He is the heir to the lands and numerous descendants whom God promised to faithful Abraham.

The Gen 26 version of the story has neither Isaac telling Rebecca what to do when they come to the land (cf. Gen 12) nor Isaac initiating what others would know about his relationship to Rebecca (cf. Gen 20). It is the men of Gerar who ask Isaac about the woman; to them he responds that she is his sister. The narrator then quotes Isaac's thinking that led to his answer, thinking very similar to what Abraham told Sarah in Gen 12:7.

In contrast to the accounts in both Gen 12 and 20, God does not here intervene, either with punishments or with a dream. Abimelech is the one who discovers that Rebecca is Isaac's wife. He witnesses their caressing (v 8). But similar to the Gen 20 incident, he summons the male who has deceived him and asks why. Isaac responds honestly. He feared that because of her he would be killed (v 9). Abimelech replies to Isaac, indicating that, fortunately, no one has yet slept with Rebecca. Otherwise, guilt, in this case, undeserved punishment, would have come to the people of Gerar (v 10).

The narrator tells us how Abimelech acted in response to this new knowledge. He ordered his people not to harm either Isaac or Rebecca (v 11; cf. v 29). The episode may end there, or may continue through v 30 which announces Isaac's prosperity in Gerar.

Interpretation

From a feminist perspective, this story more closely resembles Gen 12 than Gen 20. Isaac lied, risking his wife to secure his own well-being. He was more important than her, and if one should suffer, quite logically it should be the woman. Isaac is not punished for his lie. On the contrary, Abimelech is grateful that none of his people has followed through on the implications of the lie, violating Rebecca whom, because of Isaac's lie, they understood to be fair game. That would have been a grave offense against Isaac, and the patriarchal culture, and would have resulted in misfortune for Gerar. Rebecca never speaks, never has a choice, never makes a decision. She is a passive character, passed between men, a tragic example of patriarchal culture.

Summary

Three stories, similar and yet different. They are not intended to be about women. Interpreters tell us they are about God's protection of his people; that is, of his important people, Abraham and Isaac. But when one reads a story, one tends to identify with the character most like oneself. And women have come to read these stories as testimonies to a terrible injustice in the past, an injustice grounded in historical circumstances, not in God's will, an injustice whose contemporary expressions can no longer be tolerated.

Two Women Compete for One Man:
Sarah and Hagar; Leah and Rachel
(Genesis 16; 30)

The Pentateuch's themes have already suggested the presence of polygamy in ancient Israel and the importance of a man's continuing his life after he died through his male offspring (and therefore, the importance of a fertile woman to make such progeny possible). The episodes which follow are narratives about four, or even six, women who are the sexual partners of the prominent patriarchs, Abraham and Jacob.

The Story

Genesis 16 details what happened when Abraham's wife, Sarah, did not have children. As the texts now stand Abraham had already been promised many descendants by God (e.g., Gen 12:2). But Abraham had no fertile sexual partner so how could there be descendants? Sarah decided that she would try to solve the dilemma. She had as her possession and at her disposal a maidservant (hierarchy!), the Egyptian Hagar. She told Abraham to sleep with her maidservant so that perhaps she could build a family through her (vv 1–2). The narrator reports that Abraham agreed to Sarah's scheme, that he slept with Hagar, and that she conceived (vv 3–4). But the narrator then comments that the pregnant Hagar began to "despise her mistress." The hierarchical ordering had been irrevocably altered. Sarah had power over Hagar (e.g., she could order her to sleep with Abraham) but Hagar had more power than Sarah (she could conceive).

Sarah's response to the situation is to blame Abraham for Hagar's new attitude. One gathers from this that Sarah's giving Hagar to Abraham had been a decision made somewhat reluctantly. Under the circumstances of her own infertility, did she really have a choice? Sarah, well schooled in patriarchy and hierarchy, finds Hagar's more assertive attitude intolerable (v 5).

Abraham's reply to Sarah's complaint comes as an affirmation of hierarchy. Hagar is, after all, Sarah's, and Sarah can do with her what she thinks appropriate. The narrator tells us what Sarah does and how Hagar responds: Sarah treats Hagar cruelly and Hagar flees (v 6).

The scene changes to the desert near a spring. An angel of the Lord finds Hagar and asks her origin and her destination. She replies honestly. She is fleeing her mistress, Sarah (v 8). The angel tells Hagar to return to her mistress and submit to her. The angel, however, adds words which in that patriarchal culture Hagar would want to hear because of their ability to increase her value and prestige: the angel will generously increase her descendants (v 10). The angel gives Hagar more details about her pregnancy. She will bear a son. She is to name the child "Ishmael," a name that embodies her experience: God has heard her. The angel predicts, however, that the child, like Hagar herself, will not live in harmony with his own (vv 11–12).

The narrator concludes the scene with Hagar's naming God out of her experience; "he" is the one who saw her and she saw "him," and acknowledging that, the spring is now named after what happened there; it became known as "the well of the one who sees and lives" (vv 13–14). The narrator concludes the episode with the notice that Hagar bore a son whom Abraham named "Ishmael" (v 15).

Interpretation

Was Sarah jealous that another woman had slept with her husband? Was she upset that Hagar had, after all, become pregnant, because pregnancy was a woman's road to whatever power and prestige she could attain in the culture? Or was the real reason Sarah was upset because Hagar, a servant and an inferior, had communicated an attitude toward Sarah, now that she was pregnant, that was less than fully subservient? Or was Sarah's resentment of Hagar based upon a combination of these reasons?

A twentieth-century critic of the narrative may ask why the women were ever put in this competitive situation in the first place. The historical critic responds that the point of the narrative is not the women—it was, after all, a patriarchal culture. The point of the story is to determine whether Yahweh's promise to Abraham of descendants can be fulfilled. How can it be fulfilled if his wife is barren?

In fact, this segment is part of a longer promise and fulfillment narrative; the verses studied here function within a larger framework, according to the literary critic, to "retard the action" and thereby generate suspense. The obstacle of Sarah's barrenness must be overcome if the promise is to be fulfilled. The obstacle is overcome—Sarah's maid bears Abraham a son. But is this sufficient? Only the students who read on in the biblical text will know.

The Story

Genesis 30:1–24 deals with two women not yet discussed, the two wives of Jacob, Leah and Rachel. A little background (see Gen 29:14b–35) prepares us for Gen 30. Jacob worked for his uncle Laban. He wished to receive as his wages Laban's daughter Rachel for a bride. Rachel was the more beautiful of Laban's two daughters, but she was the younger. Laban deceived Jacob and gave him Leah. Because Jacob still desired Rachel, he agreed to work another seven years for Laban in exchange for Rachel; he then married her. As fate, or luck, or God, would have it, Rachel remained barren while Leah produced four sons. With each new son, she had hoped to win her husband's love. It is at this point that our narrative opens.

The narrative informs its readers that the barren Rachel became jealous of the fertile Leah (v 1). Her frustration led her to beg Jacob for children. His response, however, was anger. He had no power to control or change her situation (v 2).

The narrator then records that Rachel did what Sarah had done. She gave to Jacob her maidservant, Bilhah, so that through her she might have children (v 3). The narrator reports the outcome: Jacob slept with Bilhah, Bilhah became pregnant, Bilhah gave birth to a son (vv 4–5). Rachel's response is far different from Sarah's, however. The text omits any mention whatsoever of Bilhah's attitudes and behavior in all this—whether she would accept or reject Jacob if she had a choice and how she responded after her pregnancy and motherhood—and there is no mention of any antipathy of Rachel toward Bilhah (v 6). In fact, Bilhah again conceives and bears another son (v 7). Rachel's response to this son is again not directed to Bilhah but directed to Leah: she had been competing with her sister and she had won (v 8). (She had not been competing with Leah for Jacob's affection; he had preferred Rachel from the beginning. But she had been competing with Leah for what would give her husband continuing life—his progeny—and what would give her greater prestige in the patriarchal culture: children. The children were hers because they were the fruit of her husband and of a woman who belonged to her.)

The competition rises. Leah has had four sons and Rachel two. Leah is no longer having children. The narrator reports Leah's response to these developments. She gives Jacob her maid, Zilpah, and Zilpah has for Leah two more sons. Leah's response is telling: "The women will call me happy." (She has done what women are supposed to do; she has fulfilled her role well; she—and her maid-servant—have borne for her husband six sons and she has won the respect of the other women who measure their success by the number of their children.)

The following verses chronicle an exchange between Rachel and Leah. Leah has mandrakes, a fertility potion, and Rachel wants some of them. Leah resents Rachel so why should she share the mandrakes. Rachel offers to buy them from Leah. With what? With Jacob! Rachel will arrange that Jacob and Leah sleep together in exchange for some of the mandrakes (vv 14–15). Jacob complies (v 16). The narrator informs the reader that the mandrakes worked. Leah conceived and bore Jacob two more sons. With each new child she hoped to win her husband's favor (vv 17–20). Almost as an afterthought, the narrator records that Leah gave birth to a daughter (v 21). But the story does not end there. The mandrakes worked for Rachel also. She finally bore to Jacob her own son.

Interpretation

That there was some historical basis for the kind of situation detailed in Gen 30 is evident from reading Deut 21:15–17. The law recorded there protects the rights of a man's firstborn son, when the man has two wives who both bear him sons, and the firstborn is the son of the woman he loves less. In such a case the law requires that the man give the double share of his possessions to his firstborn and not to the first son of the preferred woman. Feminists note how the law is designed to protect the male and, only secondarily, his mother.

Often scholars interpret Gen 30 as the origin of Israel's twelve tribes. The chapter gives Jacob twelve children, though only eleven are sons (cf. Gen 35:18). Such an explanation accounts for the later geographic locations of the tribes as well as the sibling rivalry (e.g., Gen 37). The passage is therefore identified as an aetiological narrative.

Feminists, however, though respecting such an interpretation, recognize that limiting one's understanding of the text to that interpretation blinds one to the patriarchal prejudice behind the text, to the patriarchal culture which produced this kind of story to explain Israel's tribal origins. Competition between two women for one man has thus been historically legitimated as having biblical foundations.

In contrast, feminists point to the victimization of all the women in the story. What choices do they have? What decisions are they really free to make? Neither Bilhah nor Zilpah is ever asked if she wishes to become her master's sexual partner. And if either does so wish, is it because pregnancy is the only possibility for her of human recognition? Do Rachel and Leah really have a choice to offer or not to offer other women to the man whose they are? Is not remaining barren a greater risk? Is not another son the most valuable gift Leah can offer Jacob in her effort to win his affection? Feminists conclude that this aetiological narrative recounts Israel's tribal origins at the expense of Israel's women.

Summary

A careful look at these two narratives betrays similarities and differences. The competitors differ—a free woman and a slave (Sarah and Hagar) and two free women (Rachel and Leah) for whom the slaves are merely fertile possessions and useful objects. The stakes and the emotions are similar. Men's wars are most often fought on battlefields with foreign enemies for control of lands and resources; women's wars are fought in their homes with other women, for "control over" the men who are their husbands and the males who will become their sons. The stage is here set for far too much of the history of the last two millennia.

God on the Side of the Oppressed:
Sarah, Hagar, Rebecca, Leah
(Genesis 16; 21; 27; 29; 49)

The Stories

Before we leave the narratives which tell us about Sarah and Hagar, and Rebecca and Leah, it is necessary to look at another aspect of their stories, one which allows the portrait of a caring God to emerge from the lives of these characters whom their patriarchal culture continually oppressed. Each of these women's stories helps to reveal Israel's understanding of its God, a God who was consistently on the side of the oppressed.

Hagar as Vindicated Victim

Genesis 16 has already been examined (see pp. 33–38), but certain aspects of the narrative have not yet been highlighted. Notice that the angel of the Lord appeared to Hagar (vv 7–8) and gave her a promise (v 10). Hagar is the first woman in the Old Testament who receives an apparition. She also receives a blessing, the same promise—of descendants—that Abraham had received. Yahweh makes no such explicit promise to Sarah. Though God sends Hagar back to Sarah who abuses her, Hagar will be compensated. Yahweh hears her misery (v 11), and God sees her (v 13). (Later in the narrative, when Sarah directs Abraham to expel Hagar and Ishmael [21:8–20], God consoles with a reaffirmation of the promise first given to Hagar about Ishmael's descendants [Gen 16:10, 18]. In the latter scene life-giving water in the desert [a fertility symbol?] also plays a significant role.) God does vindicate Sarah's rejection of Hagar. The God who provided Hagar with a son will provide for that son a great nation and, in Israel's patriarchal culture, what more could Hagar ask?

Sarah as Vindicated Victim

Sarah's suffering, too, is overcome. Hers had been not the tragedy of rejection, but the tragedy of barrenness. The Lord provides that she bear a son (21:1–3). His name, "Isaac," like the name of Hagar's son, symbolizes the situation: laughter (17:17, 19; 18:12; 21:3, 6). Sarah laughs; others will laugh. What greater oppression could a woman feel than barrenness? But "the Lord was gracious to Sarah" (21:1). A close feminist reading of the narrative uncovers an interesting irony. Though the culture and the narrative are patriarchal, it is the woman who determines the outcome. Abraham had begotten a son Ishmael by a slave girl Hagar, but the fact that Ishmael was Abraham's son did not make him the heir to the promise. Sarah had hoped that, since she did not seem to be able to conceive, her maid's son would suffice to fulfill the promise. In fact, Sarah was the one who bore a son, Isaac; her son was to be the heir to the promise. The crucial character in the story, viewed from this perspective, is neither Abraham nor Isaac, Hagar nor Ishmael, but *a particular woman,* Sarah. God gave Sarah her vindication.

Rebecca as Vindicated Victim

Rebecca, like Sarah, had been passed off by her husband as his sister in order to secure his well-being in a foreign land (cf. Gen 12; 26). Though neither woman had been violated, it was no thanks to their husbands. The men had taken no risks to guarantee their wives' safety. Now (Gen 27) Rebecca is given the opportunity both to cooperate with God in fulfilling the divine will (cf. 25:23) and to secure Isaac's blessing for the son she preferred, Jacob (vv 6–10). That Rebecca's choice of Jacob over Esau coincided with the Lord's choice made possible the execution of her will instead of her husband's (v 4). Rebecca had been victimized by her culture and by her husband, but God had favored her favored child. Rebecca was able to exercise to the full the only control a woman could have—domestic control.

Some interpreters have understood Rebecca as a character who schemes with her son (vv 6–10), who deceives her husband and gets away with it, and they have condemned her accordingly. They have understood Jacob as a son who cheats his brother and who deceives his father (vv 21–29, 35) and gets away with it. They have pitied the aged and blind Isaac (vv 1–2). Many of these same interpreters would pass over—or whitewash—Abraham's deceit of the Pharaoh (Gen 12) and Isaac's deceit of Abimelech (Gen 26), perhaps betraying their own patriarchal bias.

Other interpreters, ignoring the specific details of the story, see in it an explanation for later history—Jacob had superseded his brother and this in contrast to the law of the firstborn. The story would then legitimate the reality with a divine explanation (the prediction to Rebecca at the twins' birth). Such an interpretation, which presumes the patriarchal period during which the text was composed, relegates Rebecca to a minor role. Her role is minor, yet ironically she gets her way; she achieves what is important to her.

Leah as Vindicated Victim

We have already considered Leah's contest with Rachel to win Jacob's approval. The ugly duckling's (29:17) only hope was children. By the end of Gen 29, the character Leah had borne to Jacob four sons while Rachel had borne none. By the end of Gen 30, Leah, herself and through her maid, had borne eight sons and one daughter, while Rachel, herself and through her maid, had borne only three sons. Each time Leah bore a son, she hoped that he would be able to succeed in turning her husband to her. Unfortunately, by the end of the chapter, we have no indication that Leah's hope has been fulfilled. What is stereotypically true even in the twentieth century finds early expression here: men desire body beautiful.

The Lord, however, vindicates Leah through one of her sons. It is Judah from whom the scepter will not depart (Gen 49:8–12). Though Rachel's son Joseph went to Egypt, saved his family from famine, and brought them to the place from which Moses would later deliver them (cf. Gen 37—50), still, it is Judah who emerges as the ancestor of King David. Leah may not have been Jacob's favorite, but she did achieve the only real power and prestige then available to a woman, the power and prestige which came to her through motherhood.

Summary

By now a careful reader of the biblical texts and of this text realizes that how one reads a story very often depends on the perspective of the reader as well as the content of the words read. If one presumes that the culture which produced these texts is patriarchal, it is not difficult to uncover indicators of patriarchal prejudice. But fairness to that culture and fairness to the narratives demands as well that we bring to our reading more than our own prejudices. The texts we read have been understood to contain God's revelation to human beings. Such revelation can be found in the fact that the texts, including Gen 16, 21, 27, 29, and 49, reveal a God who is always on the side of the oppressed. In these cases, and in much of patriarchal history, the oppressed are women.

Dinah: Raped Daughter of Jacob
(Genesis 34)

The Story

We have already indicated that Jacob's wife Leah gave birth to a daughter (Gen 30:21). According to the texts it was the last child she bore. A careful reader might recognize that such a notice is unusual. Genealogies chronicle the birth of sons. Transfer of property almost always takes place between men (but see Num 26—27; 36; and pp. 58-62 below). In the patriarchal culture of ancient Israel inclusion in the text of the comment that Leah gave birth to Dinah must be a foreshadowing of things to come. And so it is.

Dinah is not named explicitly again until Gen 34 (cf. Gen 32:11) when a narrator informs us that Shechem, the son of the ruler of the land, violated her (v 2). The narrator is quick to add, however, that Shechem loved the girl and sought to marry her (vv 3-4).

Marriages were usually arranged by fathers for their sons (cf. Gen 24), and Shechem here asks his father to acquire Dinah for him. Moreover, a raped girl was to marry the man who had violated her, though this recorded law (Deut 22:28-29) dates from a later period and refers, anyway, to a marriage between Israelites.

The narrative informs the reader that when Jacob heard about his daughter's rape, he waited till his sons returned from the field to say anything (v 5). (Some interpreters suggest that the narrator is portraying here a weak Jacob—he needs his sons to act—while others see this note as quite logical. Knowing what their concern would be for their father's honor, he did not want his sons to learn this news from strangers.) The narrator would lead the reader to believe that it was while Jacob's sons were still in the field—ignorant of the rape—that Shechem's father approached Jacob (v 6). Verse 7, however, contradicts this. Jacob's sons did learn about the rape while they were still in the field, and when they heard the news, they returned to their father. They were furious, implicitly because of the injury done to their father and less directly to them, but explicitly because of the offense Shechem had committed "against Israel."

Both Hamor, Shechem's father, and Shechem himself plead with Jacob and his sons for Dinah. The narrator reports that Hamor spoke as a father and as a king to Jacob and his sons. Hamor attested his son's love for Dinah and he invited the Israelites to share all his people's resources—both daughters and sons, land, and other possessions (vv 8–10). Shechem spoke as a heartsick lover. He was willing to give anything if only he could have Dinah (vv 11–12).

The narrative now very skillfully engages the reader. It first tells the reader that Jacob's sons lied to Hamor and Shechem. Then it tells the reader what the sons said, and what the sons said makes perfect sense. Neither Shechem nor Hamor and his people were circumcised. The Israelites could only intermarry with Hamor's people if they would be willing to be circumcised (vv 13–17; cf. Gen 17:14).

Verses 18–24 detail what happened next. Shechem was keen to satisfy Jacob's sons' request. Both he and Hamor went to the city gates and convinced the men, by pointing out to them what they had to gain from the merger, to submit to circumcision. They did. So far so good. Where is the deception v 13 alerted us to?

The narrative then informs the reader that the condition of circumcision had been a way to trick Hamor's people. Two of Jacob's sons, Simeon and Levi, use the opportunity of the men's weakened condition to attack and kill all the men, including Hamor and Shechem, and to take all their possessions, including Dinah and the other women, their flocks, cattle, and other wealth (vv 25–29).

Jacob's response to his two sons was a reprimand, not because what they had done was unjust but because of the possible deleterious consequences of their action. They were few in number and in a foreign territory. Aggravating those who surrounded them was not in their best interests (v 30)! The brothers' reply to their father, in direct address, was to appeal to Dinah's rape, to use her plight to justify their retaliation, to use her as an excuse for their murder and pillage: Shechem should not have violated her in the first place (v 31).

Interpretation

Many English translations preface this narrative with a subtitle (e.g., "Dinah and the Shechemites") and Gen 33:19 alerts the reader to the fact that Jacob purchased land in Canaan near the city Shechem (cf. Gen 12:6). Historical-critical scholars suggest this as an aetiological narrative—one which artfully explains why the city is called Shechem, why there was hostility between the Israelites and a people known as Shechemites (but cf. Num 26:31)—as well as a narrative which reinforces the Israelites' belief that they should not intermarry with foreigners. Interpreting this text as an aetiological narrative also explains why Simeon and Levi, the chief perpetrators of the crime, are tribes scattered throughout the land (cf. Gen 49:5–7). Such interpretations may well be historically accurate, in which case the story has very little, if anything, to do with Dinah. Dinah's very existence as a character may simply be the occasion to explain the Israelites' relationship with the Shechemites and the relationship of the tribes of Levi and Simeon to the others.

For feminists, however, the historical explanation—and the likelihood of its accuracy—is just another insult against women, and an insidious one at that, because, on the pretext of defending a woman, hostility between peoples is justified. Dinah never speaks. She is victim, first of Shechem who rapes her, then of her brothers who both deceive her would-be spouse and then use her as an excuse for murder and pillage. A close literary analysis of the text notes how the author justifies the men's actions because of the rape. Whereas in vv 1, 3, and 7 Dinah is identified as "the daughter Leah had borne to Jacob" and "the daughter of Jacob," in vv 13,

25, and 31 she becomes "the sister of the sons of Jacob," and "their sister," and Simeon and Levi become "Dinah's brothers." This language implies a close sibling relationship. (Very rarely in the Old Testament are children identified by their relationship to siblings and even more rarely are men identified by their relationship to women.) Moreover, two of the verses (13, 31) refer to Dinah's rape. The juxtaposition of the sibling relationship and the rape may lead a reader to infer that the actions of Dinah's brothers against the Shechemites were on behalf of their violated sister, to vindicate her. Is this really the case, however? Does the term "deceitfully" (v 13) imply not only that the sons of Jacob lied to Shechem and his father about their intent, but also that they were using their sister's rape deceitfully? If Dinah's well-being was really their intent, why did they not let Shechem marry her? Dinah would have been better off marrying her rapist who "loved" her (v 3; cf. Deut 22:28).

The female character Dinah is never vindicated; she is forgotten. What happened to raped women who did not marry their rapists? Was her fate the same as Tamar's (cf. 2 Sam 13:20)? Remember that Jacob had more than twelve sons, "the twelve sons of Jacob." Jacob had thirteen children, including a daughter, Dinah.

Tamar: Faithful, Childless Widow
(Genesis 38)

The Story

Judah, while visiting his friend Hirah, saw a nameless Canaanite woman whom he married and through whom he fathered three sons, Er, Onan, and the youngest, Shelah. Judah arranged for Er to marry Tamar. Because Er was evil, the Lord punished him with an untimely death. Judah then requested that Onan fulfill the Levirate law, that is, that he beget a child with Tamar for the sake of his deceased brother. Onan was unwilling to, however, so he spilled his seed. The Lord punished this evil deed of Onan's with an untimely death. Judah then feared to give his third son to Tamar, lest he too die. But Judah led Tamar to believe that, as soon as

Shelah was old enough, Judah would give him to her. However, he did not.

Sometime after Judah's own wife died, Tamar heard that Judah was going up to Timnah to shear sheep. She took advantage of the opportunity. She exchanged her widow's garments for a harlot's and, disguised, sat at the entrance of the city. Judah sought her services; she requested a fee; he agreed to send her a kid from his flock and to leave as a pledge his signet and cord and staff. Tamar conceived with Judah.

Judah, according to his contract, sent a kid to the harlot of Timnah but no such harlot could be found. There was no such harlot. Judah, then, kept the kid, and the woman, her identity still unknown to Judah, kept the signet and cord and staff.

When Judah discovered that his widowed daughter-in-law was pregnant, he ordered that she be burned. Tamar then brought forth the signet and cord and staff. Their owner was her child's father. Judah could only acknowledge the faithfulness of his daughter-in-law to her dead husband. He admitted, "She is more righteous than I, inasmuch as I did not give her to my son Shelah" (v 26).

Interpretation

Traditional interpretation of this text emphasizes either the Levirate marriage law or the twin offspring of Tamar, Zerah and especially Perez, the ancestor of David (cf. Ruth 4:18–22). Occasionally Judah is contrasted with his two evil sons. Er and Onan are evil and both die—childless. In contrast, Judah is the caring father who cannot risk the death of his third son. Since both Er and Onan had died while "involved" with Tamar, Judah does not give Shelah to her. Further, it was only after his own wife had died that Judah sought out the harlot. Since the text makes certain that the reader knows this, one can only conclude that the author wants to assure the reader of the appropriateness of Judah's sexual act. Finally, Judah made every effort to pay his just debt to the harlot; he sent the kid in fulfillment of the pledge.

When Tamar is praised, she is lauded for persisting in her efforts to fulfill the Levirate law. Though Judah is not condemned for obstructing its fulfillment, for withholding Shelah from Tamar,

Tamar is rarely analyzed with the thoroughness accorded Judah. Though she was not responsible for either Er's evil or Onan's, she would have been prevented—by both her brother-in-law and her father-in-law—from raising up a child to her dead husband. She herself would have lived her days as a widow and died childless. Tamar was as sensitive to appropriate behavior as Judah. She wore the garments of a widow; only the necessity of the particular occasion prompted their change; she returned to them.

Tamar was not only a clever woman but also a courageous one. To fulfill the Levirate law—to act "righteously" according to her situation—she chose the time, the place, the circumstances. Had she not thought ahead to keeping Judah's pledge, she would have had no way to prove his paternity. Tamar was also willing to take risks—to disguise herself, to remove her widow's garments, to act as a harlot, the possible consequence of which was to be burned. Tamar might have remained a victim of unfortunate circumstances, a childless widow, had she not used initiative to effect change.

Summary

Tamar is a childless woman destined to remain so. She is not childless by nature, a barren woman; she is childless by circumstance, a widow with no relative of her dead husband willing to perform the obligation of a kinsman. While many women of patriarchal cultures accept their lot, receptive and passive, Tamar does not. Her situation is changeable and, if the men who should intervene—Judah and Shelah—do not willingly do so, she will think of something. She does! And as Judah himself testifies, Tamar proves to be "more righteous than" Judah.

Shiphrah and Puah: Courageous Midwives
(Exodus 1)

The Story

The Book of Exodus opens with a list of the names of the twelve sons of Jacob who went down to Egypt (vv 1–5). The narrator gives the reader a sense of the passage of time. Jacob's sons had all died, but their many offspring filled the land (vv 6–7). For a long time, one concludes, all went well.

When a Pharaoh came to power who did not know Joseph—that is, who did not know how Joseph had saved Egypt from famine, a Pharaoh for whom Joseph's deliverance was merely a vague ancestral memory—he became concerned that the increasing numbers of Israelites could pose a threat to national security. Something had to be done (vv 8–10).

What the Egyptians decided was to relegate the Israelites to forced labor. But their scheme backfired. The harder the Israelites worked, the more numerous they became (vv 11–14). (Oppressed people tend to be fruitful even today! What other sources of stimulation, pleasure, and human accomplishment do they have?) The Egyptians became desperate.

The Pharaoh spoke to Shiphrah and Puah, the Hebrew midwives, with this command: kill the male babies whom the Israelite women bear; let the females live (vv 15–16; note the inequality and the irony: Shiphrah and Puah could allow the female infants to live because women could never become powerful enough or important enough to threaten Egyptian security).

Verse 17 strongly contrasts with the verses which precede. The women take on the Pharaoh. They do not speak; they just act. They disobey the Pharaoh and let the males live. Pharaoh then summons the women and demands an explanation (v 18). The midwives give him one, a lie, but a lie which affirms the strength of women (even of Hebrew women over Egyptian women) and ironically, a lie which they get away with: because of their strength, the Hebrew women have already given birth before the midwives arrive (v 19).

The narrator reports that God was "good" to the midwives. (God's goodness is associated in the Old Testament with covenant fidelity.) They had both gotten away with the lie and, because they had feared God, God gave to them their own children (vv 20–21).

Just as the Hebrews had succeeded in increasing when the Egyptians were seeking their diminishment, so the midwives had succeeded in preserving the Hebrew males when the Pharaoh was seeking their elimination. Having failed twice, the Egyptians must think of some other way of guaranteeing their control over the Hebrews. Verse 22 closes chapter 1 and prepares for chapter 2: Pharaoh orders the male infants, successfully born thanks to Shiphrah and Puah, to be thrown into the Nile.

Interpretation

Analysis of Exod 1 usually concentrates on the fact of the Hebrews in Egypt, their ever-growing numbers, the passage of time, the Pharaoh who did not know Joseph, and the Hebrews' persecution. This sets the stage for the birth of Moses (chap. 2), his call (chap. 3), and Israel's deliverance (chaps. 4—15). Rarely do traditional commentaries point to the midwives, and certainly their names died with them. (The name "Shiphrah" occurs only once in the entire Old Testament; the name "Puah" occurs four times, but the midwife is named only once.) Few celebrate the courage of their decision—to bring forth life rather than death. The commentators who do notice them place the women's heroism under the umbrella of God's favor for Israel; everything worked to thwart the purpose of the Pharaoh to the benefit of the Hebrews.

Yet the careful reader dare not ignore these women. Shiphrah and Puah—as well as fertile Hebrew women generally (1:12), and Moses' mother (2:2), and Moses' sister (2:4), and even Pharaoh's daughter (2:5)—are the very instruments God chooses, according to the narrative, to build the people who become Israel. They are the people who save the child Moses who becomes Israel's deliverer.

Zipporah: The First Ruth?
(Exodus 4: 18)

The Story

Moses, after killing an Egyptian (Exod 2:12), had to flee Egypt and was living in Midian. There he married Zipporah, the daughter of a Midianite priest. Zipporah bore to Moses a son, whom he called "Gershom," the name symbolically describing Moses' own fate: he had become a sojourner in a foreign land (2:21-22).

Exodus 3 records the call of Moses by Yahweh to become God's servant in delivering the Hebrew people from Egyptian bondage. Accepting this call demanded a courageous return to the land from where he was a fugitive, back to Egypt and the land of his birth. Moses had lived in Egypt as an Egyptian; he had been raised at the court. Now he returned there as a Hebrew. He had solidly identified with his oppressed people by killing an Egyptian oppressor. He had cast his lot with the Israelites and now, through Yahweh, would deliver them. Yet, Moses had not been circumcised, and by the time this narrative was written, circumcision was essential in order to be a part of the Israelite people. Who would circumcise Moses? The Midianites in whose land he dwelt could not; they themselves were not circumcised. But who else was there? Vicariously, Moses' son, a true Hebrew, the son of a Hebrew father, accomplished it. (In these times, a Hebrew father made a Hebrew; today, a child is considered Jewish if she or he has a Jewish mother.) Zipporah circumcised her son Gershom, still a small child no doubt, and then Zipporah touched Moses' feet (a euphemism for the genitals) with Gershom's foreskin (4:25). Her act was equivalent to the circumcision of Moses (4:26).

Interpretation

A close reading of Exod 4:24–26 couches the vicarious circumcision of Moses in the comments that the Lord was about to kill Moses (v 24) and the Lord let him alone (v 26). What Zipporah did appeased the Lord, and prepared Moses to assume his role as the Israelites' deliverer. Most students of the Pentateuch, reading this text for the first time, cannot understand why the Lord, having just called Moses, would want to destroy him. The answer lies in his lack of circumcision and the importance of circumcision for the author of this text and the period in which it was composed.

What commentators fail to note, however, is Zipporah's role. Just as Shiphrah and Puah and Moses' mother and Moses' sister and Pharaoh's daughter had kept Moses alive, though unknowingly, for his future mission, so now Moses' wife keeps him alive also for that mission. Six women each play significant roles in the narrative, to bring Moses to the brink of Israel's exodus.

The narrative about the Moabite woman Ruth occurs much later in the Bible (see pp. 205–10 below). She, too, however, though a foreigner, proved by her actions that she was faithful to—even exemplary regarding—the demands of Israel's covenant partner, Yahweh.

The Story

After the Israelites' successful exodus from Egypt, the narrator tells us that Moses is again reunited with his wife and children, whom he had sent back to his father-in-law during the struggle in Egypt. The reader learns also of a second son, Eliezer, this child named for the fact that the God of Moses' father had saved him from the sword of Pharaoh (18:2–6). (Moses' God had saved him through Moses' courageous mother: Exod 2:2–3!)

When Jethro (and Zipporah and Gershom and Eliezer) met Moses, Moses embraced Jethro (and the others too?). The narrator tells us that the men went apart, into the tent, to talk, and that Moses shared with Jethro all that had happened (vv 7–8). The narrator continues with Jethro's response to Moses, Jethro's confession that the Lord is greater than other gods, and Jethro's sacrifice (vv 9–12).

Interpretation

From a patriarchal perspective, there is nothing unusual in the episode here recounted. Zipporah's father had filled in as his daughter's "protector" while Moses was involved in Egypt. Now that the Israelites have been successfully freed, now that they are safe in the desert, the woman's father can return her and her husband's sons to Moses. He does so. Then the men talk about the public sphere, about Pharaoh, about God's mighty acts and the liberation; the men initiate a sacrifice.

Summary

From a feminist perspective, the narratives are another example of writing women out of history. By seeing to Moses' circumcision, Zipporah has made a significant contribution to the success of the exodus. But she is excluded from the victory. Irony of ironies! A Midianite male makes Moses a better conversation partner than his wife. The Midianite priest brings a sacrifice *after* the Israelites' deliverance when he is thoroughly convinced of the power of Moses' God. The Midianite female, on the other hand, had acted in accord with the demands of Moses' God *before* the liberation. The woman has the faith but the man gets the credit (see also the remainder of Exod 18)!

Miriam: Her Song and Her Leprosy
(Exodus 15; Numbers 12; Deuteronomy 24)

The Story

Exodus 15 has been singled out by many historical critics as one of the earliest pieces of literature in the Bible, dating back perhaps to the twelfth century B.C. One reason for this opinion is its poetic form; another reason, the fact that some of its phrases are closely related to similar phrases in Ugaritic, a Semitic language closely related to Hebrew but about one thousand years older. The poem contained in the chapter parallels closely the content of Exod 14 which chronicles in prose the final stages of Israel's deliverance from the Egyptians. A close scrutiny of the text of Exod 15 raises an important question: Who did the singing?

Verse 1 of the chapter informs us that "Moses and the Israelites" sang this song (vv 1–21) to the Lord. The opening words of the song are:

> I will sing to the Lord,
> for he is highly exalted.
> The horse and its rider
> he has hurled into the sea.

Verse 21, which concludes the poem, cites Miriam as the speaker:

> Miriam sang to them:
> "Sing to the Lord,
> for he is highly exalted.
> The horse and its rider
> he has hurled into the sea."

Before proceeding further one must look into the identity of this Miriam. She is here identified as Moses' sister. Buried in the

Septuagint translation of the genealogy of Exod 6:13-25, and translated into the New American Bible (NAB), is, remarkably enough, a woman, Miriam, and she is there identified, with Moses and Aaron, as a child of Amram and Jochebed (v 20). She is also so identified in two other genealogies, in Num 26:59, and in the later text of 1 Chr 5:29. Since Miriam is so identified, and since no other sister of Moses or Aaron is elsewhere named, it is logical to conclude that she is the unnamed sister of Moses referred to in Exod 2:4, the girl who saw to it that Moses' own mother would nurse him (2:7-8).

Finally, Miriam is here identified as a prophetess (Exod 15:20). Up to this point in the narrative of the Pentateuch, the only other persons to have been explicitly associated with prophecy are Abraham (Gen 20:7) and Aaron (Exod 7:1).

Interpretation

Traditional interpreters have taken the names—Moses (v 1) and Miriam (v 21)—at face value. They allow that Miriam was implicitly included "among the Israelites" in v 1. Perhaps vv 20-21 initiate the repetition of the song, this time with music and dancing. Women often led the music and dancing. Miriam probably was leading the women. Though historical critics, reading the other texts (Exod 3—14), struggle to determine the relationship of Moses to Aaron (was Aaron originally, in a separate source, the leader instead of Moses?), and may even suggest that originally Miriam had more influence than the combining of sources has left her, still these commentators do not probe the discrepancy in names here.

Some feminist interpreters—Elisabeth Schüssler Fiorenza for one—suspicious of the patriarchal bias which produced the texts, suggest that, originally, Miriam was the subject of v 1 as well as of v 21. Though King David is associated with music (e.g., 1 Sam 16:18) and late texts depicting temple singers presume their male sex (e.g., 1 Chr 25), still, many women are also associated with that role, especially after a victory (e.g., 1 Sam 18:7). Feminists also use the work of the historical critics to suggest a more significant role for Miriam behind the present text. They point to the fact that both Aaron and Miriam have prophetic roles (Exod 7:1 and 15:20). (Why, then, do most historical critics suggest a more important role for Aaron but ignore the data which suggests a more important role for Miriam?) They point, also, to the genealogies which include Miriam along with Moses and Aaron. Women were so rarely included in genealogies that, for one to be included, she must have held a major role and been a vivid memory for the communities of the texts' authors.

Finally, feminist interpreters point to a text, written no earlier than the eighth century B.C. and probably considerably later, Mic 6:4. The prophet Micah is speaking the word of the Lord against Israel, and reminding them of what Yahweh had done for them: God had brought them up out of Egypt and redeemed them from the land of slavery. Yahweh had sent Moses—and Aaron and Miriam—to lead them. The verse clearly puts Miriam on a level of importance at least equal to Aaron, if not also equal to Moses!

Interpreters will never know for certain whether the original form of Exod 15 had Miriam as the subject of v 1 or whether the present form is the original. In either case, however, Miriam does emerge as having played a significant role in the exodus.

The Story

Numbers 12 adds to our knowledge of the character of Miriam; this time quite explicitly she is a victim of patriarchal bias. Verses 1 and 2 present the reader with jealousy and sibling rivalry. Moses had married a Cushite woman and this became the occasion for Miriam and Aaron to criticize him. (Were they criticizing his polygamy—Zipporah was also his wife—or were they pointing to the fact that the Cushite was a foreigner [cf. Gen 28]? Most likely the text reflects the period when marriages to foreign women were prohibited, and it is used here as an excuse to reprimand Moses.)

Miriam and Aaron's criticism takes the form of resentment, of assertion of their own equality with Moses. The Lord had spoken to them, too (cf. Exod 7:1; 15:20). Verse 3 is parenthetical, describing the humble character of Moses, and implying a contrast with the proud characters of Aaron and Miriam. The narrator reports that the Lord intervened. First, God called together the three siblings; then, God became present in a pillar of cloud at the entrance of the Tent of Meeting; and finally, God called apart the two,

Miriam and Aaron (vv 4–5). God, speaking in direct speech, proceeded to explain to Miriam and Aaron how they differed from Moses. They were prophets and God did speak to them, but in visions and dreams. In contrast to this, God spoke to Moses face to face. Aaron and Miriam should have been afraid to challenge their brother (vv 6–8).

The encounter with God ended there; the cloud lifted from the tent. But the consequences of that encounter did not end for Miriam. God was angry and God punished her; she became leprous (vv 9–10). Since the pillar of cloud was no longer present in their midst, Aaron turned to Moses to entreat him on Miriam's behalf. He asked that Moses not hold their sin against them (vv 11–12). The narrator reports that Moses heeded Aaron's request and asked God to heal Miriam (v 13).

The Lord's reply to Moses is curious. Nowhere in the entire Old Testament is there a similar comment. God told Moses to leave Miriam outside the camp for seven days. Seven, a symbolic number for completion, refers to the duration of an appropriate time after which Miriam could be rehabilitated and return. But God seems to put before Moses a rhetorical question, explaining or even justifying his punishment of her. Would she not likewise have been in disgrace for seven days if her father had spit in her face (v 14)? The narrator concludes the episode with a report that the Israelites did not break camp until after Miriam returned (vv 15–16).

Deuteronomy 24:9, clearly a later text, is parenthetically included among the laws Israel is to follow in the land, and in this instance, what provisions to follow for cases of leprosy. The verse functions as an incentive; the Israelites are to remember what the Lord did to Miriam, both the affliction and the cure.

Interpretation

Numbers 12, interpreted from a patriarchal perspective, may serve an aetiological function: how did such a horrible disease as leprosy ever come into existence in the first place? The verses also function to verify the uniqueness of Moses; whereas others are prophets, he is in a class by himself.

Viewed from a feminist perspective, the text is one more incident of prejudice against women. Both Aaron and Miriam had challenged Moses; both Miriam and Aaron had appeared before the Lord; both the man and the woman, therefore, should become victims of leprosy. Why, then, is Miriam singled out? Why is she the only one to suffer? Is the answer to be found in the hierarchical way the narrative is told and in Miriam's inferior status? When God is on the scene—in the pillar of cloud—the three siblings appear before him; when the pillar of cloud is gone, then the two appear before Moses. But even between the two, there is a hierarchy. Only the woman becomes leprous. This creates the situation where the one brother, Aaron, intercedes before the other brother, Moses, for sake of the third sibling, the men's sister, Miriam.

Is there another answer to why Miriam is singled out, why she is the only one to suffer? Perhaps the answer can be found in God's reply to Moses when he intervenes on Miriam's behalf. Did the author here intend to trivialize her affliction, betraying that it was a common practice to hold a woman in disgrace for seven days, betraying also that it was a father's prerogative (and perhaps a husband's as well)—and not an uncommon occurrence at that—to spit in one's daughter's face. We have no way of knowing whether such treatment was a common practice since this is the only place in the Old Testament where there is mention of spitting in a woman's face. If such treatment was in fact common practice, then the text is sad testimony to a degrading custom in Israel's patriarchal culture.

Summary

Miriam, as the texts of the Old Testament present her, is a complex character. She is a prophetess; she ranks equally with her brothers in accounts of both her birth and her death (cf. Num 20:1). But she is also very much the product of a patriarchal society. Though she celebrates the victory of the exodus, she is not given full credit for the song of victory. Though she shares responsibility with Aaron for their challenge to Moses, only she must pay the penalty. The text betrays its patriarchal prejudice, and Miriam serves as an excellent example of the patriarchal culture that produced the text.

Ministering Women
at the Tent of Meeting
(Exodus 35; 38)

The Story

Exodus 35:1—38:20 details the building of the "Tabernacle of
the Tent of the Presence" according to all the directions that Yahweh had commanded Moses (Exod 25—30). Historical critics as-
cribe this text to the Priestly source; it is usually considered
anachronistic, that is, it details Israel's temple, which dates to the
monarchy, ascribing its specifications to the original tabernacle
and to Yahweh's directive.

A careful examination of 35:20–29 reveals women's contribu-
tions, as well as men's, to the construction of the tabernacle and the
fulfillment of Yahweh's command. "Men and women alike"
brought some of their valuables, including gold, for the tabernacle
(v 22). The men, specifically, brought copper, silver, and acacia
wood (v 24); those women who could brought spun yarn, fine linen,
and goats' hair (vv 25–26). "Every Israelite man and woman" who
wished to contribute did so (v 29).

Though the tabernacle (and later the temple) is clearly associated with men, this text does acknowledge that both men's and
women's offerings were needed and used to build the Tabernacle
of the Tent of Presence. Both men and women contributed with
such generosity that they even had to be told to stop giving (36:6).

Interpretation

Traditional interpretation of these chapters is concerned with
sources and the suggestion that perhaps the tabernacle and the tent
each represent a separate source from Israel's past. Each had, in its
own time and its own locale, represented that place where Yahweh
was especially present in their midst. The development of the Pentateuch effected the combining of sources so that eventually the
tabernacle came to be understood as being housed in the tent.

Of concern to feminists is the fact that women are, indeed, included; they contribute to the tabernacle's construction. Whereas

Exod 25:2–4 would, for example, allow us to believe that men provided the yarn and linen and goats' hair, and all of the gold, the text of Exod 35 contradicts this and credits women with these gifts. Though most of the gifts provided by the women are from the "domestic sphere," nevertheless, without their offerings there could have been no veil for the tabernacle (36:35), no screen for its entrance (v 37), and no curtains (36:8–13).

The Story and Interpretation

The chapters continue to detail the execution of Yahweh's plans for the tabernacle. Exodus 38 records the building of the acacia-wood altar, with horns overlaid in bronze at each corner (v 1). The narrator reports that bronze vessels for the altar—including pots, shovels, tossing bowls, forks, and firepans—were cast (v 3), as well as a bronze grating which had bronze rings at each corner for the acacia-wood poles with which to carry the tabernacle (vv 5–7).

The narrator continues with a report about a bronze basin and stand which were made, but the stand and basin—in contrast to the other vessels described—had been made from "the bronze mirrors of the women who were on duty at the entrance to the Tent of the Presence" (v 8). This text reveals at least two insights.

First of all, not only did women contribute gold and yarn and linen and goats' hair, for which the text has previously credited them, but they also contributed bronze. Whereas Exod 25 could have given the reader the impression that men possessed all the valuables, chap. 35 makes the reader aware of some valuables which were held by women. Chapter 38 now adds to that picture.

Second, who are the women whose duty it was to be stationed at the entrance of the Tent of the Presence? Were they women of means, the upper class who because of their wealth—and potential for donations to the tabernacle—could command such an honor? Were they prostitutes (cf. 1 Sam 2:22)? But surely the chapters which cite the details of the Lord's temple could not include, and thereby tacitly approve of, that role! We are left with an unanswered question. What role—or roles—did women play vis-à-vis Israel's tabernacle and temple? Does the text here present its reader with a brief allusion to a function and a place for women in worship which—because of the patriarchal culture which produced the text—historians will never be able to uncover adequately?

Summary

Segments of the Book of Exodus which historical critics attribute to the exilic or postexilic Priestly source, and which are, therefore, thought to be historical reconstructions of Israel's early tabernacle from the memory of Israel's first temple, contain brief references to women. Their importance lies in what the verses say about women's contribution to the tabernacle and in what the verses fail to say—what roles women could play vis-à-vis Israel's worship. That women played only a very small part in Israel's worship is suggested historically by the patriarchal culture; that Exod 25—40 makes little mention of women is a logical consequence. Nevertheless, what little is said needs to be remembered, especially since the references may be unwitting indications of women's greater influence.

**Mahlah, Noah, Hoglah,
Milcah, and Tirzah:
Zelophehad's Docile Daughters
(Numbers 26; 27; 36)**

The Story

Numbers 26 records a census of the whole Israelite community by families—the clans of the twelve sons of Jacob (v 1). Among those named is Zelophehad, a descendant of Manasseh who bore no sons. A reference is made here, however, to Zelophehad's daughters and each of the five is named: Mahlah, Noah, Hoglah, Milcah, and Tirzah (v 33). Their inclusion is unusual since women are rarely named in genealogies, and when they are, it is usually a single exception. When one reads further, however, one realizes that this insertion was made in light of the narrative about Zelophehad and his daughters which follows.

Reading Num 27:1–11 carefully, one observes peculiarities right from its outset. Verse 1 gives a very detailed legitimation of

Zelophehad. He is the son of Hepher who is the son of Gilead who is the son of Makir who is the son of Manasseh who is the son of Joseph. In other words, he is a true blue blood. Because Zelophehad has such a noble lineage, his daughters, too, are named. They are Mahlah, Noah, Hoglah, Milcah, and Tirzah.

The narrator informs the reader that these daughters stationed themselves at the entrance of the Tent of Meeting before Moses, before the priest, and before the leaders of the assembly, and presented their case (v 2). Their father had died in the desert without having begotten a son (v 3). His daughters did not think it right that their father's name should perish (a son continued to keep alive the name of his father, which was why—at a time when there was no belief in life after death—sons were of such importance; see the Levirate law, p. 17; cf. Gen 38, pp. 44–46). They therefore requested that they be the recipients of property among their father's relatives (v 4).

The narrator informs the reader that Moses took the matter to the Lord, who confirmed the women's position (vv 5–7). Further, the Lord proposed a general ruling: if a man should die without having first begotten a son, then his property should be turned over to that man's daughter. If the man shall have died without having begotten either a son or a daughter, then his inheritance should be given to his brothers. But if the deceased does not have any brothers, then the inheritance should go to his uncles on his father's side of the family. Failing that, the property should go to his nearest kinsman in his clan (vv 8–11). The context clearly indicates that males are the normal inheritors of property.

Interpretation

To better understand this text, one should recall the Levirate law (see p. 17 above). It requires that a woman who had not borne a son to her husband before the husband died should be taken by the husband's brother, and the first child born to that union should be raised up for the dead man. That son would then serve to guarantee that the deceased's name would not be forgotten in Israel (cf. Deut 25:5–10). The text of Num was most likely composed before the text in Deut. There are similarities but also differences. The major difference in the Num passage is that daughters qualify to inherit their father's property. They cannot, however, carry forward his name. That may be the reason why the later text makes no provisions for daughters' inheriting from their fathers. If there is no son, the property of a deceased man—including his wife—must go to the man's brother (or closest kinsman) in order to guarantee a son for the dead man and thus a future for his name in Israel.

Feminists reflecting on the text from the vantage point of the twentieth century remark how, at least in most Western countries, a man's name is still carried on through his sons, whereas a woman's name, which is her father's, is lost when she marries and takes on the name of her husband.

The Story

Numbers 36 returns to the narrative of the inheritance of the daughters of Zelophehad. The family heads of the clan of which Zelophehad had been a part, the clan of Gilead who was the son of Makir who was the son of Manasseh who was the son of Joseph, approached Moses and the leaders (v 1). They had a problem, even possibly a contradiction in their understanding of the will of God. The problem was this.

God has assigned to each of the Israelite tribes a part of the land which is to remain always within the tribe. God has also assigned to the daughters of Zelophehad the portion of land which belonged to their father. When the daughters of Zelophehad marry, the property belonging to them will cease to be theirs and will become the property of the men they marry. But, if the daughters marry men who are not members of their own tribe, that will mean that the daughters' property will cease to belong within the tribe. It will at the time of the marriage or at least at the Year of Jubilee be transferred to another tribe. But that will violate the provision that had allotted the land to Gilead in the first place (vv 2–4).

The narrator reports that God, through Moses, offers the solution to the problem. Yes, daughters may inherit their father's property if there are no sons, as in the case of the daughters of Zelophehad. However, the land allotted to the tribes must remain within the tribes. Therefore, daughters who have inherited property will be permitted to marry only within their tribe, only from those men who belong to the tribe of their father. That way the land will not be transferred from one tribe to another at the time of any marriage (vv 5–9).

The narrator concludes with a report that the daughters of Zelophehad—Mahlah, Noah, Hoglah, Milcah, and Tirzah—obeyed the Lord's command. They married their cousins on their father's side, within their clan and tribe. They saw to it that their inheritance remained within the family (vv 10–12).

Interpretation

Just as women belonged to men, so also did property—especially the precious land. If a daughter's father were living, her future husband would be determined between her father and the family or man who wanted her. If a father were deceased, one might suppose that the daughter had more control over whom she would marry. She could, after all, own property (chap. 27). However, there were always laws to restrict women. Without the restriction of obedience to one's father in the selection of a husband, fatherless daughters now had another restriction imposed. This property law narrowed the options considerably. She might have had more say in choosing a husband, but she had considerably fewer men from whom to choose. As part of what had been her father's property, *she* must remain—with the property—within his tribe.

Summary

Together Num 27 and 36 present the reader with interesting insights into patriarchy. Within patriarchy itself, there are degrees of the superior/inferior relationship. Women do have some freedoms, some opportunities to exercise control. If one stops reading the Book of Numbers somewhere between chap. 27 and chap. 36, one may rightly conclude that some women, at least, held the kind of power and prestige that comes from owning land and other property. If one reads through Num 36, however, one realizes that even this is limited and carefully controlled. A daughter was expected to marry; that was a given of the society. It was also a given of the society that a propertied daughter must relinquish her property to the man she would marry. The result was that a daughter who had inherited her father's property was only temporarily in control of it. And though she may have had some say in whom she married, she would—ironically enough, and in contrast to our society!—have had considerably fewer potential suitors than her unpropertied counterpart.

**Circumcising the Heart:
Potential for Women?
(Deuteronomy 10; 30)**

The Story

The Book of Deuteronomy is understood to be a compilation of those laws that came to be important to the Israelites once they had entered the land of Canaan (mid-thirteenth century B.C.). Most of the laws, though projected back into the mouth of Moses, are products of the monarchial period (the tenth through the sixth centuries B.C.). They spell out in detail the Israelites' relationship to Yahweh—what it means in practice that Yahweh is their God and they are Yahweh's people—and their relationship to one another, as well as to foreigners and aliens. Historical critics suppose Deut 12—26 to have been, originally, independent laws formed into an ancient core, the earliest source, then combined somewhat later with the contents of Deut 4:44—11:32. Finally, Deut 4:44—26 was joined to Deut 1:1—4:43 and to the final chapters of the book, texts thought to have been written by the Deuteronomist(s). The "Deuteronomist(s)" is the name given to that editor or school who joined, by means of a unifying theological perspective, the contents of the Book of Deuteronomy to the contents of Joshua—2 Kings to form what now is called the "Deuteronomistic History."

Within each of the two major sections of the Book of Deuteronomy one finds the curious and yet very significant phrase: "circumcise your hearts." These texts deserve close examination.

Deuteronomy 10:12–22 is an exhortation by Moses to the Israelites to persevere in covenant fidelity. The Israelites are to fear the Lord, to walk in God's ways, to love God, to serve God with all their heart and soul, and to observe the commands and decrees which Moses was giving them for their own good (vv 12–13). Moses' method of persuasion is to remind the Israelites of who God is and of their unique relationship to God: the heavens and the earth and everything in them belong to God, and yet, among all that is God's, Israel is special. God has chosen them above all others (vv 14–15). Buried in this exposition is the exhortation that the Israelites are to circumcise their hearts and be stiff-necked no longer (v 16).

Returning to who God is and the Israelites' unique relationship with God, Moses affirms that Israel's God is God above other gods, the God of gods, the Lord of lords, the mighty, awesome God (v 17). How does this great God, Israel's God, act? God shows no partiality; God accepts no bribes; God defends the cause of the fatherless and the widow; God loves aliens and gives them food and shelter (v 18). The implication is that Israel is to be like their God. They are to show no partiality (cf. Lev 19:15; Deut 16:19); they are to accept no bribes (cf. Exod 23:8; Deut 16:19); they, too, are to defend the cause of the fatherless and the orphan (e.g., Exod 22:22; Deut 14:29; 24:19–22; 26:12–13). The Israelites are to love the aliens; Moses gives them additional motivation. God loves the aliens, that is true. But the Israelites are to remember their own experience and how God loved them: they themselves were aliens in Egypt (v 19; cf. Exod 22:21; Deut 14:29; 24:17–18).

Moses continues his directives: the Israelites are to fear and serve their God (v 20; cf. v 12). They are to hold fast to God and swear in God's name. Again, Moses returns to who it is who commands this kind of response from them: God is their praise and their God. Their God performed great wonders on their behalf which they themselves saw (v 21). One such wonder was the fulfillment of the covenant made to Abraham: from a small number they have become as numerous as the stars in the sky (v 22; cf. Gen 15:5).

Interpretation

This text gives the reader a clear illustration of how God was understood to observe the laws which the Israelites also were to obey.

In fact, God's so acting provided the reason for men's so behaving. In this patriarchal society, God was understood to be male; here the male God is understood to be like the best of men; "he" does what men are supposed to do; "he" practices what "he" preaches. It is God's behavior which provides the pattern for human action.

Many feminists use this text as another illustration of how the biblical author depicts God as a God of the oppressed. This text (and it is similar to many others) stresses Israel's responsibility to the powerless of the society. Though the passage represents Israel as a hierarchical society—with its judges at one end of the scale and its fatherless, widows, and aliens at the other—it nevertheless calls that society to provide for those on the bottom rung of its socioeconomic ladder.

Buried in this text (which is artfully composed of exhortation, motivation, and obligation) is the directive: Circumcise your hearts. The author here transfers a physical act, possible only for males, to a symbolic one, possible for all human beings. The author thus transforms an essential sign of covenant partnership (cf. Gen 17:10–14; Exod 4:24–26) from one which can include only males to one which can include both men and women. Though historical critics may be right in believing that the text, as a product of its culture, is intended only for men, still, a text such as this leaves a door open for women. All the people—men, women, children, aliens—are to learn to fear the Lord and faithfully follow God's laws (cf. Deut 31:12).

The Story

Deuteronomy 30:1–10 presupposes a different historical situation. The author envisions not Israel's entrance into the land (Deut 10), but Israel's return to the land after exile. Most historical critics date this text to the late sixth century B.C.

Verses 1–3 speak, from retrospect, of what "will" inevitably happen to Israel. They will experience the Lord's blessings and they will experience the Lord's curses (cf. Deut 28). The blessings will have provided them with prosperity and progeny in the land; the curses will have resulted in Israel's loss of the land. The all-knowing author tells them their future. In exile they will do a lot of thinking about their past (v 1). They will regret their unfaithfulness to the Lord and come again to obey God (v 2). Then the Lord will act on their behalf. The God who had punished them by removing their good fortune will now restore it. God will act compassionately and bring the dispersed people together again (v 3). The speaker is Moses and he assures the Israelites that "even if" the people have been scattered all over everywhere, God will renew the covenant; God will return them to the land which belonged to their ancestors and will again bless them with progeny and prosperity. In fact, they will be "even more" prosperous and fruitful than their ancestors (vv 4–6).

Verse 6 transforms the phrase of Deut 10:16, "circumcise your hearts." It is now not they, the Israelites, who are to do it (an imperative), but rather the Lord who will do it for them. The Lord will circumcise their hearts and the hearts of their descendants so that they may love the Lord with all their heart and soul, and so that they may live (cf. v 19). In contrast, Israel's enemies—those who have hated and persecuted them—will receive the curses, that is, death (cf. v 19).

When Israel obeys the Lord and follows God's commands (v 8; cf. v 2), then the Lord will increase their prosperity (v 9; cf. v 5). The Lord will have the same posture toward them as God had toward their ancestors if they obey fully and turn to the Lord with all their heart and soul (v 10; cf. v 2).

Interpretation

Historical critics point to the importance of this text. It is a key reference in the Old Testament to the exile and one of the most explicit ones in the Pentateuch (cf. Lev 26:43–45; Deut 31:16–18). Deuteronomy 30:1–10 is considered to be an interpolation, inserted as an addition or updating into an already-existent passage. In addition, historical critics are intent to identify the lands to which Israel has been scattered (vv 1, 3–4; Egypt, Babylonia, etc.), as well as Israel's enemies on whom the Lord's curses will fall (v 7; e.g., Babylonia, Edom).

Literary critics point to the author's emphasis on obedience (vv 2, 8, 10), and they remark upon the relationship of past to present in the passage. The laws are being given today (vv 2, 8); they will be violated (what the author knows did happen but what his character Moses predicts). The author addresses his present as though he were addressing the speaker's future. From a literary perspective, the author has chosen a skillful and unthreatening method of exhortation.

Feminists reflect on the text's patriarchal presuppositions. The land belonged to Israel's "fathers"; the Israelites, once restored, will become more prosperous than their "fathers" (v 5). The Lord will take delight in them as "he" had taken delight in their "fathers" (v 9). Feminists agree that it is important to uncover this patriarchal bias because the term occurs so frequently with respect to Israel's most treasured assets—the covenant, the land, progeny, and prosperity. They disagree, however, about what to do once the bias is recognized. Some emphasize the historical setting of the texts, a patriarchal culture, and render a literal translation of the Hebrew preserving the masculine form for God. Others, conscious of the Bible's place in the prayer of believing twentieth-century communities, translate the text naming God without sexual specification and the "ancestors," choosing an English rendering that includes females (as this text can).

Again, it is important to emphasize that the Lord will circumcise the hearts of the present Israelites (Moses' audience and the exiles!) and of their descendants (the exiles more explicitly). The Lord will establish a new covenant (cf. Jer 31:31–34), not only restoring the people to former favor but improving upon that favor (cf. vv 5, 9). Again, making circumcised hearts rather than circumcised bodies the appropriate sign of the covenant relationship with Yahweh makes that relationship more directly available to women; access to that relationship is no longer only through the penis of father and husband.

Summary

The reader should not be so naive as to think that Deut 10 and 30, with the "circumcision of hearts," were, when they were originally composed, meant to include women on a equal footing with men in the covenant relationship with Yahweh. Though it is true that many of the demands of the covenant also applied to women, it was primarily to men that the laws were directed. Then, as heads of houses, it was their job to see that the women obeyed. Yet the texts stand, and the fact that they transform a one-time physical action into a lifetime personal posture, the basis of which is not sex-defined, can bear abundant fruit for women in the present.

CONCLUSION

The first five books of the OT, the Torah, stand for Jews as the primary religious text. Traditionally, these words were understood to have been given by God to Moses; all else—the Prophets, the Writings, the Talmud—were considered to be commentary on the Torah. For Christians, too, this text has held a special place of honor; the Pentateuch contains the beginnings—the exodus and the covenant.

Though the text of the Pentateuch is a product of many hands over several centuries, most of the hands throughout this period were influenced by patriarchal biases. This does not mean that all of the texts are equally patriarchal, or that all expressions of patriarchy are equally oppressive. What it does mean is that these texts, though believed by communities of faith to be inspired writings, were nevertheless influenced by the culture which developed them. This section has tried to show how patriarchy is present in the particular texts known as the Pentateuch (and their subsequent interpretation). Patriarchy should not be ignored; rather, it should be recognized for what it is, a product not of divine inspiration but of historical conditioning. The section has also tried to show how the Pentateuch has also incorporated texts which are open to non-patriarchal interpretation by contemporary believers.

RECOMMENDED READINGS
The Pentateuch

Adler, Rachel. "A Mother in Israel: Aspects of the Mother Role in Jewish Myth." In *Beyond Androcentrism,* edited by Rita M. Gross. Missoula, Mont.: Scholars Press, 1977.

Allen, Christine Garside. "Who Was Rebekah?" In *Beyond Androcentrism,* ed. Gross.

Aitken, Kenneth T. "The Wooing of Rebekah: A Study in the Development of the Tradition." *JSOT* 30 (1984): 3–23.

Bal, Mieke. "Sexuality, Sin and Sorrow: The Emergence of the Female Character (A Reading of Genesis 1—3)." *Poetics Today* 6 (1985): 21–42.

Beeston, A. F. L. "One Flesh." *VT* 36 (1986): 115–17.

Bird, Phyllis A. "'Male and Female He Created Them': Gen 1:27b in the Context of the Priestly Account of Creation." *HTR* 74 (1981): 129–60.

Brenner, Athalya. "Female Social Behavior: Two Descriptive Patterns within the 'Birth of the Hero' Paradigm." *VT* 36 (1986): 257–73.

Brock, Sebastian. "Genesis 22: Where Was Sarah?" *ExpTim* 96 (1984): 14–17.

Carmichael, Calum M. "Forbidden Mixtures." *VT* 32 (1982): 394–415.

Crawley, Joanne. "Faith of Our Mothers: The Dark Night of Sara, Rebeka and Rachel." *RR* 45 (1986): 531–37.

Eslinger, Lyle. "More Drafting Techniques in Deuteronomic Laws." *VT* 34 (1984): 221–26.

Exum, J. Cheryl. "The Mothers of Israel: The Patriarchal Narratives from a Feminist Perspective." *BRev* 2/1 (1986): 60–67.

———. "'You Shall Let Every Daughter Live': A Study of Exodus 1:8—2:10." *Semeia* 28 (1983): 63–82.

Frymer-Kensky, Tikva. "The Strange Case of the Suspected Sotah (Numbers 5:11–31)." *VT* 34 (1984): 11–26.

Hamill, Thomas. "The Bible and Its Imagination: A Modest Sounding of Its Harlot's Evaluation." *ITQ* 52 (1986): 96–108.

Hanson, Paul D. "God Metaphors and Sexism in the Old Testament." *ER* 27 (1975): 316–24.

Higgins, Jean M. "The Myth of Eve: The Temptress." *JAAR* 44 (Dec. 1976): 639–47.

Horowitz, Maryanne C. "The Image of God in Man—Is Woman Included?" *HTR* 72 (1979): 175–206.

Houtman, C. "Another Look at Forbidden Mixtures." *VT* 34 (1984): 226–28.

Jagendorf, Zvi. "'In the Morning, Behold, It Was Leah': Genesis and the Reversal of Sexual Knowledge." *Proof* 4 (1984): 187–92.

Kromminga, Carl G. "Remember Lot's Wife: Preaching Old Testament Narrative Texts." *CTJ* 18 (1983): 32–46.

Lipinski, E. "The Wife's Right to Divorce in the Light of Ancient Near Eastern Tradition." *JLA* 4 (1981): 9–27.

McKeating, Henry. "A Response to Dr. Phillips." *JSOT* 20 (1981): 25–26 (see below).

———. "Sanctions Against Adultery in Ancient Israelite Society, with Some Reflections on Methodology in the Study of Old Testament Ethics." *JSOT* 11 (1979): 57–72.

Mendes, Rui de. "Social Justice in Israel's Law." *BibBh* 11 (1985): 10–16.

Milgrom, Jacob. "The Betrothed Slave-girl, Lev 19:20–22." *ZAW* 89 (1977): 43–50.

———. "On the Suspected Adulteress (Num 5:11–31)." *VT* 35 (1985): 368–69.

Phillips, Anthony. "Another Look at Adultery." *JSOT* 20 (1981): 3–25.

Pilch, John J. "Biblical Leprosy and Body Symbolism." *BTB* 11 (1981): 108–13.

Rendsburg, Gary A. "Notes on Genesis xxxv." *VT* 34 (1984): 361–66.

Scharbert, J. "*Bēyt 'Āb* as a Sociological Unit in the Old Testament." In *Von Kanaan bis Kerala. Festschrift für Prof. Mag. Dr. Dr. J. P. M. van der Ploeg O. P. zur Vollendung des siebzigsten Lebensjahres am 4 Juli 1979*, edited by W. C. Delsman et al. AOAT 211. Kelevaer: Butzon & Bercker, 1982.

Schierling, Marla J. "Primeval Woman: A Yahwistic View of Woman in Genesis 1—11:19." *JTSoA* 42 (1983): 5–9.

Schungel-Straumann, Helen. "Tamar." *BK* 39 (1984): 148–57.

Selvidge, Marla J. "Mark 5:25–34 and Leviticus 15:19–20: A Reaction to Restrictive Purity Regulations." *JBL* 103 (1984): 619–23.

Sharp, Donald. "In Defense of Rebecca?" *BTB* 10 (1980): 164–68.

Steinberg, Naomi. "Gender Roles in the Rebekah Cycle." *USQR* 39 (1984): 175–88.

Tosato, Angelo. "The Law of Leviticus 18:18: A Reexamination." *CBQ* 46 (1984): 199–214.

Trible, Phyllis. *God and the Rhetoric of Sexuality.* OBT. Philadelphia: Fortress Press, 1978.

———. *Texts of Terror.* OBT. Philadelphia: Fortress Press, 1984.

Turner, Mary Donovan. "Rebekah: Ancestor of Faith." *LTQ* 20 (1985): 42–49.

Vogels, Walter W. F. "'It Is Not Good that the "Mensch" Should Be Alone; I Will Make Him/Her a Helper Fit for Him/Her,' (Gen 2:18)." *EgT* 9 (1978): 9–35.

Wander, Nathaniel. "Structure, Contradiction, and 'Resolution' in Mythology: Father's Brother's Daughter Marriage and the Treatment of Women in Gen 11:50." *JANESCU* 13 (1981): 75–99.

Wenham, G. J. "Leviticus 27:2–8 and the Price of the Slaves." *ZAW* 90 (1978): 264–65.

———. "The Restoration of Marriage Reconsidered." *JJS* 30 (1979): 36–40.

_____. "Why Does Sexual Intercourse Defile (Lev 15:18)?" *ZAW* 95 (1983): 432–34.

West, Angela. "Genesis and Patriarchy." *TNB* 62 (1981): 17–32.

_____. "Genesis and Patriarchy: Part II. Women and the End of Time." *TNB* 62 (1981): 420–32.

Zarovitch, Yair. "The Woman's Rights in the Biblical Law of Divorce." *JLA* 4 (1981): 28–46.

Ziderman, I. Irving. "Rebecca's Encounter with Abraham's Servant." *DD* 14 (1985/86): 124–25.

⇻ PART II ⇺

THE DEUTERONOMISTIC HISTORY

INTRODUCTION

For many Christians the Books of Joshua through 2 Kings were associated with the "historical books" of the Old Testament, precisely because their contents were believed to contain an accurate account of past events. They were thus distinguished from the books of the Prophets and the wisdom literature. The Jewish community, on the other hand, distinguished between the Torah—the five books of Moses—and the Prophets.

The Former Prophets

The Jewish tradition, meditating on the words of the Books of Joshua through 2 Kings, concluded that the books could not adequately be interpreted without serious consideration being given to the role played by Israel's prophets in effecting that history. After all, is not Joshua the messenger of God, commissioned by Yahweh to take Moses' place and to bring the people into the land? And who can ignore the prophetic role of Samuel, who inaugurates the kingship when he anoints Saul and who afterward, in Yahweh's name, rejects Saul in favor of David? And can the reader ignore Nathan, who predicts to David that he will have a dynasty and that his son will build the Lord's temple (2 Sam 7)? The prophet Ahijah warns of the division of the kingdom into north and south (1 Kgs 11), and the prophetess Huldah predicts Jerusalem's fall (2 Kgs 22). And there are Gad, and Elijah and Elisha, and Micaiah, and Isaiah, and the

71

others. Surely these books tell the story of God's interaction with Israel through divinely appointed mediators whose power exceeds that of kings and priests and people! It is not difficult to see why the Jews, reading their sacred history as recorded in Joshua through 2 Kings, came to understand it as the account of God's word and action to and for the people through chosen messengers, the prophets.

Historical Considerations

In 1944 the German biblical scholar Martin Noth put forth the hypothesis that the Books of Joshua through 2 Kings were compiled by someone (or several persons of similar perspective) whom Noth named the "Deuteronomistic Historian." This writer, using ancient sources—already-collected accounts of military leaders, excerpts from the chronicles of the kings of both Israel and Judah, miracle stories, legends, and so on—edited his sources into a unified whole through the careful inclusion and exclusion of available information as well as by the creation and addition of unifying materials. The final redacted product tells the story of Israel's past from the perspective of fidelity or infidelity to Israel's covenant with Yahweh as specified in the Book of Deuteronomy, hence the name "Deuteronomistic History."

Though most historical-critical scholars accept Noth's thesis of a unified History, they differ as to the dating of that History, the setting where it was produced, the reasons or occasion for its having been composed, whether or not there are two major redactions—an exilic and a postexilic one—and the purpose of the History. Was it written to explain why Judah fell, from a rather pessimistic perspective, with no other purpose than to account for the present situation? Was the History written for a positive purpose, as an incentive for the present and the future? Depending on when one determines that the text was compiled, and how many redactions one thinks it had, one may deduce the purpose for its having been written in the first place.

Deuteronomistic Theology

Regardless of its authorship, date, or setting, anyone reading the literature contained in the Books of Joshua through 2 Kings will recognize the prominence of a controlling theological perspective: if you are good, God will bless you; if you sin, you will be cursed. This theology is most noticeably expressed in the Book of Judges. There, the people are portrayed as being faithful to Yahweh, as long as a judge provides them leadership. When the judge dies, however, the people begin to worship idols. This angers Yahweh who sells them into the hands of their enemies. Oppressed, they cry out to the Lord for deliverance. Yahweh hears their prayer and sends a savior to deliver them. While the savior/judge lives, all is well. When the judge dies, however, they again fall into sin and the pattern repeats itself (e.g., Judg 3). Though less fully elaborated elsewhere, it is this theology—obedience brings the Lord's favor; disobedience brings rejection and consequent punishment—that permeates these books.

Deuteronomistic Additions

The Deuteronomistic Historian is thought to have accomplished his purposes—unification of the sources and a controlling theology—by composing appropriate texts himself. These include "farewell speeches," including Moses' in Deut 31, Joshua's in Josh 23, and Samuel's in 1 Sam 12. They also include interpretive segments of texts, such as those explaining the fall of Samaria (2 Kgs 17) and Judah (2 Kgs 24—25), and verses added to texts which record particularly critical events (Solomon's role in temple building in 2 Sam 7, and later temple interpretation in 1 Kgs 8). Interspersed throughout the History are key words and phrases that focus the reader's attention on the theology which, for the Deuteronomistic Historian, directs the History.

Literary Considerations

Most literary studies of this segment of the Old Testament have centered on major characters and their activities—for example, on Samuel, Saul, David, and Solomon. Other studies have included analyses of "The Succession Narrative" (2 Sam 7 [or 9]—20; 1 Kgs 1—2) and works dealing with the *function* of any one of a number of chapters in the History as a whole. The poetic version of Deborah's defeat of Sisera (Judg 5) has been compared and contrasted with its prose counterpart (Judg 4). The genre of miracle story found in 1 Kgs 17—2 Kgs 9, the legends of the prophets Elijah and Elisha, has been analyzed. However, most of the studies of the content of Joshua through 2 Kings as literature which have been made in the past couple of centuries have been closely related to and dependent on historical criticism.

THEMES FROM A FEMINIST PERSPECTIVE

The Deuteronomistic History contains the same basic patriarchal prejudice as the Pentateuch, but this perspective is specified in the History by the particular historical content and literary genre which compose it. It is therefore necessary to look again at the themes to see how they work themselves out in the Deuteronomistic History.

Patriarchy and Hierarchy

Patriarchy has many expressions but one exceptionally common in the Deuteronomistic History is the theme of the unnamed woman. She is attached to someone else (usually a named man) or something (usually a particular place) or she is given a precise description or a symbolic significance. She, however, is anonymous; she herself has no name. There are at least twenty-three such characters alluded to in the Deuteronomistic History:

Gideon's unnamed concubine (Judg 8);
Jephthah's unnamed daughter (Judg 11);
Manoah's unnamed barren wife (Judg 13—14);
Samson's unnamed Philistine wife (Judg 14);
Micah's unnamed mother (Judg 17);
the unnamed victim of Benjamite rape (Judg 19);
Phineas's unnamed wife (1 Sam 4);
the unnamed maidens who brought together Samuel and Saul (1 Sam 9);
the unnamed female medium who recalled Samuel for Saul (1 Sam 28);

the unnamed female nurse who saved Mephibosheth (2 Sam 4);
David's unnamed wives and unnamed concubines (2 Sam 5; 17);
the unnamed wise woman of Tekoa (2 Sam 14);
the unnamed maidservant who saved David (2 Sam 17);
the unnamed woman who secured Sheba's death (2 Sam 20);
the unnamed daughter of Pharaoh who became Solomon's wife
  (1 Kgs 3);
the unnamed widow of Hiram's father (1 Kgs 7);
the unnamed sister of Tahpenes (1 Kgs 11);
the unnamed wife of Jeroboam (1 Kgs 14);
the unnamed widow of Zarephath (1 Kgs 17);
the unnamed prophet's wife (2 Kgs 4);
the unnamed Shunammite woman (2 Kgs 4);
the unnamed Israelite maid of Namaan's unnamed wife
  (2 Kgs 5);
the unnamed wife or concubine of Zedekiah (2 Kgs 25).

In addition to the category of unnamed women, women usually identified by men, there is an even more buried category—women who exist in the texts only by inference. The fathers are named and the sons whom they begot are named, but what about the women who bore the sons? What about, for example,

the woman who bore Joel and Abijah to Samuel (1 Sam 8);
the woman who bore Saul to Kish (1 Sam 9);
the woman who bore David to Jesse (1 Sam 17);
the woman who bore Mica to Mephibosheth (2 Sam 9);
the woman who bore Tamar to Absalom (2 Sam 14)?

Moreover, who are the women who bore children to Ahab (1 Kgs 20) and the woman who bore two sons to Zedekiah (2 Kgs 25)?

Ancient Israel condemns harlots. Moreover, harlotry (prostitution) is associated with idolatry in both the Pentateuch and the Deuteronomistic History. Though harlotry is not a sin confined to women, patriarchal culture and the biblical texts most frequently portray it that way (e.g., 2 Kgs 9:22; Judg 2:17; 8:27–33). Harlots washed themselves in the evil Ahab's blood (1 Kgs 22).

Foreign women are also associated with idolatry (e.g., 1 Kgs

11:2–4, 8; 14:21, 31; 16:31; 18:19; 2 Kgs 9:22). From a historical perspective, it is quite possible that these women brought with them to Israel their faith in and worship of their own native gods. To the extent that their husbands and children joined in worshiping these gods, the Israelites violated Yahwism—the religion which accepted Yahweh not only as Israel's God but also as the only God—and practiced idolatry. Extraordinary circumstances were created to prevent the Benjaminites from marrying foreign women (Judg 21).

Sexual intercourse was somehow understood as making men unholy. When the priest Ahimelech offered David the temple bread for himself and his men who were fleeing Saul, the priest's only concern was whether or not David's men had lain recently with women. If they had, they would not have been able to eat the holy bread (1 Sam 21:4–5). The subtle implication here is that contact with women contaminates men!

In ancient Israel woman's value most obviously lay in her role as fertile female and mother of sons, yet a woman who had had sexual relations was, in a sense, damaged goods. She was not of equal value with the woman who was still a virgin. When the Israelites smite the inhabitants of Jabesh-gilead, they kill all the men and the women who have had sex; the four hundred young virgins who have not yet had sex, however, they keep alive, so that these may become wives for the Benjaminites (Judg 21:11–12, 14). This practice betrays a hierarchy among women. Just as today a used car is to be valued less than a new car, a used woman was perceived to be of less value. There is sad irony in the fact that the reason special women had to be sought for the Benjaminites in the first place was that the Benjaminites had been guilty of rape; the rape of which they were guilty involved the sacrifice of a woman to save a man (cf. Judg 19).

Israel's History as Men's History

The Deuteronomistic History lacks the extended genealogies contained within the Pentateuch. Nevertheless, with rare exceptions, its characters are identified as the sons of their respective fathers and, if the characters are to assume major roles, then the paternal grandfathers, great-grandfathers, and other famous forefathers are also named (e.g., Josh 7:1; Judg 10:1; 1 Sam 1:1).

Only two kinds of exceptions to this pattern occur in the Deuteronomistic History. The first occurs in Judg 9, a reference to Abimelech's "mother's kinsmen" and "his mother's family" (vv 1, 3). These persons are contrasted with his "father's house." The evil Abimelech uses his mother's family to destroy his father's household (v 5), but, ironically, he is destroyed by a woman (vv 53–54). The second type of exception includes those verses where a person is named as the son of a person whose name occurs only once in the biblical text. The reader, presuming the patriarchal culture of ancient Israel, may conclude that the reference is to a male.

The Deuteronomistic History is similar to the literature of the Pentateuch in naming fathers as the heads of households (e.g., Josh 2:12; 14:1; 1 Sam 2:27), and in specifying houses which belonged to men (e.g., Saul: 2 Sam 3:6; David: 2 Sam 7:26; Abinadab: 2 Sam 6:3; Obededom: 2 Sam 6:10; Machir: 2 Sam 9:4; Absalom: 2 Sam 13:20; Joseph: 2 Sam 19:20; Hiram: 1 Kgs 5:11; Baasha: 1 Kgs 16:3; Jeroboam: 1 Kgs 16:7; Ahab: 1 Kgs 21:29; Judah: 2 Kgs 19:30).

Moreover, just as the covenant in the Pentateuch was cut with the patriarchs, so this same covenant became a touchstone in the Deuteronomistic History: the covenant with Abraham, Isaac, and Jacob (e.g., Josh 24:3–4; 1 Kgs 8:21; 2 Kgs 13:23). And the Lord made another covenant with another man: David (e.g., 2 Sam 7:12). The Deuteronomistic History also understands the land to have been promised to Israel's "fathers" (e.g., Judg 2:1; 1 Kgs 8:34; 2 Kgs 21:8). Men benefited by the exodus (e.g., Josh 24:6), and it is men whose burials are worth remembering (e.g., Josh 24:29; Judg 16:31; 1 Kgs 1:21; 2 Kgs 8:24). Men are even the appropriate worshipers (e.g., Judg 13:19–20; 1 Sam 2:15–17; 9:9; 16:5; 1 Kgs 8:2; 15:15).

Israel's history as recorded in the Old Testament has predisposed the reader to expect that proper names refer to men unless otherwise specified. A more objective analysis, however, requires the reader to wonder if our interpretation has been even more biased than some texts. For example, 2 Sam 5:13 records that daughters were born to David. Which of the children born to David in Jerusalem—including Shummua, Shobab, Nathan, Solomon, Ibhar, Elishua, Nepheg, Japhia, Elishama, Eliada,

Eliphelet (vv 14–16)—were girls? The fact that these children, with the exception of Solomon, are never named again—as contenders to the Davidic throne or otherwise—suggests that some of them could be females!

One might also ask whether Shisha is the mother rather than the father of Elihoreph and Ahijah (1 Kgs 4:3); and Abda, the mother, not the father, of Adoniram (1 Kgs 4:6); and Paruah, the mother of Jehoshaphat (1 Kgs 4:17); and Ela, the mother of Shimei (1 Kgs 4:18); and Mahol, the mother of Heman, Calcol, and Darda (1 Kgs 4:31); and Abishalom, the mother of Maacah (1 Kgs 15:2, 10). Since each of these names occurs only once in the biblical text, one cannot know with absolute certainty which parent is being named. It is possible that the names are references to the children's mothers (cf. Zeruiah, pp. 116–18 below), though in the patriarchal culture which produced the texts, identification through one's father was much more common. The same principle applies to Imlah as mother of Micaiah (1 Kgs 22:8–9), Chenaanah as the mother of Zedekiah (1 Kgs 22:11, 24), and Kareah as the mother of Johanan (2 Kgs 25:23). Since Abijah is used as both a man's (1 Kgs 3:10) and a woman's (2 Kgs 18:2) name, may not other names also be so used?

Language: Masculine by Preference and a "God of the Fathers"

All too frequently the Hebrew language, just like the English language, uses the term "man" or "men," either to specify "male" or "males"—women are included in the term only insofar as they are attached to men—or as a generic term which also "implies" "woman" or "women." The Books of Joshua, Judges, 1 and 2 Samuel, and 1 and 2 Kings each contain many examples. The same holds true for the Hebrew words for "father" or "fathers," "brother" or "brothers," "son" or "sons"—women are subsumed—even when the true implication of the term is "ancestor" or "ancestors," "parent" or "parents," "sibling" or "siblings," "fellow Israelite" or "fellow Israelites," "child" or "children." Unfortunately, often the Hebrew language (and sometimes, though less often, also English) does not have appropriate "generic" terms. The writer had to choose between using either the masculine or the feminine form. One should not be surprised that the patriarchal culture of ancient Israel is reflected in its language, that almost always the masculine form was preferred (e.g., Josh 2:19; 1 Sam 2:9; 2 Sam 15:6).

The RSV, as well as other versions, has continued to use the masculine forms, even though an English generic equivalent is available. For example, one finds "man" for "person" (e.g., Josh 2:11); "men" for "people" (e.g., 1 Sam 5:7); "sons" for "descendants" (e.g., 2 Kgs 8:19). The linguistic remnants of patriarchy continue, even in the text's use of manslayer (e.g., Josh 20:3, 5, 6) and our own use of manslaughter!

Another aspect of expressions of patriarchal culture in language is the attribution of God to "the fathers" (e.g., Josh 18:10; Judg 2:12; 2 Kgs 21:22), and the attribution to God of activities stereotypically attributed in history to men (i.e., war and destruction). God has an army (Josh 5:14–15), and is the God of Israel's armies (e.g., 1 Sam 17:45). The Lord fights for Israel (e.g., Josh 10:14, 42; 23:3, 10), and God destroys Israel's enemies (e.g., Josh 24:8). God is "the God of Israel" (e.g., Josh 24:2; 1 Kgs 8:17) and, lest we forget, the name "Israel" derives from Jacob, patriarch and son of Isaac from whom came a tribe and a nation!

Finally, God is named as the father of David's offspring (2 Sam 7:14) and David's offspring is named son of God (2 Sam 7:14). The metaphorical language of father-son to describe the relationship between God and Israel's king is one significant example of how the patriarchal culture of ancient Israel transformed belief in a personal God, Yahweh, into expressions which presumed the maleness of God (at least by the men who produced the texts).

Just as masculine forms are used to describe the Israelite God Yahweh, feminine forms are often used to name and describe idols. This usage originates historically in the fact that the other nations practiced polytheism, claiming both male and female gods, while Israel's faith, in contrast, was monotheistic. In practice what this meant was that while Yahweh was understood in male terms (there were also male idols), any god understood in female terms had to be an idol. Ashtoreth, the goddess of the Sidonians, is one example (e.g., 1 Kgs 11:5, 33; cf. 15:13; 16:33; 18:19; 2 Kgs 13:6; 17:16; 18:4; 21:3, 7; 23:4, 6–7, 13, 15).

Women as Men's Possessions

The centuries which produced the Pentateuch also produced the Deuteronomistic History and during those centuries patriarchy prevailed. One expression of patriarchal culture was the identification of women by their fathers or husbands or sons (e.g., 1 Sam 14:49–50; 18:27; 2 Sam 3:2–5; 17:25; 1 Kgs 4:11, 15; 11:19; 14:21, 31; 16:31; 22:42; 2 Kgs 12:2; 14:2; 15:2, 33; 18:2; 21:1; 22:1; 23:31, 36; 24:8, 18).

Another even more explicit articulation of the fact that ancient Israel understood women to be men's possessions is the marriage agreement: a man (a girl's father) gave his daughter to another man (her future husband). Texts such as Josh 15:16; Judg 1:12–13; 12:9; 21:1, 7, 18, 22; 1 Sam 17:25; 18:17, 19, 21, 27; and 2 Kgs 14:9 presuppose this situation. Twice the Deuteronomistic History records a father reclaiming his married daughter from one husband and giving her to another man (i.e., Judg 14:20—15:2, 6; 1 Sam 25:44; cf. 2 Sam 3:16). Three times also a man—Abner, Absalom, and Adonijah—would violate the concubines of another man to exercise his own power (i.e., 2 Sam 3:7–8; 16:21–22; 1 Kgs 2:13–18, 21). A dowry along with the woman (as an incentive to take her?) was often given by the father to the future husband (e.g., 1 Sam 18:25; 1 Kgs 9:16). Not only was it inconceivable for a woman to choose not to become a wife, a woman had no say in whose wife she would become. The decision was arrived at by the men involved.

In addition, whereas a woman could usually belong to only one man (cf. 1 Sam 25:44), one man could usually possess many women. Gideon, for example, had many wives (Judg 8:30); Elkanah was married to both Peninnah and Hannah (1 Sam 1:2); both David (1 Sam 18:27; 25:42–43; 2 Sam 5:13; 11:27) and Solomon (1 Kgs 3:1; 11:3) had many wives and concubines.

Finally, when men's possessions are enumerated, their wives are included in the list (e.g., Josh 1:14; 1 Sam 30:22; 2 Sam 19:5; 1 Kgs 20:3, 5, 7). Women are included among the spoils of war (e.g., Judg 5:30; 21:14, 21; 1 Sam 30:2–3, 5; 2 Kgs 25:4, 19). Also, they can be disposed of by the men who possess them: to be raped and murdered (Judg 19) and to be sacrificed in fulfillment of a father's vow (Judg 11). The text even legitimates the taking of women by force (Judg 21:21–23). Neither self-identity nor self-determination were appropriate to the women of the patriarchal culture of ancient Israel; most of the women portrayed in the texts, with a few significant exceptions, lack both.

When women's identity is defined by men, their role as mothers takes on major significance. Women bear children, preferably sons, for their husbands. Children are considered to be a blessing from the Lord. The priest Eli blesses Elkanah and Hannah with a prayer that the Lord will give Elkanah children by Hannah (1 Sam 2:20). The wife of Phineas is told, on her own deathbed, not to fear: she has borne a son (1 Sam 4:20). Each of the two harlots who present themselves to Solomon claims that she is the mother of the living son (1 Kgs 3:16–17). In one instance the "maternal instinct" even wins out over the instinct of "self-preservation" (2 Kgs 6:29).

Barrenness, on the other hand, is considered a curse from the Lord. Michal, for example, must bear it because she publicly reprimands David (2 Sam 6:23). When Hezekiah describes Sennacherib's siege of Jerusalem, he speaks of a day of distress, when children have come to the birth but there is no strength to bring them forth (2 Kgs 19:3). Death and miscarriage are equated as the possible results of polluted water (2 Kgs 2:21). Killing people is described as the act of making women childless (1 Sam 15:33). The fact that the daughter of Jephthah laments her virginity further testifies to the importance of maternity within the patriarchal culture of ancient Israel (Judg 11:38–39).

The Deuteronomistic History records several rapes. The Levite's unnamed concubine is raped (Judg 19); Saul's concubine Rizpah is raped (2 Sam 3:7–8); perhaps Bathsheba is raped (2 Sam 11); David's concubines are raped (2 Sam 16:22); David's daughter and Absalom's sister, Tamar, is raped (2 Sam 13). In each instance, the violation is understood to be against the man to whom the woman belongs—and Abner, at least, considers "a fault concerning a woman" to be of little moment (2 Sam 3:8); she herself has no recourse.

A word needs to be said about the practice of calling cities and mountains "daughters." Though the Deuteronomistic History contains this technique considerably less frequently than the prophetic writings or the wisdom literature, nevertheless even here the reference occurs. The city Abel is described as "a mother in Israel" (2 Sam 20:19). It is "the virgin daughter of Zion"—that is, Jerusalem—which despises Assyria; she, the daughter of Jerusalem, wags her head (2 Kgs 19:21). Just as patriarchal culture understands women to be men's possessions, so cities can also be understood in the same way. It is thus quite common within patriarchal cultures for nouns such as "city" to be replaced by synonyms which are feminine and the feminine forms of personal pronouns.

That women are men's possessions has several implications within the culture of ancient Israel:

definition by men;
dependence on men;
primary role as mother;
passivity;
lack of participation in decision making;
lack of personal choice;
the possibility of having to share one's husband with other women;
rape understood as violence against the man to whom a woman belongs;
women, like silver and gold and cities, treated as things—acted on and controlled.

Role Stereotyping and Sexual Discrimination

One way of discriminating between the sexes is to stereotype men's roles and women's roles, men's work and women's work, men's interests and women's interests, and so on. The Deuteronomistic History clearly associates men with war (e.g., Josh 8:1; Judg 6:16; 20:2; 1 Sam 13:2; 2 Sam 17:8; 1 Kgs 20:34; 2 Kgs 8:12; 25:19). Yahweh fights and they fight with Yahweh. Where war is concerned women are only the innocent victims (e.g., Judg 16:27; 2 Kgs 8:12; 15:16) or the spoils (e.g., Judg 5:30; 2 Kgs 15:4, 19).

Men are city builders (Josh 6:26), temple builders and palace builders (1 Kgs 5:18), altar builders (Josh 22:28; Judg 6:27), and idol builders (2 Kgs 17:30), spies (Judg 18:2, 4, 9, 14, 17), horsemen, farmers, and weapon makers (1 Sam 8:11–12). Women, on the other hand, are seamstresses (1 Sam 2:19), perfumers, cooks, and bakers (1 Sam 8:13). Women serve at the entrance to the Tent of Meeting (1 Sam 2:22) and are doorkeepers (2 Sam 4:6); they were singers (1 Sam 18:6–7; 21:11; 29:5).

Role stereotyping allows one to presume that separate is equal. To justify specific roles and activities appropriate to men and to distinguish these from other specific roles and activities appropriate to women is subtle sexual discrimination. Such a perspective allows one to deny that the role and activities of one sex are superior to that of the other, while at the same time not allowing persons to choose their role and activities. The superior or dominant sex—in a patriarchal culture, the male—would rarely choose to assume the roles and activities deemed appropriate for the female, while the female, though she might choose to assume the roles and activities deemed appropriate for males, is not permitted to do so.

Exceptions within a Patriarchal Culture

The Deuteronomistic History allows for some expressions of sexual equality within the patriarchal culture it portrays. For example, both men and women are victims of *herem* (destruction as an offering to God during a holy war; Josh 6:21) and of Saul's anger (1 Sam 22:19); both are servants (2 Kgs 5:26) and slaves (1 Sam 8:16); both are victims of war (Josh 8:25); both are called to listen to the reading of the law (Josh 8:35) and to celebrate the ark's arrival in Jerusalem (2 Sam 6:19); Aachan's daughters as well as his sons become victims of their father's sin (Josh 7:24); evil Israel sacrifices both daughters and sons to idols (2 Kgs 17:17) while the good king Josiah defiles Topheth lest anyone of Judah burn "his" son or daughter as an offering to Molech (2 Kgs 23:10).

The literature of the Deuteronomistic History portrays children whose concern for their mother equals that for their father. Rahab, for example, is intent on saving her mother as well as her father (Josh 2:13, 18; 6:23); Elisha wishes to kiss both his mother and his father goodbye (1 Kgs 19:20). The Deuteronomistic Historian accuses Ahaziah of walking in the way of both his mother (Jezebel) and his father (Ahab; 1 Kgs 22:52). Gideon speaks of his brothers as "sons of my mother" (Judg 8:19).

In 1 Kgs 10 an episode is described which celebrates the wisdom of Solomon. The Queen of Sheba comes to see for herself if Solomon is as wise as his fame suggests. Why is there no mention of a king of Sheba? Perhaps Israel's patriarchal culture would find it hard to imagine a king visiting another king out of curiosity and bringing gifts; after all, kings stood either in alliance or in competition with one another. Or perhaps Israel's memory contained the recollection of a woman doing such a thing.

Had a king approached Solomon in the manner attributed to the Queen of Sheba—whether as historically verifiable fact or at least as literary construction—the biblical text would thereby give stronger testimony to the wisdom and fame of Solomon. Yet the text as it now exists is constructed to give the greatest possible credibility to the woman. Though deprived of a personal name, she nevertheless exhibits a certain power of self-determination and choice. The Queen, for example, has valuable possessions which she can afford to give away; she can and does travel at will. She is smart enough to want to pursue wisdom and to recognize it when she sees it!

Several women whose characters seem to be exceptions to general patriarchal expectations are studied below (pp. 85–89; 116–18; 124–26). One is Rahab, the heroine of Jericho (Josh 2; 6); another is Zeruiah, the mother of Joab, Abishai, and Asahel (e.g., 2 Sam. 2:18); a third is the wise woman of Tekoa (2 Sam 14). One should remember, as one reads specific biblical texts, that outstanding female characters, to whatever extent they become their own persons, have triumphed in no small way over the dominant patriarchal culture which produced them.

TEXTS FROM A FEMINIST
PERSPECTIVE

Rahab: Heroine of Jericho
(Joshua 2; 6)

The major action that takes place in the Book of Joshua is the occupation of the land of Canaan by the Israelites. According to deuteronomistic theology, if the Israelites are faithful to Yahweh, Yahweh will be faithful to them. God will "fight for them" and bring them into the land which Yahweh "swore to give them." After the Israelites crossed the Jordan from the east into Canaan (a symbolic reenactment of the exodus crossing?), the Book of Joshua records that they set about taking the southern part of the land. The city of Jericho was first on their list.

The Story

The first thing Joshua did was to send out two spies to investigate the city. They came to the harlot Rahab's house and lodged there (Josh 2:1). When it became known that Israelites had come into the city, representatives of the king came to Rahab's house to fetch them. The account tells us twice (vv 4 and 6) that Rahab hid the men. Between these statements—the latter specifying precisely how and where she had hidden them—are included Rahab's words to the men seeking the Israelites: she pleads ignorance of their origin and of their present whereabouts; she knows only that they went out of the city gates. The narrator records that the men, believing Rahab's words, went out after the Israelites.

The next scene takes place on the roof of Rahab's house where the men were hiding. Rahab tells them—again direct address—that she is convinced that the Lord has given the Israelites the land. She explains why she thinks so—the Lord had dried up the Red Sea for them when they were fleeing Egypt; the Israelites themselves had been able to destroy the two Amorite kings, Og and Bashan (v 10); Israel's God is *the* God (v 11). She asserts again twice, probably for emphasis, that her own people are very much afraid of the Israelites (v 9). Rahab then makes a covenant with the two messengers from Joshua; she promises her help and her silence in exchange for the safety of herself and her father's house. The men agree (vv 12–14).

The narrator then records the aid Rahab provided: a rope and good advice (vv 15–16). The two Israelites now become true dialogue partners. To Rahab's words they answer: they will be innocent of any wrongdoing if she either makes known their situation or fails to clearly mark her house and to keep her family whom she wishes to save within it (vv 17–21). Rahab agrees and complies (v 21).

The narrator closes this episode of the story reporting that the spies obeyed Rahab's advice (v 22). Subsequently they returned safely to Joshua (v 23). Their report to him included Rahab's words: the Lord would give them the land; its people feared them (v 24).

Interpretation

The first thing one notices in reading this story is that its major character is a woman. She is named, in sharp contrast to the two Israelite spies who remain anonymous. One notes also that references are made to "her house," not to the house of her father or her husband, which would normally be the case.

Of course, the reason for these irregularities is the fact that Rahab is a harlot. She lives no longer in the house of her father, yet she is not in the house of a husband either; she is neither wife nor concubine. Precisely because the culture was a patriarchal one, there was tolerance in the society for harlots. They satisfied men's physical needs when neither wife nor concubine was available (cf. Gen 38).

Though a man was allowed to use a harlot, one wonders what ramifications there were for a woman in being one. Certainly, if this text is any indication, a harlot had more independence than a daughter or a wife or even a concubine. She had her own house and she could choose whom she would house there, including men (v 1). She could make a binding promise without needing her husband's endorsement of it (cf. Num 30:10–14). The text clearly indicates, though this might well be an anomaly, that her harlotry did not in any way prevent her from assuming an almost prophetic stance; she proclaimed Yahweh's future for Israel (v 9; how could she know it?) and her actions, at least in this part of the story, to the extent that she harbors the Israelites and secures their safe escape, help to effect it (vv 4–6, 16).

The "scarlet cord" (v 18) would serve as a sign to the invaders that that house was to be preserved, that the people therein were their allies. Has history, however, seen in the scarlet cord a sign of her harlotry (cf. Gen 38:28)? The color scarlet, of course, became a symbol of the loose woman (cf. Nathaniel Hawthorne's novel *The Scarlet Letter*).

The Story

The account of the fall of the city of Jericho to the Israelites, recorded in Josh 6, is one of the most famous in the Old Testament. Many Americans are certainly familiar with the spiritual "Joshua Fit the Battle of Jericho." The narrator opens the biblical account with an affirmation of what Rahab had already alerted the Israelites to: the people of Jericho greatly feared them (v 1; cf. 2:9). The Lord then tells Joshua what Rahab had told the spies: the Lord will give the land to the Israelites (v 2; cf. 2:9).

The Lord continues to direct how the Israelites will take the walled city. The soldiers are to march around it once each day for six days. On the seventh day, the soldiers are commanded to march around the city seven times with seven priests carrying seven trumpets followed by the ark of the covenant (vv 3–4). (In many biblical texts, seven is a symbolic number for completion.) Finally, the Lord tells Joshua that when the people hear the priests blowing their trumpets, they are to shout and the consequent result of the noise will be that the city walls will collapse. The Israelites are then to invade the city (vv 5–6).

The narrator reports that Joshua ordered the people to do what the Lord had commanded. The soldiers were to head the procession, followed by the seven priests blowing their trumpets, followed by the ark, and then, finally, a guard bringing up the rear (vv 7–14). This was to take place around the city once each day for six days. The seventh day was to be different. On the seventh day they were to march around seven times and finally Joshua would tell the people to shout, for the Lord had given them the city. Joshua would then remind the Israelites of the rule for their holy war: all the spoils of the war were to be destroyed and all the gold, silver, bronze, and ivory were to be placed in the Lord's treasury, because these truly belonged to Yahweh. Since God was the true victor of the battle, all the spoils belonged to God. Joshua's command to the people included words concerning Rahab. Identified as a harlot, she and everyone who was "her house" were to be spared, because she had harbored the two Israelite spies (vv 15–19).

The narrator reports the same basic information a third time. This time, the report is of what did happen. Everything went as the Lord had told Joshua it should, and as Joshua had commanded the people (vv 20–21). The narrator adds that the same two men who had investigated the land went into Rahab's house, at Joshua's order, to get Rahab and her family out of the city before the Israelites destroyed it. They brought them to outside the Israelite camp and then executed the city's total destruction (vv 22–24).

The narrator repeats Rahab's fate. She, and this time her "father's household," Joshua saved, because she had saved the Israelite spies. Rahab came to dwell in Israel (v 25).

Interpretation

In this segment of the story, the harlot Rahab never speaks. She is named three times, however: when Joshua explains to his forces the battle plan (v 17); when Joshua tells the spies to fulfill their promise and save her and her family (v 22); and when the narrator reports that Rahab and her family were, in fact, saved (v 25).

The narrator carefully suggests that when Rahab and her family were saved, they were taken to "outside the camp of Israel" (v 23) and later, that she and her family "dwelt in Israel" (v 25). The detail may be a subtle allusion to her identity as a harlot. Since the men of Israel were to have no sexual relations before going into battle (cf. 1 Sam 21:5), the safest thing to do was to keep a harlot out of their midst. The allusion may also underline the "civilian" character of Rahab's family—separated from the soldiers but accepted into the people. The statement that "she dwelt in Israel to this day" (v 25) may be an aetiological reference, justifying the presence of "foreigners" in Israel, foreign women even, who, rather

than being a threat to the Israelites (cf. Josh 23:12), had functioned
as a real asset.

Summary

The story of the fall of Jericho places a foreign woman in a
prominent position. In fact, Rahab and Joshua are the only characters named in the two chapters. Rahab emerges as a foreign woman
who recognizes that Israel's God is *the* God, and that God has
given the land to Israel. Because she knows this, she dares to hide
the Israelite messengers and to lie to the messengers of her own
king. In return for saving the lives of the spies, she wishes only to
save her own life and the lives of her family.

The Book of Joshua schematizes the taking of the land of
Canaan into three major advances—to the south (Jericho), to the
central region (Ai), and to the north (Hazor). The text describes
how the cooperation of a woman—the very lowest on the totem
pole as foreigner and harlot—is crucial to that first success.

Deborah and Jael:
Saviors of the Israelites
(Judges 4—5)

The Book of Judges is believed to contain stories of the mighty
warriors who defended their tribes and of respected elders who
settled disputes among tribal members. The stories of these persons are bound together by deuteronomistic theology—a judge
provided the leadership to guarantee the people's covenant fidelity. The absence of a judge led to the Israelites' idolatry, and
then the Lord's anger, and then the people's oppression, and then
cries to Yahweh for deliverance, and finally, the gift of another
judge. The Book of Judges provides the portrait of twelve such
persons, one of whom is a woman.

The Story

Deborah is introduced as the judge who will rescue the Israelites
from Jabin, the king of Hazor. She has an identity as a wife but also
as a prophetess (4:4). She is first depicted in the role of respected

elder, one who provides judgment for the people of Israel (v 5), and then in her role as prophetess. She conveys the Lord's command to Barak. Barak is to gather his men—the reader concludes that Barak heads up an army—and to prepare to meet the forces of Sisera, the commander of Jabin's army. The Lord promises Barak, through Deborah, that the Lord will make Barak the victor (vv 5–7).

A dialogue then follows between Barak and Deborah in which Barak tells Deborah on what condition he will obey the Lord's command: Deborah must accompany him (v 8). Deborah agrees to Barak's condition, but she tells Barak that the outcome of the battle will not be as he anticipates. Sisera will fall "into the hand of a woman" (v 9), not precisely into "your hand" (v 7). The narrator reports that Deborah accompanied Barak, who followed the Lord's order (v 10).

The narrator interjects parenthetically a comment which the reader will need in order to understand the later action of the story: the Kenite Heber was living near Kedesh (v 11). The story then proceeds with the report that Sisera, having learned of Barak's move, prepared his troops. The armies readied, and Deborah gave Barak the signal to advance; the time was ripe for the Lord's giving Sisera into his hand (v 12; cf. v 7). When the two armies met, the Israelites totally defeated the Canaanites, except for Sisera who had fled (vv 15–16).

In the next scene the reader finds Sisera at the tent of Jael, Heber's wife (cf. v 11). The conversation which ensues allows the reader to believe that Jael will protect Sisera (vv 18–20). This is not the case, however. Jael kills him (v 21). When Barak, who was pursuing Sisera, reached Jael's tent, she showed him Sisera's body (v 22).

Interpretation

Judges 4 presents us with four major characters—Deborah, Barak, Jael, and Sisera. Deborah is portrayed as performing both functions ascribed to the judges: she rendered judgment and she helped to deliver Israel. Deborah also functioned as prophet, proclaiming the word of the Lord to Barak. Barak's role was clearly inferior to Deborah's. He was to obey the Lord's word through the prophet, to function as commander of the army. The fact that he would not go into battle without Deborah makes clear his dependence on her.

Barak successfully accomplishes his mission—the Canaanite army is destroyed—except that the symbol of the army, its commander, Sisera, still lives. The victory cannot be complete until Sisera has been destroyed. That Jael, not Barak, effects this final blow to the Canaanite army fulfills Deborah's words to Barak that the glory would not be his, but a woman's. Verse 9 had presented us with a double-entendre. The reader presumed that the woman being referred to was Deborah; in fact, it was *implicitly* Deborah but *explicitly* Jael! Credit for the final defeat of the enemy fell to a woman.

A closer look at Jael reveals a foreigner, yet not one who obstructs Israelite well-being with her gods, but rather one who helps to fulfill the word of the Lord (v 7). She is particularly unusual in that her action does not correspond to what one might expect in a patriarchal culture; her relationship to Hazor's king does not conform to her husband's. The reader would expect from Jael that she would provide Sisera with protection—the protection Sisera expected from her. In order to fulfill the Lord's word through Deborah, she contradicts those expectations. Sisera, though important to the story, never speaks.

The Story

Historical critics believe Judg 5 to be an older poetic version of Judg 4. Literary critics believe it to be repetition, with variation. The genre is a song of praise and thanksgiving to God for Israel's victory. Women are often portrayed as singers in Israel (e.g., Exod 15:21) and here Deborah and Barak join voices.

This version of the story introduces Jael as one in whose days "caravans ceased and travelers kept to the byways" (5:6); it was a dangerous time. In contrast, Deborah is described as a "mother in Israel," one who made possible the restoration of the peasantry (v 7). Deborah utters a song; Barak is victorious in battle against the mighty (vv 12–13). The poetry seems to emphasize the role of certain tribes in the victory—Zebulun and Naphtali (5:14, 18; cf. 4:6), and Issachar (5:15). The stars and the River Kishon also fought against Sisera (vv 20–21). In contrast, the Reubenites, the Danites, and the tribe of Asher did not participate (vv 16–17).

The poetry of Judg 5 clearly lauds Jael as "the most blessed of tent-dwelling women" and describes in clear detail her protection and then destruction of Sisera (vv 24–25). The chapter also introduces additional characters—all females. Sisera's mother and her wise ladies all conclude that the reason Sisera's return is delayed is because he has been victorious; his men are dividing the spoils. These women imagine more women, those who have become spoils of war (vv 28–30).

Interpretation

Though this version makes reference to Deborah (vv 7, 12), Jael clearly has the major role. Deborah is not here named as a prophetess; there is no reference to her communicating God's orders to Barak. On the contrary, she is the one who has the support of the people and who can, with Barak, rally the forces. Perhaps Jael stands in the limelight because Deborah is doing the singing (v 1), or more likely, Jael wins the credit because she was the one who actually killed Sisera. From a poetic perspective the addition of Sisera's mother creates a pathetic contrast. She gave Sisera life; Jael gave him death. Her son was her glory; the reader should not be surprised that she can imagine only his victory. In truth, in the patriarchal culture which produced the text, her glory died with her son.

Summary

Judges 4 and 5 tell the same story but from two slightly different perspectives. One reason for the shift in emphasis is historical. The earlier poetic version emphasizes the victory and the woman who effected it. Though Barak's military prowess is celebrated and Deborah's collaboration recognized, the climax of the poem makes Jael the real victor. In contrast, the latter version emphasizes the woman-prophet-judge who proclaims Yahweh's word and thus legitimates the unusual character of the Israelite victory. Jael is given no less credit, but her role is incorporated into a larger divine plan. Careful examination of both these texts, in spite of their slightly different emphases, clearly illustrates an early historical memory of the role women played both in the relationship of the Israelites with Yahweh and in their military victories, a perspective all too often either ignored or minimized by later interpretation.

Two Women Compete for One Man: Gilead's Harlot and His Wife; Peninnah and Hannah; Two Harlots (Judges II; I Samuel I; I Kings 3)

The Story

Gilead begat many sons, at least one of whom was born to an unnamed harlot; other sons were born to Gilead's wife, whom the narrator also left unnamed. The disparity in women led to a perceived inequality among the sons. The sons of Gilead's wife cast out the son of Gilead's harlot. The only advantage the son of Gilead's harlot seemed to have was that, being singular, the text names him, Jephthah.

The story as so far described might lead the reader to recall the account in the Book of Genesis of Abraham's son Ishmael by the slave woman Hagar as contrasted with that of his son Isaac by his wife, Sarah, and the consequent strife between the two women. An equally appropriate comparison, also contained in the Book of Genesis, is the jealousy of Joseph's brothers. This text, however, gives the reader neither indication of Gilead's preference for Jephthah nor indication that his mother, as "the other woman," was in competition with Gilead's wife.

Interpretation

Literary critics would make little of Jephthah's origin, concluding that this detail functions to introduce why Jephthah had the relationship he did with the other Gileadites. He was one of them and as such, he was an appropriate warrior and leader for them. But what would single him out from the others? The technique of "special circumstances surrounding his birth" is an oft-used biblical tool. Whereas many texts suggest sons destined for great things by their birth from previously barren women (e.g., Gen 11:30; 29:31)—and the surroundings of Moses' own birth were unusual—Jephthah's singularity is established by the lesser status of his mother. The sons of harlots were not disowned in ancient Israel but neither did they have equal rank with the sons of wives. What is most unusual about this text, however—a point which most often goes unnoticed—is the fact that the son of the harlot was destined for greater things than any of the sons of Gilead's wife. In patriarchal terms, though the harlot was by her own situation inferior, she won superior renown, precisely because of the success of her son.

The Story

In 1 Sam 1 two women are portrayed who seem to have an equal relationship vis-à-vis one man. Both are wives. The difference between the two emerges, however, when one considers the primary role, in patriarchal culture, of women as wives: to become mothers. Whereas Peninnah had children, Hannah did not (vv 1–2). Each year when Elkanah went to Shiloh to sacrifice, the discrepancy between the two women became most obvious. Elkanah gave Peninnah several portions from the offering, one for herself and one for each of their sons and daughters. Elkanah gave Hannah only one portion, for herself. To add salt to Hannah's wound, Peninnah used these occasions to lord her fertility over her barren counterpart (vv 3–6).

Irony enters when Elkanah, with the best of intentions, tries to console Hannah. Instead of obviously preferring the fertile woman, and shunning the barren woman who did not give him sons, Elkanah made no reference to his deprivation because of Hannah's condition. And since he was not troubled by her situation, why should she be? He determined that he should be of more value to her than ten sons (vv 7–8).

Interpretation

The relationship between Peninnah and Hannah resembles that between Rachel and Leah. The fertile woman uses her children as a lever against her "fellow wife." In this case, however, Elkanah does not so evidently love Hannah more and Peninnah less; he just does not love Hannah less because she is barren! On the other hand, he chauvinistically presumes that if she has him, what more should she want? The character Elkanah fails to appreciate the character of Hannah in a patriarchal culture. Her stature was measured by the person of her husband but also by the number of her offspring.

The Story

Two other women, both unnamed, and both unconnected to husbands are portrayed in 1 Kgs 3 (vv 16–18). The women are harlots. Each has borne a son, which means that each has recently grown in prestige. The two women were living in the same house. Unfortunately, however, one of the children died; the mother had unwittingly lain on the child while she was sleeping. Each woman accused the other of being the mother of the dead child, claiming herself to be the mother of the living child. Who could determine which woman was telling the truth and which was lying? Who could distinguish the mother of the living child from the mother of the dead child? The women came to King Solomon so that he might settle the matter (v 16).

When the two arrived before the king, one woman presented her side of the story, only to be contradicted by the other. The king called for a sword to decide the matter (v 24). He ordered the living child to be divided into two halves, and each woman to be given one of the halves. If the women's testimonies had been similar, the women's reactions to the king's judgment were not. The mother of the living child protested. Rather than kill her child, she agreed to sacrifice it to the other woman, to give her living son to the mother of the dead child. The mother of the dead child, however, not having equal maternal attachment to this living child, agreed with the king's decision that the child should be divided in two (vv 25–26).

The king then intervened. The women had betrayed their true colors. She who would preserve the child's life—even at the cost of relinquishing that child—had to be its true mother. The king ordered the living child to be awarded to her (v 27). The episode concludes with an acknowledgment of Solomon's wisdom in rendering such a judgment (v 28).

Interpretation

Most scholars interpreting this passage place it in its larger context and see the episode as helping to establish Solomon's wisdom. They refer back to an earlier verse in the chapter where Solomon requests from God "an understanding mind to govern his people, and the ability to discern between good and evil" (v 9). They likewise refer forward to Solomon's achievements in building the temple and his own palace (chaps. 5–8) as well as to the Queen of Sheba's testimony about Solomon's wisdom (10:7). Viewed in this light, the harlots become instruments of a larger message, useful details at best.

Feminists recognize in this narrative another example of woman as means to man's end. In the patriarchal culture of ancient Israel where women's identity depended on father or husband, and where "fulfillment" depended on one's fertility, the harlots are here competing for a slightly higher rung on the ladder of Israel's hierarchy. As they compete with each other for the child, they vicariously compete for themselves.

Summary

The Old Testament presents clear examples of situations in which two women compete against each other for one man. In Gen 16 and 30, Hagar and Sarah compete for Abraham, and Leah and Rachel compete for Jacob; an unnamed harlot and an unnamed wife compete for Gilead in Judg 11; Peninnah and Hannah compete for Elkanah in 1 Sam 1; and two unnamed harlots compete for one living son in 1 Kgs 3. Though this phenomenon is not confined only to women (both David and Paltiel wish to have Michal as their wife: 2 Sam 3:14–16), it does occur more frequently among women. Perhaps there were simply more women than men, but a more likely explanation is that men were more prized than women. Women competing against other women for men is to be expected both in patriarchal cultures and in the literature they produce.

An Unnamed Daughter Submits
to Fulfill Her Father's Vow:
Do with Me according to Your Word
(Judges 11)

The Story

We have already examined the first verses of the chapter, those which explain why Jephthah is different from his brothers, why he was forced to flee, and so on. His mother was not their mother. The text introduces Jephthah when Israel is at war with the Ammonites. They need a military leader and call on him. Jephthah, once rejected by his own people, sets up stipulations according to which he will agree to their request. If he comes back as their military commander, and if the Lord gives him victory, then the people must acknowledge his headship over them. They consent (vv 4–11).

The narrator then reports a dialogue which takes place between Jephthah and the Ammonite king. Jephthah wants to know why the Ammonites are attacking and the king responds that they are seeking to regain territory which the Israelites took from them. They want the land back and suggest that Israel return it to them peaceably (vv 12–13). Jephthah's answer details how Israel came to possess the land, what lands they bypassed, what lands they would like to have passed through but were unable, what lands they conquered to traverse. Jephthah's ultimate defense is that Israel's God has given them the land (vv 14–27). The Ammonite king, however, rejects Jephthah's explanation, and war ensues. Jephthah then makes another bargain, this time with God. If God gives him victory, he will offer to the Lord whomever emerges first from his house on his return (vv 28–31). The narrator reports that the Lord delivered the Ammonites into Jephthah's hand (vv 32–33).

The writer has built up the reader's suspense. Will Jephthah fulfill his promise to the Lord, and if so, how? Who will emerge from his house when he returns victorious? Who is within to emerge? The narrator quickly gives answer: his daughter, his only child (v 34). The woman emerges with instruments of celebration, to which

Jephthah responds with gestures of mourning. He explains the dilemma to his unnamed daughter (v 35).

The girl speaks, addressing her father with a posture of humble submission. The Lord has fulfilled his part of the agreement; her father can do no less. She asks only that she be given a brief period of time—two months—in which to bewail her virginity. Her father consents (vv 36–38). The narrator concludes the story. Everything transpired as expected. The girl spent the time lamenting her virginity; she then returned and her father's vow was fulfilled (v 39).

Interpretation

Though the first part of the episode is necessary for understanding the whole, it is the second part which most concerns the feminist reader. A named father makes a promise to God, bargaining another person's life—he knows not whose—in exchange for a military victory that will "legitimate" him, that will secure for him a place of honor among his people. Somebody will be expendable to achieve his goal. Yet many interpreters ignore this shadowy side of Jephthah's personality and concentrate on his victory.

The person sacrificed turns out to be Jephthah's only daughter. He, too, must pay a price; his price is increased by the fact that he had no sons and not even any other daughters. She was less of a loss than an only son would have been, but more of a loss precisely because there were no sons. Though her father grieves, he does not retract his part of the bargain. (He can have other children?!)

Turning one's attention to the girl, one sees a portrait of unquestioning filial obedience—is this why the reader admires her and feels sorry for her? She asks a small favor—small in comparison to her future fate—and he magnanimously agrees. That the story is thus portrayed betrays the patriarchal culture in which it was produced; that interpreters have praised the girl betrays their own patriarchal culture. The text is probably an early one—it does not condemn human sacrifice (cf. Gen 22; 2 Kgs 21:6).

The favor that the girl asks also betrays the patriarchal culture. Her regret is her virginity. How much more ready to die she would have been had she been able to fulfill her own destiny. Her father fulfills his vow at the cost of her fulfillment.

Historical critics look to the last verses of the episode for its meaning (vv 39–40). There is a custom in Israel that women go for four days each year to lament Jephthah's daughter's virginity. Why was there such a custom? Why did women have an occasion to lament virginity formally? Can the practice be grounded in history and explained with a story? The story of Jephthah's daughter serves this function well—but feminists would say at the price of the female victim!

Summary

Feminist interpretation has compared this episode with the account of Saul's vow which his son Jonathan violates (1 Sam 14). Though Saul is willing to have his vow fulfilled, that is, to allow his son to die (vv 39, 44), the people are not. In the first place, they protest the appropriateness of Saul's vow (vv 24–26); second, they do not allow Jonathan to become its victim (v 45). In contrast, the companions of the daughter of Jephthah do not protest. Rather, they too are submissive. They support the victim by their presence, but they do not challenge the girl's fate.

The episodes narrated in Judg 11 and 1 Sam 14 both involve vows made to God. They both involve consequences for their children. Both fathers are willing to have their vows fulfilled. What distinguishes the two stories are the responses of the children's constituencies and the stories' outcomes. The female companions of the daughter of Jephthah are typical products of patriarchy; the "sons of Israel" are also, but differently! One response leads to life; the other to death. Interestingly enough, there is no penalty placed on the people for obfuscating Saul's vow and securing Jonathan's life. May we conclude similarly that no penalty would have ensued had the girl's companions had the courage to challenge Jephthah?

Trust in God:
Manoah's Unnamed Wife
(Judges 13)

The Story

The narrator reports that Manoah has a wife but she is childless. "The angel of the Lord," however, appears to her with word that she will conceive and bear a son. The angel stipulates the special precautions the pregnant woman should take and the special treatment the boy should receive (vv 2–5).

In direct address, the woman tells her husband about the apparition. Manoah's response is directed to God. He takes the apparition one step further. Manoah asks for another apparition, this time one which will explain to the parents how to deal with the child. God hears Manoah's prayer and the messenger again appears, again to the woman rather than to Manoah. The wife calls her husband and brings him to the messenger. A dialogue ensues. Manoah asks his question and the messenger's response is again directed to the woman. She is to execute carefully the directives the messenger had previously given her (vv 6–14).

Manoah wishes to prepare food for the man but he transfers this gesture of generosity toward him into a gesture of thanksgiving to God. The man would not eat food if Manoah were to prepare it for him; on the other hand, Manoah could render that which he offered the man as a sacrifice to God. Manoah does not recognize that the "man" with whom he speaks is the "angel" who had appeared to his wife (vv 15–16).

Manoah then asks the man's name. Again, the messenger's response points to, but does not define, his identity. With a play on words—virtually untranslatable from Hebrew to English—the messenger suggests his name/identity as "wonderful." Manoah then performs the sacrifice the man had suggested to the God who does "wonderful" things. While the flame is ascending from the burning sacrifice, the angel also ascends; Manoah and his wife look on, amazed.

There are no more apparitions. When Manoah finally realizes the messenger's identity, he fears greatly. He tells his wife that, having seen God, they will surely die. His wife contradicts him. From her perspective, the events that had thus far transpired simply do not add up to their dying. She is right. They do not die. Rather, she bears the son whom the angel had foretold.

Interpretation

Many interpreters use this passage as an illustration of the Nazirite vow. According to Num 6, the Nazirite vow consisted in the promise to separate oneself for the Lord, not to drink wine or strong drink, or vinegar made from wine or strong drink, or any drink made from grapes, or even any grapes or parts thereof. While under vow, the person was not to have his (or her?) hair cut, or to come in contact with any dead person, even a family member, who would render the person unclean. Interpreters also point to the angel's prediction about John the Baptist's not drinking wine or strong drink (cf. Luke 1:15), as well as Jesus being called a Nazarene (e.g., Matt 2:23); in accounts of the last supper Jesus asserts that he will not drink wine again until coming into the kingdom (e.g., Matt 26:29).

In the text of Judg 13, the angel twice (vv 4, 14) tells the wife of Manoah that she should not drink wine or strong drink or eat anything unclean. The son whom she shall bear must not cut his hair; he will be a Nazirite from birth; he will help deliver Israel from the Philistines (v 5; cf. v 13).

When feminists consider the Nazirite vow as it applies in Judg 13, they note that *together* the woman and her son are to fulfill its stipulations. Because he is to be a Nazirite from birth, his mother must adhere to its stipulations at least during her pregnancy. Though the description is typically patriarchal in that peculiarities involving the mother (e.g., barrenness) signal the birth of a son whose future will be significant, nevertheless, this text shows more than biological sharing. The mother is called on to act in a manner not dependent on her female anatomy in order to advance her son's future.

This interpretation is strengthened by further indications from the text. It is the unnamed woman to whom the "angel" twice appears (vv 3, 9). Only when she gets her husband does he come into contact with the "messenger." She recognizes the messenger for what he is, "a man of God" (v 6). Her husband, in contrast, recognizes the man for what he appears to be, a "man" (vv 11, 16). Because the words "angel" and "messenger" translate the same Hebrew word (*măl'āk*), it may be difficult for someone reading the text in English to comprehend fully the play on words which is present in the original text. The wife of Manoah recognizes the "angel" as a "messenger" sent by God; Manoah recognizes the "man." Manoah does not question the messenger's message, but his experience of the messenger does differ from his wife's. The messenger has to educate

Manoah to who he is—by refusing to eat and by giving as his name also a play on words. The wife of Manoah seems to need no such education. And when Manoah does get the message, he draws a legalistic conclusion (cf. Exod 10:28), one which is inappropriate to the circumstances before him. His wife, in contrast, trusting her experience, interprets the data differently. Her analysis proves correct.

Summary

When interpreters consider Judg 13—16, that segment of the Old Testament which deals with Samson and his exploits against the Philistines, they place the circumstances surrounding his birth within the larger context. They note its unusual character. What interpreters have often failed to note, however, is that although this text was produced in a patriarchal culture (the woman goes unnamed, identified only through her husband and her child-bearing role) it nevertheless draws a sharp contrast between the characters of the woman and the man. She, like Hagar (cf. Gen 16:7) but unlike her husband, receives an apparition and is commissioned. She is the one—not her husband—who, perhaps intuitively, recognizes the messenger as an angel. She is the one—not her husband—who is confident of their future. She, not Manoah—though it is his name the reader will remember—is the primary actor in the narrative. Not only because she participates in parenting—Manoah also does that—but also because she participates in the Nazirite vow, the wife of Manoah plays a valuable role in helping to deliver Israel from the Philistines (v 6).

Perseverance as Victor
over Physical Strength:
Delilah and Samson
(Judges 16)

The Story

The narrator reports that "Samson loved a woman named Delilah." Such a detail suggests his vulnerability, and yet he was famous for his great physical strength (e.g., Judg 14:6); he had proven to be every bit the Philistine threat which the angel had predicted (Judg 13:5). The Philistines now call upon Delilah to betray Samson. They offer her money (16:5).

Delilah enters into conversation with Samson. She asks him directly the source of his strength. He answers her, but with a lie. She believes his lie, and creates the very situation which he said would be his undoing. She then announces to him his defeat. He had lied, however; therefore, her efforts prove vain (16:6–9).

Delilah again asks Samson to tell her the secret of his great strength. He replies, suggesting a new source, but again he lies. She executes his directive, but again, to no avail (vv 10–12). A third time Delilah repeats her request and a third time Samson lies. A third time Delilah does as Samson suggests, and a third time her efforts bear no fruit (vv 13–14).

If Delilah is to deliver Samson to the Philistines and earn for herself monetary recompense, she must develop a new strategy. She does so when she calls on his protestation of love. How can he say he loves her, and then act in such a way that he makes a fool of her? His words and actions are not consistent and she objects. From such a perspective she day after day harasses him. Finally, he tells her the truth: he is a Nazirite, his hair cannot be cut; if it is cut, then his extraordinary strength will cease (vv 15–17).

When Delilah realizes that she has finally wrenched the truth out of him, she calls the Philistines and asks them to come, just once more—she had already subjected them to three false alarms. They come, and they bring the money. Samson, innocent of her intent, falls asleep in her lap. She has one of the men cut his hair, and then, finally, she claims victory over him. This time he had told the truth, and she acted accordingly; his extraordinary strength then left him (vv 18–20). The Philistines are finally able to capture a significant opponent.

Interpretation

Though critics doubt the historical accuracy of all of the "legends" regarding Samson, they nevertheless presume that the legends are about Samson, and they are usually read from

Samson's point of view. Samson, though not necessarily the brightest man—how could he possibly trust a woman who had thrice tried to betray him?—is nevertheless described as innocent, the victim of a deceitful woman. It has even been imagined that the combination of her physical beauty and his extraordinarily strong sexual drive was the reason for his seduction. Such interpreters, placing this story into its larger context, are quick to point out that the story does not end with the loss of Samson's hair and his capture. Though the woman had betrayed him, selling him to the enemy, still, in time, Samson's hair grew back and he regained his strength. He was thus able to triumph over the Philistines after all. Because of his renewed strength, he was able, albeit at the cost of his own life, to kill more Philistines than he had—all told—before that time. The story thus concludes, they purport, with Samson's success; despite Delilah, Samson was able to defeat the Philistines.

Feminist interpretation points to the patriarchal bias in the text. There is no indication that Delilah returned Samson's love. She may even have been a victim of his lust. If he had taken advantage of her, then, given the patriarchal culture, she was in no position to send him away. There is no mention of marriage. Yet, by the way the text is written, the reader is disposed to think that any response from Delilah—apart from her returning Samson's love—is an inappropriate one. Who stops to consider how she may have felt, why she is so willing to betray him; one often stops to consider the motives of other characters. Why is it that her willingness to betray him tends to issue in the reader's judgment against her? The text's patriarchal bias is dangerous because of its subtlety.

Actually, in contrast to Samson, Delilah tells the truth. Three times she asks Samson for the precise information she wants. She honestly admits that she is interested in finding out not only the secret of his strength, but also how he can be bound so as to be subdued. Why is it that the reader is tempted to consider her deceitful when it is Samson who has lied? And why is it that interpreters do not condemn the character of Samson for saying one thing—"I love you"—and doing quite another: bold-faced lies? Delilah may have betrayed Samson for money, but Samson was guilty of hypocrisy and deceit.

Delilah is not identified by her father but by a geographical location—the valley of Sorek. The valley is far to the west. The fact that the Philistines approached her, and trusted her, leads us to believe that either she herself was a Philistine, or at least, that she was not an Israelite. Has she been condemned for a treason of which she is not guilty?

Summary

A recent popular song portrays Delilah as an alluring woman who deceives the stupid and easily seduced Samson. It even suggests more than sexual similarity with "the temptress Eve" (Gen 3). Such songs are what form the popular imagination and reinforce patriarchy in the contemporary culture. A close reading of the text, however, highlights the inappropriateness of any interpretation that accuses Delilah of either seduction or deceit. Hers may have been courageous acts of national loyalty. In any case, a full appreciation of the pervasiveness of patriarchal bias requires the reader to be willing to consider such a possibility.

Hannah's Prayer of Reversals: New Testament Foreshadowings (1 Samuel 2)

The Story

The story of how God overcame the barrenness of a faithful woman is narrated in 1 Sam 1. Hannah made an agreement with the Lord: if God would give her a son, she would, by Nazirite vow, give that son back to the Lord. The Lord agreed to the woman's terms and Hannah gave birth to Samuel. Hannah then carried out her promise; she weaned the child and brought him to the temple that he might "abide always in the presence of the Lord."

Chapter 2 is written, against the backdrop of chap. 1, as Hannah's prayer of thanksgiving to God. The poem opens with Hannah's exuberant heart exalting in God, while her mouth is deriding her enemies. She acknowledges the uniqueness and singularity of God and, in stark contrast, her own lowliness (vv 1–3). The next verses celebrate God's judgment: whereas the weapons of the mighty are destroyed, the feeble are strengthened; whereas the full become hungry, the hungry are satisfied; whereas the mother is deserted, the barren woman becomes a mother (vv 4–5). The Lord is in control of both life and death, of poverty and wealth, of humiliation and exaltation (vv 6–7). The Lord will raise the poor and lift the needy, making the lowly equal partners with princes and granting them places of honor. In fact, everything belongs to God (v 8). Hannah then lauds God's protection of the faithful, and affirms God's expulsion of the wicked, adding the explanatory comment that might does not make right (v 9). God's enemies will be destroyed; God will give power to the king, to the anointed of Yahweh (v 10).

Interpretation

Historical critics distinguish between the literary genre of chaps. 1 and 2 and conclude that they had different authorship with centuries in between. The poetry is considered the older literature, but its inclusion here may be quite late. It is thought that the poem—general in content—is only "applied" to Hannah, put into her mouth, appropriate but hardly particular.

Christian literary critics and New Testament scholars point to the close similarities between 1 Sam 2 and Luke 2:46–55, better known as Mary's Magnificat. When Mary discovers that Elizabeth has recognized the uniqueness of the child she is bearing, Mary proclaims God as Savior, as the one who had, not ignorant of her low estate, transformed it. God is mighty, and holy, and merciful. God has scattered the proud, dethroned the mighty, exalted the lowly (cf. 1 Sam 2:4). God has filled the hungry and allowed the rich to be empty (cf. 1 Sam 2:5). God has been faithful to the promises to Israel. (Whereas the final verse of Hannah's prayer alludes to a monarch, the final verse of Mary's poem alludes to the Messiah.)

Feminists note precisely the appropriateness of Hannah's

prayer—to her own experience as the narrative records it, and to the experience of many women. Hannah herself had enemies, including barrenness and a competitor who ridiculed her because of her barrenness. She also knew what it meant to be powerless. For one thing, she was a woman in a man's world; but worse, she had been a barren woman in that world, lacking even the fulfillment that children could provide. Her recognition that she could do nothing to change her situation, but that God could and, in fact, did alter it, might surely lead to Hannah's easy acknowledgment of God's power and mercy. Her experience might readily give birth to the conviction that God strengthens the feeble, that God provides for the needy, that God who is fully in control raises up the lowly and places them on an equal footing with the others. Had this not been Hannah's own experience? The once-barren Hannah had been vindicated and she, now raised to the fullness of Peninnah, was likewise both wife and mother. God *could* and *had* done this, and God was the kind of God who *would*. Before such a God, what could Hannah do but render praise?

The Deuteronomistic History is not replete with formal prayers. Occasionally one or another of the main characters prays, for example, David in 2 Sam 7, and Solomon in 1 Kgs 3 and 8. Who has noticed that Hannah ranks with the kings, but that unlike David's and Solomon's prayers, hers is one lacking further request? She is grateful for God's action in her life, and experiences that action as a paradigm of God's action in history. The reader is called upon to learn from Hannah's experience and to learn to recognize in it his or her own experience.

Summary

Just as Miriam sings of God's victory for Israel over the Egyptians, and Deborah sings of God's victory for Israel over Sisera's army (and Mary will eventually exalt in God's Messiah), so here Hannah praises God's victory over her enemies—over powerlessness, and barrenness, and inferiority—and likewise, she gives thanks to God. She is part of the long-unsung tradition of women who remember to give thanks (cf. Luke 17:11–19).

David's Female Saviors:
Michal; Abigail;
an Unnamed Maidservant;
an Unnamed Wise Woman
(I Samuel 19; 25; 2 Samuel 17; 20)

The Story

Anyone who knows anything about Western culture has at least heard of the great king David. Some have heard of his wife Bathsheba, though often what they have heard about her is distorted. Few have heard of his other wives, and almost none have heard about the four women who saved David from disaster and death. The first of these, Michal, a daughter of King Saul, became a wife of David. She loved David (1 Sam 18:20), and once, when Saul was seeking to kill David, her courageous actions preserved his life. The episode is recorded in 1 Sam 19:11–17.

Saul had for some time been seeking David's life. He himself had, at least twice, unsuccessfully thrown a sword at David (1 Sam 18:11; 19:10); he had also created a trap—which had proven unsuccessful—whereby the Philistines would kill David (18:27). Moreover, Saul had alerted his son Jonathan and all his servants that if any one of them saw David, they were to kill him (19:1). Saul was desperately jealous.

In order to guarantee David's death, Saul sent messengers to watch David's house. Saul intended to come in the morning to kill David (19:11). Saul's plan might have worked, had not his own daughter betrayed her father for the sake of her husband. Michal warned David. She said that tomorrow would be too late. David must flee immediately. Michal helped David out a window so that he might successfully escape (v 12).

But Michal's work did not end there. She made a dummy and put it in his bed. The next morning when Saul's messengers came for David, she stalled them with a lie; she told them that he was sick. They reported this back to Saul. His reply was to bring the bedridden David to him so that he might kill him (vv 13–15).

When Saul's messengers approached the bed, they found only the dummy. Saul then asked Michal why she had deceived him and let his enemy escape. Michal's response was another lie, a crafty one which would save her as the other lie had helped to save David. She led her father to believe that she had no other option (vv 16–17).

Interpretation

Historical critics unanimously agree that 1 Sam 16—2 Sam 5 chronicle David's rise to power. David is the main character. Structuring the text thus, they interpret Saul as being David's chief adversary, Samuel as being the Lord's prophet who anoints David, and Jonathan as being the son of Saul who enters into a covenant with David. The others are lesser characters. Michal is one of these. Her role is also defined vis-à-vis the character of David, but is less significant. Though in many ways her character has much in common with Jonathan's—a child of Saul who transfers her loyalty to David—she is never the subject of David's praise (cf. 2 Sam 2).

This text portrays a woman who takes initiative on her husband's behalf at personal risk. Had she not exerted leadership and persuaded David to flee, Saul's messengers might have captured him; had she not intervened, David's history—and Israel's—as the texts portray it, might have been very different. Yet if Michal is remembered at all, it is because of deception; she lied. Or else she is remembered because she refused to tolerate David's "uncovering himself" before the servant girls (cf. 2 Sam 6:20), a gesture for which she was severely punished (v 23).

Feminists wish to rehabilitate Michal. In true patriarchal fashion she was here faithful to her husband. She had belonged to her father, Saul, but she now belonged to David. Later, her father would give her over to another husband, Palti (1 Sam 25:44), but because she had not been Saul's to give, David could demand her return (2 Sam 3:13–14). As David's wife, she used prudence, courage, and cunning to save him from her father's pursuit and from almost-certain death. Interpreters are accustomed to laud the character of men who act with such bravery; readers must begin to laud the character of such women also.

First Samuel 19 is devoted to Jonathan's saving David from Saul (vv 2–7), Michal's saving David from Saul (vv 11–17), and Samuel's saving David from Saul (vv 18–24). Why is it, then, that so much more has been made of Samuel's and Jonathan's roles than of Michal's?

The Story

Abigail is introduced as the wife of Nabal in 1 Sam 25. Immediately the reader is given a character contrast: she is "of good understanding and beautiful" while he is "churlish and ill-behaved." The reader can only anticipate that she will somehow surpass her husband.

Nabal is next contrasted with David. When David was in the fields, he had generously provided for the well-being of Nabal's shepherds. Now, when David seeks a similar favor, Nabal refuses. David's instinctive response to this rejection is to fight.

Nabal's men make known to Abigail Nabal's refusal of hospitality. One concludes that they count on her to intervene to change her husband's mind. As the episode continues, Abigail does intervene— but not with Nabal. Abigail seeks out David who has, in the meantime, sworn to destroy Nabal. She offers him provisions which she has brought and pleads with him not to take vengeance. When the Lord has made David a house—which God surely will since David is fighting the Lord's battles—David will not want to have committed any evil, including the shedding of blood without cause. Abigail asks that David remember her when the Lord has appointed him prince over Israel.

David's response both to God and to Abigail is one of gratitude. Her words are the vehicle of God's promise for David's future. Had she not warned him, he would have rashly acted out his anger and massacred Nabal's household.

Abigail returns home to a drunken husband. When she tells him what has happened, he becomes despondent and shortly thereafter he dies. David takes the news of Nabal's death as his own vindication. Nabal was fittingly punished. Abigail, however, had saved David from being the one to inflict the punishment. Nabal now dead, Abigail was free to become David's wife.

Interpretation

Traditional interpretation centers on vv 28 and 30, the promise made to David through Abigail that the Lord will make him a sure house and appoint him prince over Israel. The rest of the story is interpreted as little more than the setting for this promise.

Feminists protest. The character Abigail becomes an overlooked literary tool to accomplish male ends—men's history. The literary context is worth closer scrutiny. Beside her husband Nabal, Abigail stands tall. She has "understanding," while he is "ill-natured." She is respected by her husband's shepherds who appeal to her, confirming that David is owed recompense for the hospitality he had shown them. She is assertive; she recognizes Nabal's limitations (perhaps that it would be futile to try to change his mind or his behavior toward David's men) and acts accordingly. She seeks out David on her own, without even telling her husband that she is leaving. She becomes the messenger of God's revelation to David (the text anticipates 2 Sam 7). Moreover, she is upright; she returns to her husband, though everything one knows of him would not make that a desirable thing to do. Yet, despite her beauty, her intelligence, her assertiveness, and her role as an instrument of promise, Abigail is very much situated in a polygamous patriarchal culture. She who had saved David from bloodguilt becomes, after Nabal's death, one of David's many wives.

The Story

Buried in 2 Sam 17 is the story of a maidservant who risked her own well-being, if not her very life, to save David from Absalom. Two counselors tell Absalom how to defeat his father, David. Ahithophel's advice is sound. Hushai, who is secretly loyal to David, however, offers that advice which Absalom will follow, advice which will allow the Lord to bring evil on Absalom (v 14).

Hushai's advice calls for Absalom to wait until morning before pursuing David. This will give Hushai a chance to send messengers to David, to tell him what both he and Ahithophel had counseled Absalom and to tell David what he should do. Hushai informs the priests who in turn will relay Hushai's message to messengers who will report to David (vv 15–17). However, the process of transferring the information includes a woman. The priests and the messengers need a go-between, someone who will not arouse Absalom's suspicion. An unnamed maidservant performs this function (v 17).

The plan might have gone smoothly had not a lad seen the two messengers and informed Absalom. The messengers, realizing they were being pursued, sought hiding in a well. The woman then covered the well and disguised it. When Absalom's servants came to the house where the well was, they asked the woman where the messengers were. She lied. She told them that the messengers had crossed the brook. They believed her and their pursuit was therefore unsuccessful (vv 18–20).

Interpretation

This narrative is usually interpreted from the perspective of David's loyal counselor, Hushai. Though his son betrayed him and would even kill him, David's friend was loyal. And God used Hushai's counsel to bring evil upon Absalom (v 14). The event is thus explicitly interpreted, within the text itself, as God's judgment in favor of David.

A close examination of the text reveals that the narrative names all the men involved—David and Absalom, Ahithophel and Hushai, the priests Zadok and Abiathar (v 15), the messengers Jonathan and Ahimaaz (vv 17, 20)—but the maidservant, whose cleverness and whose lie saved the messengers and indirectly saved David, remains anonymous. Had she perhaps not been a "maidservant," but rather, either the daughter or the wife of a prominent male character, the reader might know her name. As the text now stands, however, she is an unsung heroine, another unnamed victim of both patriarchy and hierarchy.

The Story

Another insurrection against David is narrated in 2 Sam 20: this one under the leadership of the Benjaminite Sheba. The northern tribes joined Sheba, while Judah remained staunchly loyal to David (vv 1–2). David needed to get the upper hand against Sheba quickly.

Any delay would allow Sheba time to gather more men. Joab and Abishai lead David's forces out to meet Sheba's, which they do at the walled city of Abel (v 15). While David's men are battering the wall, a woman calls out from within the city. She wants to talk to Joab. She tells him that she is a loyalist, and that she does not want the city destroyed. Joab assures her that he is not interested in destroying the city; he only wants to get at the traitor Sheba. She tells Joab that Sheba's head will be thrown over the wall (vv 16–21).

The woman then proceeds to convince the people that Sheba's head is less a loss to them than their city. Consequently, they cut off Sheba's head and throw it over the wall to Joab. Sheba's death puts an end to the revolt (v 22).

Interpretation

Placing this episode in context, it is another example of David's difficulty in maintaining the kingship over all Israel (cf. 2 Sam 15). The story also illustrates, at one level, Joab and Abishai's loyalty to David, though later Joab's killing Amasa (2 Sam 20:10) will be an excuse for Solomon to rid his kingdom of a potential military coup (cf. 1 Kgs 2:5, 28–34).

The unnamed woman is twice called wise (vv 16, 22). Had she not intervened, Sheba's rebellion might not have been crushed, or might have been crushed only at the cost of countless innocent victims and a city's destruction. That she did intervene may even have saved David's life. Certainly it saved some of his power and prestige. David and Sheba have names; Joab has a name; Abishai has a name; even Amasa has a name. All the men who have individual identities have names; only the woman remains nameless.

Yet the woman proves to be wiser than any of the men. Sheba tries a revolt which leads to his death. David, Joab, and Abishai would end that revolt, but not before many deaths. Amasa's action occasions his own death (vv 5, 10). The wise woman saves lives—ultimately David's, but also the lives of many of the people in her city, and the lives of many of Joab and Abishai's forces. Sheba was stupid; David, Joab, Abishai, and Amasa were "not too smart"; the woman was wise!

Summary

Rarely do introductions to the study of the Old Testament high-light those women whose efforts saved David and secured his well-being, including Michal (1 Sam 19), Abigail (1 Sam 25), an unnamed maidservant (2 Sam 17), and a likewise-unnamed wise woman (2 Sam 20). Yet the narratives report that these women acted on David's behalf with courage and cunning, with prudence and shrewdness, and often even at personal risk. One does Israel's history a disservice and these female characters an injustice if one fails to render them their rightful recognition.

Cursing by Making Reference to One's Mother
(1 Samuel 20)

The Story

Rarely in the Old Testament is it recorded that a father curses his son, especially when that son could be the future king of Israel! On the contrary, David continues to love his son Absalom even though he proves to be a traitor to his father (2 Sam 18). Yet Saul curses Jonathan. A close reading of the texts surrounding 1 Sam 20:30–31 may lead the reader to the conclusion that Saul's primary interest lay not with Jonathan's future but with his own jealousy of David. Nevertheless, regardless of motive, Saul does curse his own son.

Traditionally men are proud of their sons, claim them as their own, and render the mothers who bore them little recognition. When a son fails to meet his father's standards, however, then the father may disown his son, denying the paternal relationship and blaming the son's behavior on his mother. Such is the case in 1 Sam 20. Whereas Saul hated David and had tried to kill him, Jonathan loved David and would seek to protect him. Further, Jonathan would even bestow on David his own robe and armor (1 Sam 18:4). Such a posture infuriated Saul. What he needed in his son was an ally against David, not an ally of David. When it became clear to Saul that Jonathan would remain loyal to David, Saul's anger against his son grew. This is the setting for Saul's curse.

Saul identified Jonathan as the son of "a perverse, rebellious woman" (yet not one so important that she is ever named!). Somehow, that his mother was perverse and rebellious seems to account in Saul's mind for Jonathan's perversion and rebellion. Certainly Saul himself could not be the cause of these traits! And there was no doubt in Saul's mind that Jonathan was perverse and rebellious. From Saul's perspective it was downright shameful that Jonathan should support David. Did he not realize that David was a contender with him for his father's throne? How could he then—if he were not perverse and rebellious—protect David? By protecting David he shamed himself and "his mother's nakedness," that is, his mother's role in conceiving him. Saul stooped to insulting Jonathan's mother in his effort to change his son's attitudes and behavior toward David.

Interpretation

A popular contemporary form of cursing accuses the person cursed of being an offspring out of wedlock. He—whether male or female!—is the son of a woman who had not been married at the time of the child's conception. Those who speak English rarely reflect on the pejorative character of the curse, not just to the person cursed, but to the woman who bore that person. There is no similar curse accusing the person cursed of being the offspring of an unmarried male! Obviously this contemporary curse is an expression of patriarchy!

Should the reader be surprised then that the patriarchal culture of ancient Israel possessed a curse which accused the person of having a "problematic" mother? A closer examination of this curse reveals an accusation, not that Jonathan was conceived out of wedlock—that accusation might be inappropriate for a potential monarch—but an accusation that Jonathan's mother was perverse and rebellious. The accusation, in the contemporary curse, of conception outside marriage is often a false one; might the reader conclude that the accusation of perversity and rebelliousness is equally false? Or, if Jonathan's actions which Saul uses to explain the curse are any indication, Jonathan's mother's only real fault was that she did not silently submit to Saul!

Saul perceives Jonathan's attitude toward David to be disgraceful. He thus concludes that it is also, implicitly, a cause of shame to his mother's "nakedness." In other words, Saul believes that Jonathan's actions not only do not exalt his existence, they call the very legitimacy of that existence into question. Perhaps it would have been better—less shame to his mother—had he not been born! Since childbirth made women unclean, it was a mixed blessing. Offspring were a blessing for women, to be sure, but a perverse and rebellious child . . . Was it worth it? Saul uses the woman, his own sexual partner and the mother of Jonathan. He baits Jonathan with her in an effort to secure his own will against David and perhaps in favor of his son.

Here again the woman is a nameless victim. Who knows what she thinks, whether she has been portrayed justly or has herself been perverted by the very character who accuses her of perversion?

Summary

Verses such as 1 Sam 20:30–31 rarely merit comment in an introduction, or even, for that matter, in a commentary on 1 Sam. Yet precisely because cursing by making an insulting reference to a person's mother is not new—it is as old as ancient Israel—has the incident been included here.

Not Just Any Mother: Zeruiah
(2 Samuel 2; 17—19; 21; 23;
1 Kings 1—2)

The Story

Genealogies are one expression of patriarchal culture. A line of descendants is traced from father to son, from son become father to a new generation, and so on for centuries. While a son is identified by his father but himself becomes the means whereby his son is identified, a daughter is identified by her father until such time as she is identified by her husband. Only very rarely is a child identified by its mother. Nevertheless, in no fewer than eight chapters of the Deuteronomistic History, three significant characters are identified, not by their father but by their mother.

They are Joab, Abishai, and Asahel; their mother is Zeruiah (2 Sam 2:18).

Asahel is only once identified as Zeruiah's son; he is a minor character who is killed by Abner (2 Sam 2:23). Zeruiah's other two sons, Joab and Abishai, however, play more significant roles. David places each of them over one-third of his army (2 Sam 18:2; cf. 23:18). Twice Abishai is particularized as the son of Zeruiah (2 Sam 19:21; 21:17). He suggests to David that Shimei be put to death, but David rejects the "sons" of Zeruiah's revengeful stance. Later he defends David from the spear of Ishbibenob.

Narrative style may dictate which texts describe Joab as the son of Zeruiah. One names Joab's armor-bearer (2 Sam 23:37); two others report that Joab supported Adonijah over Solomon as David's successor (1 Kgs 1:7; 2:22). Another text notes that he avenged Asahel's death by killing Abner (1 Kgs 2:5; cf. 2 Sam 2:23). Abigail is identified once as the sister of Zeruiah (2 Sam 17:25).

Interpretation

Though Asahel functions as a minor character—his death helps to justify Solomon's eventual rejection of Joab—both Joab and Abishai are prominent characters. This makes their identification as sons of a mother both unusual and significant. It also justifies the speculation that other men may be similarly identified—as sons of their mother—but that our prejudiced reading has presumed that the proper name refers to a male. (Because some names occur in the biblical text only once, it is impossible to know for certain whether they refer to a man or to a woman.) In any event, Zeruiah is identified as a woman, a mother, and the sons whom she bore are identified not through a father but through her.

One may hypothesize that Asahel, Joab, and Abishai are identified as sons of their mother either because their mother was herself the daughter of a prominent father, or else because she was a harlot and their father is unknown. If the former suggestion is preferred, then the texts represent a lesser form of patriarchal prejudice in a nevertheless patriarchal culture. If, on the other hand, the latter suggestion is preferred, then one is faced with another instance of a harlot who, as such, is a victim of patriarchy but whose very bondage brings its own kind of liberation (cf. Rahab in Josh 2; 6).

Summary

The verses which name Zeruiah are buried in episodes which report the activities of men. For this reason, and because the woman is identified not as person but as mother, in relationship to sons, they may be considered patriarchal narrative reports. Nevertheless, a woman, Zeruiah, replaces a man in the identification of three sons and that small detail needs to be recognized as an exception to the pervasive custom of the culture.

Bathsheba: David's Victim
(2 Samuel 11—12)

The Story

It is the custom of kings to go out to battle during the spring but David does not do what kings normally do. He lets his general and his people go out to war, but he stays home (11:1). While at home, after his afternoon siesta, he goes for a stroll on his roof and looks out at a beautiful woman bathing (v 2). David wants the woman. Though she is possessed by another—she is identified as the daughter of Eliam and the wife of Uriah—he takes Bathsheba and lies with her (vv 3–4). When the woman realizes that she is pregnant, the narrator tells us that she informs David (v 5). In the entire story the character Bathsheba never speaks.

David then plots to recall Uriah from battle and get him to sleep with his wife. The plan, however, proves unsuccessful. Uriah is unwilling to enjoy his wife while the rest of Israel is at battle (vv 6–11). Even when David deliberately gets Uriah drunk to weaken his resistance, Uriah does not submit (vv 12–13). The first plot having failed, David then schemes to secure Uriah's death in battle, a plan which succeeds (vv 14–17).

Joab executes David's will. He orders Israelite soldiers, including Uriah, to approach the enemy's city walls. Such strategy could facilitate victory but only at the cost of many Israelite lives. David might object to Joab's use of this strategy because it would cause the deaths of many Israelites, even allowing women to participate in the defense of their city and these deaths; however, David applauds the strategy once he learns that it had achieved Uriah's death (vv 18–21). David's response is just as Joab had predicted (vv 22–25).

The narrator informs the reader that the wife of Uriah—here identified not by name but by "wife"—made lament for her husband's death. When the appropriate mourning period was over, however, David sent for her and she became his wife and bore him a son. The chapter closes with a summary comment which is also an ominous foreshadowing: what David had done was displeasing to the Lord (vv 26–27).

Interpretation

Historical critics, in interpreting this text, note the absence of a similar version in the Book of Chronicles with its "whitewashing" of the hero David. They suggest some historical basis for this text, though its interpretation (2 Sam 12) is considered a deuteronomistic insertion which explains, according to deuteronomistic theology, that David was punished for his sin. His sin is there twice named as taking Uriah's wife to be his own (12:9–10) and David's punishment includes his wives being taken and given to another (v 11).

Literary critics point to the contrast between the characters of David and Uriah. Uriah is a non-Israelite, a Hittite, yet he proves more faithful than the Israelite king. David apparently thought nothing of having sexual intercourse—even with women not his own—while his soldiers were out on the battlefield; Uriah, standing in solidarity with the soldiers, sacrificed sex, even with his wife. Literary critics suggest that v 1 serves as a foreshadowing of David's inappropriate behavior: while most kings are with their soldiers on the battlefield, David has stayed home. David is portrayed as totally selfish, plotting—at all costs, even murder—to hide the fact that he had impregnated Bathsheba. In contrast, Uriah is portrayed as a man of highest integrity. There is also contained in the text the subtle implication that just as women can destroy soldiers who come too close to the city walls, a beautiful woman can destroy the great David. He takes somebody else's property, that is, Uriah's wife, and his punishment includes the fact that somebody else takes his property, his concubines (2 Sam 16:22).

Feminists are particularly sensitive to how male chauvinists have misinterpreted the character of Bathsheba. The text in no way suggests that her bathing was immodest. David was on the roof of his palace (the highest roof in Jerusalem?), looking down. From there he could see the whole city, and everyone in it. In addition, the text does not indicate whether or not Bathsheba had any choice in the matter. David sent for her and she came, but he, after all, was king. One did not lightly ignore the command of the king. And there is no reason to suspect that Bathsheba knew what David wanted before she arrived anyway. In fact, the contrary is more likely. After all, Bathsheba was a married woman; she belonged to someone else. Israel had laws regarding taking someone else's wife (e.g., Exod 20:17). Deuteronomy 22:22 even provides that "if a man is found lying with the wife of another man, both of them shall die, the man who lay with the woman and the woman." David was Israel's leader. He was to be an example of covenant fidelity!

When Bathsheba found out that her husband had been killed, she mourned for him. Whether her mourning was simply to fulfill ritual law, or whether she truly cared for Uriah and lamented his death, the reader will never know. In any case, any pregnant woman with no husband—especially a woman whose pregnancy was not due to her husband!—had every reason to mourn! She had become the truly powerless person in ancient Israel. The narrator reports that when the period of mourning had passed, David sent for Bathsheba. She then became David's wife and bore him their son.

The patriarchal culture of ancient Israel justifies Bathsheba's action in marrying David in at least three ways. First of all, if she had been raped, then, since she had become a widow, she was eligible to marry the man who had violated her (e.g., Deut 22:28). Second, a widow, with or without a fatherless son, was powerless in Israelite society. Since access came only through the man to whom she was attached, a widow's remarriage was certainly most desirable. Bathsheba would not likely refuse any man who was willing. Third, in this particular case, Bathsheba would be marrying the father of her child.

Yet the text screams out the victimization of Bathsheba. First, it is possible—even likely—that she was taken against her will;

then, she is widowed because of the manipulations of the man who will become her future husband; then she "should be happy" to marry her rapist. Most horrifying of all is the fact that many commentators not only fail to understand Bathsheba's character as victim; they denounce her as seductress. That she was bathing and that she was beautiful are given as "explanations" for David's actions, as if taking a bath and being beautiful are somehow faults she committed. On the contrary, David's greed and David's selfishness would stop at nothing—seduction, manipulation, even murder.

Second Samuel 12 addresses David's greed as a reason for the problematic future of his reign, but interpreters often fail to exploit fully the fact that what happened was his problem, not Bathsheba's! David is never accused of sinning against Bathsheba—though he may have raped her and secured her husband's death. Rather, David's sin is understood to have been against God and against Uriah, the man who possessed Bathsheba. And David's punishment is not understood to be against his concubines who become sexual objects for another man. They are given no consideration. They are possessions of David who must be surrendered to another man, in payment for his having seized the possession of Uriah!

Summary

Because of David's sin the child whom Bathsheba bore died (2 Sam 12:14). David sinned and, according to deuteronomistic theology, David was punished. But who notices that David sinned and *Bathsheba* was punished? Few commentaries point out that the loss of her son was an injustice rendered to Bathsheba. In the patriarchal culture which produced the text, there was no injustice. The woman become wife belonged to her man, and she could expect nothing but to partake of his punishment. As possessed person, she was again victim.

For the time being, Bathsheba was deprived, through no fault of her own, of that access to power which was available to woman as mother. Bathsheba did, however, bear David another son, Solomon (12:24), and Solomon, with Bathsheba's help, succeeded David as king (e.g., 1 Kgs 1:17). The reader may conclude that Bathsheba possessed more power than most women who lived in Israel during the tenth century B.C.—she was queen and then queen mother—yet Bathsheba's power was by virtue of her roles, the only roles the patriarchal culture of ancient Israel allowed women. She was the wife of King David and the mother of King Solomon. Her power derived from the influential men in her life!

Tamar: Victim of Incest and Rape
(2 Samuel 13)

The Story

In this chapter Absalom is identified as the son of David, Tamar as the sister of Absalom, and Amnon as the son of David (v 1). The way the characters are identified foreshadows what will transpire among them. Amnon loved his virgin sister Tamar (vv 1, 4). He was tormented by the passion but he could not conceive of acting on it. His friend Jonadab conceived a plan. Amnon was to pretend to be sick, and to request from his father that Tamar be sent to provide for him. Amnon did as Jonadab suggested (vv 3–6) and the plan worked.

David told Tamar to go to Amnon's tent to attend to his needs and she obeyed. Amnon, however, refused to eat the food Tamar had prepared for him until everyone had departed and he was alone with her. He then requested that Tamar come near him; when she did, he grabbed her and ordered her to lie with him. Up to this point in the narrative, Tamar has not spoken. Amnon has spoken, Jonadab has spoken, David has spoken. Tamar's first words are to reject Amnon's request. What he is asking is not acceptable behavior in Israel. By so acting, he would sin and she would be disgraced. She asks him to go about this the right way: to ask her father for her. He refuses and forces himself upon her (vv 7–14).

Amnon's love for Tamar then turns to hate and he orders her to leave. Again, she speaks and again her words plead that he not act as he intends. Sending her away would be a greater wrong than raping her. Again, he refuses her request (vv 15–16). The narrator informs the reader that Tamar had been wearing a long robe customary for virgins. To symbolize that she was no longer a virgin, she tore her robe. To symbolize the grief, she put ashes on her head, and lay her hand there. Tamar wept (vv 17–19). Her brother Absalom (cf. v 1) concluded what had happened and tried to console her. He took her in. When David heard what had happened, he was angry. Absalom's response was to hate Amnon (vv 20–22).

Interpretation

Historical critics include the chapter as part of the Succession Narrative. The text will eventually exclude two sons of David, Amnon and Absalom, from being contenders for David's throne. The text also contributes to the working out of the punishment promised David after his theft of Bathsheba and Uriah's murder: the sword would not depart from his house (12:10).

Literary critics mark the contrast between love and hate. Amnon loved his sister Tamar (vv 1, 4); after the rape, Amnon hated his sister Tamar (v 15); Absalom hated Amnon for what he had done to Tamar, a foreshadowing of things to come (v 22). They point also to the careful construction of the story. Though v 1 introduces both Absalom and Amnon as sons of David, it introduces Tamar as Absalom's sister; it is Absalom, not David, who will take Tamar in and avenge her. At this stage in the larger narrative, the two brothers are strongly contrasted. Absalom is the protector of the innocent while his brother is the evil oppressor.

Feminist interpretation points to the woman as victim of incest and rape. She obeys her father David's request to provide for her brother Amnon, but David does not later provide for her! When she speaks it is to uphold the laws of Israel. She does not reject Amnon; she will become his if he so wishes. He need only get her from her father. (She belongs to her father, not to herself; if he agrees—which she thinks he will—she will consent.) What Tamar does reject is the way Amnon wishes to take her; she loses. Amnon may, and with good reason (cf. Deut 22:22), believe that David will not consent. He does not seem to care; he wants Tamar and he will take her.

Tamar again upholds the laws of Israel when she begs Amnon to keep her after he has raped her (cf. Deut 22:28–29). Who would want to marry one's rapist, especially under the circumstances as they are here described? Yet not to do so meant an even worse fate. The culture from which Tamar's character emerges gives her no choice. Her brother rapes her; her rapist rejects her; her father neither defends her nor does he punish the one who has so abused her. In her future lies only desolation and shame.

To the extent that the text is interpreted from either a historical or a literary perspective, the horror of the victimization of women is trivialized. Interpreters quickly point out that the rape is avenged—Absalom later kills Amnon. They also note that Absalom names his own beautiful daughter "Tamar" (14:27). These vindications, however, do not make Tamar any less a victim. Her life has been irrevocably ruined. She did nothing to deserve the incest, or the rape, or the future to which the patriarchal culture relegated raped women.

Summary

The worst thing about this story is that it is still occurring, and that the judgment of interpreters still continues to be against the women who are, in fact, the innocent victims. Just as Tamar was beautiful (v 1; cf. 2 Sam 11:2), victims of rape are often accused of being "beautiful," of presenting themselves as "too attractive," even "seductive." And just as Tamar unwittingly got close to Amnon (v 11), victims of rape are often blamed for not suspecting their aggressors' intent and, consequently, for not taking appropriate preventive measures. Finally, just as Tamar's future was eclipsed because of her brother Amnon's violence against her, contemporary women who have been sexually violated continue to be regarded by many as damaged goods!

Outwitting the King:
The Wise Woman of Tekoa
(2 Samuel 14)

The Story

After Amnon had raped his sister Tamar and Absalom had killed his brother Amnon, David expelled Absalom from his kingdom (2 Sam 13). Chapter 14 then tells the story of how Joab secured Absalom's return.

Joab thought up a scheme for which he needed a wise woman. He secured one—a woman who is never named in the chapter—from Tekoa (v 2) and told her what to do. She was to dress and act as though she had been many days in mourning and she was to appear before the king with the following story (v 3). She was to tell the king that she was a widow who had had two sons. She now had only one son, however, because the two sons had quarreled and the one had killed the other. The family wanted to avenge the death by killing her other son. If that were to happen, her husband's name would cease to exist in Israel—there would be no son to have children—and she, as childless widow, would have no one (and would be completely powerless in the society). She was to beg for the king's help (vv 4–7).

In the dialogue which follows, the widow convinces the king that "the avenger of blood should slay no more" and the king agrees to protect her living son (vv 8–11). That allows the "widow" to compare her situation to David's, and to press David to recall Absalom (vv 12–17). But David is not stupid. He demands that the woman answer his questions, and then asks if Joab had put her up to this. She admits it and praises the king's wisdom (vv 18–20). David then allows Joab to recall Absalom (v 21).

Interpretation

Some historical-critical commentators locate the village of Tekoa for the reader and suggest that, whereas David might know the people of his own city, a woman from a small southern village could tell him anything—even what Joab dictated—and David would have no reason to doubt her word. Further, using this text as a springboard, they pursue the role of wisdom in ancient Israel. In contrast, literary critics point to a carefully wrought story as a way of telling truth, and compare the account with Judg 9:7–15 and 2 Sam 12:1–7.

Feminist critics point to both the content of the story and then to the use of the woman. The content of the story, which makes good patriarchal sense to the king, is the plight of a widow who is about to lose her son. The story takes for granted the fact that a woman needed a man if she were to have an identity—either a father or a husband or a son—and a dead man needed a living son if he were to have his name kept alive in Israel (cf. the Levirate law). The gravity of the woman's plight is readily understood by David. Though avenging a dead person is important, keeping one's son alive is more important. Contemporary feminists bemoan the poor woman's plight—she is fully dependent on a son for whose life she must fight. Since children were so important to a woman in the culture, the reader can presume the mother's attachment to him.

Feminists, however, also point to this text as an example of an exception within patriarchal culture. For one thing, the narrative contains sexual reversals of the story contained in 1 Kgs 3. There it was King Solomon's wisdom which determined the real mother of the living son. Here, it is the unnamed woman's wisdom which calls King David to again acknowledge his son Absalom.

Moreover, feminists note that a wise woman could do what Joab could not. Though Joab gave her most of her script, the woman proved wise indeed when David recognized its source. She was not merely a "Poll Parrot" of Joab's words; she was a courageous woman who, with composure and without fear, approached the king with Joab's agenda and successfully executed it.

Summary

The narrator names the woman who secures Absalom's return as wise (v 2) while the woman herself asserts that the king (David) has wisdom "like the wisdom of a messenger of God" (v 20). One should not fail to observe the linguistic comparisons subtly being made here. The woman is like the king, not only in significant aspects of the content of her story, but especially in her possession of wisdom. But if the woman is like the king, she is also like the messenger of God—not only because she serves as a messenger, but especially because of her wisdom. She has a patriarchal script in a patriarchal culture, but she is in no way portrayed as a victim of patriarchal prejudice. She is a notable exception.

Rizpah's Story: Violated Concubine
and Faithful Mother
(2 Samuel 3; 21)

The Story

Rizpah first appears in 2 Sam 3:7, identified as a concubine of Saul. Ishbosheth, Saul's son, accuses Abner, Saul's general, of violating Rizpah. Abner is furious. He retorts that he has been loyal to Saul and his family, protecting them from David. He interprets the taking of Rizpah, by comparison, as a minor matter, and insinuates that if Ishbosheth does not appreciate his loyalty, he will use his influence on behalf of David's cause and help him secure the kingship.

Interpretation

Traditional interpretation of this text stresses the significance of taking another man's woman—that in taking Rizpah Abner was usurping Saul's possession and Saul's place. Absalom would violate David's concubines in front of all the people as a way of asserting himself over David (2 Sam 16:21–22) and Adonijah would try, albeit unsuccessfully, to take Abishag, the late David's concubine, from Solomon (1 Kgs 2:19–22). One simply did not take another man's woman and get away with it (cf. 2 Sam 11—12). The text gives an explanation for why Abner transferred his loyalty to David, and eventually for why Joab met his end (1 Kgs 2:5).

Feminists wish to remember Rizpah. She never speaks in the episode; she never chooses; what happens is done to her, seemingly beyond her control. The patriarchal culture which produced the text does not condemn Abner for what he did to Rizpah. In fact, it hardly condemns him for what, in taking Rizpah, he did to Saul (unless one interprets Abner's death as Saul's vindication). Rizpah is, rather, the silent and overlooked detail in a male power struggle.

The Story

No mention is made of Rizpah again until 2 Sam 21. The reader is then informed that Saul, Rizpah's partner, had violated Israel's covenant with the Gibeonites. David recognized the violation and wished to know how he could recompense the people for their loss.

They responded by calling for the deaths of seven of Saul's sons, including two whom Rizpah, now a widow, had borne him. David consented and the seven were hanged.

Rizpah took the sackcloth of mourning and went to Gibeon to the place where her sons hung; she kept vigil there through the harvest, preventing the birds and beasts from harming their bodies. When David heard what Rizpah had been doing, he brought Saul's and Jonathan's remains, as well as the remains of the others, from Jabesh-Gilead to Benjamin where he buried them.

Interpretation

Rizpah cannot prevent her sons' deaths. The decision to hang them is made by men—the Gibeonites and David. She can only prevent their further violation—by birds and beasts. This she does—through the harvest season until the rain. One concludes from the text that the respect she exhibited for the dead proved an effective example to David; having heard of her loyalty, he arranged for the burial of her sons with their father. Though Rizpah does not speak, she does act, and her actions speak louder than words.

Summary

Rizpah could easily be forgotten, lost among the men who determine her life. She is a victim—violated and widowed; she is a mourning mother. She had been violated, but her sons had been violated as well. Typical of what happens in a patriarchal culture, Rizpah did not respond on her own behalf; however, she did take action to protect the bodies of her sons. Rizpah's actions were not in vain. The man who had agreed to her sons' death, David, would now at least bury them. She used what power she had.

Ahab's Named Jezebel and Elijah's and Elisha's Nameless Women (1 Kings 16; 18; 21; 2 Kings 9; 1 Kings 17; 2 Kings 4; 8)

Historical and literary scholars designate 1 Kgs 17—2 Kgs 9 as the "Legends of Elijah and Elisha." The chapters are thought to have been produced early in the history of the Northern Kingdom. Together they portray the power of Yahweh's prophets who control the history according to the plan of God. To prophets, because they speak and do the word of Yahweh, even kings must bow.

The Story

At the end of 1 Kgs 16 is a short notation regarding Ahab, the son of Omri, who succeeded his father on the throne of Israel. The deuteronomistic evaluation of Ahab's kingship accuses him of doing more evil than his predecessors. Among his monstrous offenses is to be included his marriage to Jezebel, the daughter of Ethbaal, king of the Sidonians (16:31).

Chapter 18 becomes more specific in its reference to Jezebel's sin. She cut off the prophets of the Lord (vv 4, 13) whereas she allowed 450 prophets of Baal and 400 prophets of Asherah to eat at her table (v 19). Moreover, when Jezebel learned how Elijah had humiliated the prophets of Baal at Mount Carmel and how he had overcome the drought (chap. 17), she sought to kill him (1 Kgs 19:2-3). Fortunately, however, he was able to escape.

Jezebel has Naboth killed in order to add his vineyard to Ahab's property (1 Kgs 21). Ahab had wanted the property but would not have taken it against Naboth's will. Naboth was unwilling because the vineyard belonged to the inheritance of his fathers. Property was to be passed on from father to sons and was not to be traded or sold outside the tribe (cf. Lev 25:13, 23). When Jezebel perceived Ahab's disappointment at not being able to have the vineyard he wanted, she resolved to get it for him (1 Kgs 21:7).

Jezebel usurped the power and prestige of the king. She signed Ahab's name and used the king's seal for letters that she sent to the elders of Naboth's city. They were to get base fellows who would accuse Naboth of a crime such that he would be stoned (vv 8-10). The elders did as the letters dictated and Naboth was stoned to death (vv 11-13). The nobles of the city then reported Naboth's death to Jezebel. Jezebel in turn told Ahab of Naboth's death and instructed him to take for his own the vineyard which he had wanted. This Ahab did (vv 15-16).

The prophet Elijah enters the scene to bring the Lord's word of condemnation on what has happened. Ahab will die in the very place which he had so much coveted (vv 17-19). Further, his house will be destroyed (vv 20-22, 24). Finally, Elijah curses Jezebel: the dogs will eat her in Jezreel (v 23). The narrator's conclusion echoes 1 Kgs 16:30: Ahab surpassed the other northern kings in his capacity to do evil. Yet here, the ultimate blame is placed on Jezebel, his wife; she incited him (v 25).

Jehu becomes Yahweh's instrument to fulfill God's word (2 Kgs 9). He is to avenge on Jezebel the blood of all Yahweh's servants, including the prophets (cf. 1 Kgs 18:4, 13; 21:13). The prophetic word to Jehu confirms the word of God to Elijah: dogs shall eat Jezebel in Jezreel (cf. 1 Kgs 21:23). The prophetic word goes one step further: no one shall bury her (2 Kgs 9:10). Jehu does, in fact, help destroy the house of Ahab. He smites Joram, king of Israel, assuring him that there can be no peace so long as his mother Jezebel's harlotries and sorceries persist (2 Kgs 9:22).

When Jehu arrives in Jezreel, Jezebel is unable to seduce him (vv 30-32). Rather, he persuades two or three eunuchs to throw her out the window of the city wall. Her blood spatters, and horses trample her. After a lapse of time during which Jehu ate, he ordered that Jezebel's remains be collected and buried. He explained as reason for this that she was the daughter of a king (vv 33-34). By the time they reached her, however, only her skull and feet and the palms of her hands could be found. Jehu's response when he heard was to recognize the situation as fulfilling Elijah's prophecy (cf. 1 Kgs 21:23). Dogs had eaten Jezebel's flesh; her corpse had been as dung in Jezreel so that no one could identify her (vv 35-37).

Interpretation

That Jezebel was the daughter of a king suggests that she possessed more power than most women; it is, in fact, because of this connection that Jehu was willing that she be buried (cf. 2 Kgs 9:34). That Jezebel married a king could only reenforce her filial power and prestige. That she was a non-Israelite, the daughter of a man whose name contains the very name of Canaan's god, suggests her worship of idols, and since Ahab is accused of serving and worshiping Baal (1 Kgs 16:31), one should not be surprised that she is blamed for influencing him in this direction.

Interpreters have traditionally pointed to Jezebel's propensity for evil. After all, she killed the prophets. She led Ahab astray. She was the mastermind behind Naboth's death. Her harlotries and sorceries are such that they merit Joram's death.

Yet feminist interpretation takes a different approach. Jezebel capitalized to the full on the roles that patriarchal culture allotted women: as daughter, wife, and mother. She was the daughter of a king (Ethbaal), the wife of a king (Ahab), and the mother of a king (Joram). Because of her male connections, she could exert considerable influence. Jezebel not only brought with her to Israel her own worship of Baal, she also brought prophets of Baal. Not only could she influence her husband to worship Baal, she would kill Yahweh's prophets. As queen she used her influence with Ahab, so that she persuaded him to allow her to secure Naboth's vineyard. In the process, she took over his name and his seal, and the elders reported Naboth's death not to Ahab but to Jezebel. She was thus recognized as the power behind the throne.

In naming Jezebel's sins, her strengths are often overlooked. The text reveals a self-confident woman who knows what she wants and is not afraid to do what she must to achieve her goals. Jezebel understands herself as at least equal to Ahab; she proceeds to attain what he had failed to attain. Women's access to power, especially in the patriarchal culture of ancient Israel, implied the control and manipulation of men and Jezebel succeeded in controlling both her husband and the elders.

The Story

Most of the prophet Elijah's and the prophet Elisha's miracles were done for women. Though there are notable exceptions, the miracles performed for women nevertheless form the majority. One reason for this may be that women were the powerless, especially women who were either widows or childless or both.

1. The widow of Zarephath fed Elijah during a severe drought and famine (1 Kgs 17:9-16). It was the Lord who had sent him to her (vv 8-9). When Elijah asked her for water, she agreed

(vv 10–11); when he asked her for food, she explained that there was very little left, and that what she had, she was planning to prepare so that she and her son might eat a last meal (vv 11–13). Elijah comforted the woman, telling her not to be afraid, and to do as she had originally planned, but only after first preparing him a morsel. Elijah prophesied to her that her meal and oil would last until the end of the drought. The widow obeyed Elijah and the word of the Lord through him was fulfilled (vv 14–16).

2. The son of this same widow later became ill and died (v 17). The woman blamed Elijah for punishing her sins by his death (v 18). He responded by taking the dead child up to his room and praying over him. He asked God why the child had been taken from the widow. He beseeched God to allow the child to live again; the child came to life (vv 19–22). Elijah then brought the child downstairs to his mother. Her response to Elijah came as a confirmation of his identity: he is a man of God and the word of God which he speaks is true (vv 23–24).

3. Elisha performed a miracle for a widow similar to the one Elijah performed for a widow in 1 Kgs 17; he multiplied her oil (2 Kgs 4:1–8). The occasion here is not a drought and consequent famine, but dire poverty. The widow's deceased husband had been among the sons of the prophets (vv 1–2). Now creditors were about to take away the woman's children to sell them as slaves in payment for her husband's debts (v 2). Elisha asked how he could help the woman; when he discovered that she had a jar of oil, he told her to borrow several empty vessels from her neighbors. Then he told her to go inside, and to pour oil from her jar into all the other jars (vv 3–4). She did as Elisha had directed until there were no more empty jars (vv 5–6). When she reported what had happened to Elisha, he told her to go out and sell the jars of oil. With what she earned, she could both pay her husband's debts and provide for herself and her children (v 7).

4. In addition to the miracles performed by Elijah and Elisha for the benefit of widows, Elisha performed a miracle for a wealthy married woman (2 Kgs 4:8–37). She had fed Elisha (v 8) and taken the initiative with her husband in securing Elisha a lodging (vv

9–10). Elisha was grateful to the woman and wished to repay her. He volunteered his influence with the king or the army commander (vv 11–13). She rejected his offer but Elisha's servant Gehazi pointed out to Elisha that the woman was childless. Elisha then told the woman that she would bear a son (vv 14–16). Elisha's words were fulfilled (v 17).

The scene changes. Years pass. The child grew. One day while working in the fields the child complained of a bad headache. They carried him to his mother who held him till he died (vv 18–20). She lay the child on Elisha's bed, then set off to find him (vv 21–25). When Elisha saw the woman approaching, he sought after her welfare. When she arrived, she laid bare her pain (vv 26–28). Elisha sent Gehazi to restore the child but he was unsuccessful (vv 29–31). Elisha arrived and restored the child (vv 32–35). Elisha then gave the child to his mother (vv 36–37).

5. A dialogue is recorded in 2 Kgs 8:1–6 which takes place at least seven years after Elisha restored the life of the wealthy woman's child. Elisha had warned the woman of an approaching famine and advised her to seek refuge elsewhere (v 1). She had obeyed the prophet and departed with her child to the land of the Philistines. Only after the famine had ended did she return. It was then necessary for her to appear before the king to try to retrieve the property which had been hers in Shunem (vv 2–3).

A dialogue is taking place at the time when the woman is coming before the king. Its partners are Gehazi, Elisha's servant, and the king. The king asks Gehazi to tell him about the marvels Elisha has accomplished; Gehazi sees the woman and uses the restoration of her child as an example (vv 4–5). The woman confirms Gehazi's testimony, for which reason the king restores to her most generously all her property. Though she is not a dialogue partner in the narrative, the narrative does suggest her validity as a witness.

Interpretation

Historical-critical scholars suggest that miracles now credited to Elisha were originally, in the oral tradition, credited only to

Elijah, but that as the transmission of the traditions progressed, more and more miracle stories came to be associated with Elisha. Consequently, scholars have disagreed about whether the woman portrayed in 1 Kgs 17:8–16 is meant to be the same as the woman portrayed in 1 Kgs 17:17–24. Because both accounts describe "the son of the woman, the mistress of the house" the reader might conclude that she is. A widow or a harlot may have been the head of a house by default. The same question arises regarding the wealthy woman of 2 Kgs 4:8–37 and 2 Kgs 8:1–6. Though the texts seem to imply that the reference is to the same character, the latter episode omits any reference to the woman's husband. Had he died by then? He was old several years earlier (cf. 2 Kgs 4:14). Or does the latter episode highlight the woman because she is the central figure in the former, certainly more significant than her husband?

Historical critics attempt to determine the meaning of the term "sons of the prophets" (e.g., 2 Kgs 4:1) and conclude that the term refers to the existence of schools of ecstatic prophets. Literary critics point to the widow's asking Elisha not to lie to her (v 16) as a foreshadowing of the deception she feels at the child's death (v 28). They further suggest her intuition that Elisha's servant Gehazi lacks the power of the prophet. She tells Gehazi that "all is well" (v 26), waiting to reach Elisha before pouring out her pain (v 27). Then, just as Gehazi was first to meet the woman, he is first to encounter the dead child (v 31). Just as the woman failed to reveal her mission, Gehazi failed to restore her son. The same sort of implication is made when it is the woman who validates Gehazi's testimony to the king regarding the works of Elisha (2 Kgs 8:6).

Feminist interpreters point to these women as models of faith. As widowed (1 Kgs 17; 2 Kgs 4:1–7) and poor (2 Kgs 4:1–7) and childless (2 Kgs 4:8–37), they represent the powerless people of their patriarchal culture. Yet these women possess deep faith. They obey the word of the prophet—when Elijah says to share the last morsel (1 Kgs 17:15), when he asks for the dead child (v 19), when Elisha says to collect the empty vessels and close her door (2 Kgs 4:5), and when he tells the woman to leave her land (2 Kgs 8:2).

Elijah's and Elisha's women believe that the word of the prophet will be fulfilled. The widow believes that the meal and oil will not run out before the drought and famine have ended; the prophet had said so (1 Kgs 17:15). The widow believes that the prophet will recall her child to life; why else would she have given her dead child over to him (v 19)? That he does restore her child confirms her faith (v 24). The widow believes the prophet enough to seek him out and then to obey his word—to get the vessels, and so on (2 Kgs 4:4). The wealthy mother believes Elisha's word that she will bear a child (vv 16–17); not even telling her husband that their child has died (v 23), she seeks the prophet's help (v 27). Believing the word of the prophet, the woman departs her homeland to escape the famine (2 Kgs 8:2).

Further, the woman character of 2 Kgs 4:8–37 is married. (Perhaps the woman of 2 Kgs 8:1–6 is also married.) Yet the husband plays a minor role. It is the woman who feeds the prophet, the woman to whom Elisha promises a child, the woman who seeks out the prophet when the child has died, the woman to whom Elisha restores the child. The man seems to have no function in the narrative except to beget the child. Similarly, in the episode in 2 Kgs 8, the woman is described as "the one whose child Elisha had restored to life"; she, not her husband, is the one whom Elisha warns of the famine; she goes with "her" household to the land of the Philistines. She appears before the king to request the return of "her" property. Unless her husband is deceased—and perhaps we should presume he is—her assumption of these functions is truly exceptional.

Summary

The wife of Ahab by no means remains nameless. Jezebel is infamous. Yet she is remembered not for her initiative and independence, not for her courage and strength, but for the evil she committed. She led her husband astray! In contrast, the powerless women are nameless and almost forgotten. They fall in the shadows of the prophets. The details of their characters are even blurred because they seem to be so similar. Their faith is not lauded—not unless the contemporary reader is sensitive enough to read between the lines and accord them the credit which is their due.

Thanks to a Nameless Maid
and a Nameless Wife:
Namaan's Cure of Leprosy
(2 Kings 5)

The Story

The chapter opens with a description of the characters. Namaan is a successful Syrian general who is also a leper. He has a wife and she has a maid; the maid is an Israelite, captured on one of the successful Syrian raids. The Israelite maid is the first to speak. She addresses her mistress, telling her about a Samaritan prophet who could cure Namaan. The narrator presupposes that Namaan's wife told Namaan what the girl had said, for the episode proceeds to Namaan's telling the king. The Syrian king agrees to send a letter to the Israelite king on Namaan's behalf (vv 1–5).

The letter requested that the king of Israel cure Namaan. The king was appalled when he received the letter; he cannot cure people (vv 6–7). Elisha heard what happened and told the king to send Namaan to him. When Namaan came, however, Elisha did not go out to him but sent a messenger with a seemingly useless command: go wash seven times in the Jordan (vv 8–10). Namaan was unhappy. Why did Elisha not come out to him, pray over him, and so on? Namaan knew several Syrian rivers in which he could have washed (vv 11–12). His servants persuaded Namaan to obey the prophet's word. When he finally obeyed the word of the prophet, he was cured.

Interpretation

The story is not about the nameless maid of Namaan's nameless wife, nor is it about Namaan's nameless wife herself. The story is about Elisha, the prophet of God with the power of God, and then about Namaan, the named man whom the prophet of God cures. Any literary analysis would so concur. (Recall that the women for whom the prophet of God acted—see pp. 131–35 above—are not named, evidencing their inferior role in their patriarchal culture.) The function of the kings in the story is to show their respective powerlessness before the power of Yahweh's prophet. Nevertheless, the two nameless women in this episode make the story happen. Had the Israelite maid not had faith in the prophet of God and had she not spoken to her mistress and had her mistress not spoken to her husband, Namaan would have remained a leper!

Summary

Both historical criticism and literary criticism relegate the two women of 2 Kgs 5 to insignificance. A feminist reading, however, finds such analysis inappropriate. The women are the nameless heroines who do what needs to be done, yet are forgotten when the credits are rendered!

Female Power in Judah: Jehosheba and Athaliah (2 Kings 11)

Athaliah was the daughter of Ahab, who had been king of Israel, and the wife of Jehoram, king of Judah. The Deuteronomistic Historian explains that the evil which Jehoram was guilty of was ultimately due to his wife (2 Kgs 8:18). The son of Jehoram and Athaliah, Ahaziah, succeeded his father as king. He also was evil (8:26–27). Ahaziah was murdered during Jehu's rebellion (2 Kgs 9:27).

The Story

The narrative opens with Athaliah's recognition that her son, the king, is dead, and her consequent action: she murdered the rest of the royal family! Attention then turns to another named woman, Jehosheba, who is identified by father and brother; she is the daughter of King Jehoram and the sister of King Ahaziah. Jehosheba rescued Joash, her nephew, the son of Ahaziah, from Athaliah. She successfully hid both Joash and his nurse in a bed-chamber and kept them safe there for six years, during which time Athaliah was reigning over Judah (vv 1–3).

In the seventh year the priest Jehoiada worked through the temple guards to bring Joash to his rightful place as king. He planned how they would surround Joash in the temple while Jehoiada crowned him and gave him the testimony. They anointed Joash and clapped their hands and shouted, "Long live the king!" (vv 4–12).

The noise sent Athaliah into the temple. When she realized what was happening, she accused the people of treason. Jehoiada, however, commanded the guard to take her out of the temple and kill her and to kill also anybody who followed her (vv 13–16). The priest made a covenant between the Lord and the king and the people; Baal's altars were to be destroyed and the worship of Yahweh restored. Verse 20 notes that the city was quiet after Athaliah's death.

Interpretation

Historical critics seek to explain that the Joram of 2 Kgs 11:2 is the Jehoram of 2 Kgs 8:16, 25. This is not a unique instance; in other texts also, different sources have attributed variant names or spellings of names to the same person (e.g., Joash and Jehoash). These same interpreters also often fail to list Athaliah among the rulers of the kingdom of Judah. She was not herself, after all, a descendant of David! Literary critics often describe Athaliah as an ambitious, power-hungry woman who becomes a conniving murderer.

Feminist interpreters see the narrative about Athaliah as a realistic portrayal of the lengths to which a woman, in the patriarchal culture of ancient Israel, would have to go in order to attain independence and the opportunity of significant decision making. Only when all the males by whom she is possessed have been killed does she have a chance. Only when the king and potential kings have been eliminated can a queen come to the throne.

Both historical critics and literary critics too frequently ignore the character of Jehosheba and the character of Joash's unnamed nurse. And when historical critics do mention Jehosheba, it is only to comment that the account of this incident in 2 Chr (22:11) makes Jehosheba the wife of the priest Jehoiada. Though historically unlikely, such a detail would serve as a logical link between Jehosheba, who saved the prince's life, and Jehoiada, through whose efforts the prince was crowned king.

Regardless of Jehosheba's connection to Jehoiada or lack thereof, Jehosheba, at the risk of her own life, saved her nephew's life, and with it, the Davidic dynasty. Had Joash died, the history of Kings Joash, Amaziah, Uzziah, Jotham, Ahaz, Hezekiah, Manasseh, Amon, Josiah, Jehoahaz, Jehoiakim, Jehoiakin, and Zedekiah would never have been written. The Davidic dynasty would have lasted a mere 150 years instead of the 400 years with which it is credited. Only eight Davidic kings, including David, preceded Athaliah, while thirteen followed. Jehosheba's courage made the continuation of the dynasty possible, yet virtually no one knows her name!

And what of the nameless nurse? Patriarchal culture is hierarchical and she was doubtless a servant. Yet she was needed for Joash's survival, and Jehosheba saved her too. The nurse was needed during those six years Joash was hidden; she too participated in his being saved. The nameless nurse deserves remembrance.

Summary

Sometimes Jezebel and Athaliah are compared; both are portrayed as queens, Jezebel in the north and Athaliah in the south. No queens of either kingdom—except maybe Bathsheba—have such delineated characters. Yet both do evil things; between them, they murder prophets and potential kings. Few interpreters defend their brains, their risk-taking courage, their independence from male domination. Yet these aspects of their characters should not be forgotten.

In spite of how they are interpreted, at least Jezebel and Athaliah are named women with identities. Jehosheba falls between the cracks. Though named, she is forgotten, and Joash's nurse is likewise relegated to oblivion. The reader must not allow this to happen. Jehosheba perpetuates the dynasty, every bit as much as the Davidic kings! She is worthy of history's recognition and gratitude; her fame deserves to surpass that of Athaliah.

Huldah: Spokesperson for Yahweh; The Fall of Judah (2 Kings 22)

Josiah is portrayed as one of the good kings of Judah who walked faithfully in the way of David. One of Josiah's achievements as king was to order the repair of the temple. According to deuteronomistic theology, an evil king, unconcerned for Yahweh and Yahweh's dwelling, stripped the gold and silver from the temple in order to give it to the kings with whom he had contracted foreign alliances. Foreign kings were valued more than Yahweh. Not only did evil kings allow the removal of temple ornaments, they permitted the worship of foreign gods within the temple. On the contrary, good kings took care to enhance the Lord's dwelling. They did this either by adding silver and gold, often the spoils of their successful campaigns, to the temple treasury, or by purifying the temple after its desecration by evil kings. Josiah, a good king, set about the restoration of the temple after the abominations practiced by his predecessor Manasseh.

The Story

King Josiah sent Shaphan to the temple to commission the repairs on the temple. The high priest Hilkiah was put in charge of the restoration. He was to appoint appropriate workmen and give them the monies necessary to accomplish their respective tasks (2 Kgs 22:3-7). Hilkiah informed Shaphan that the book of the law had been found in the temple. Shaphan read it. Shaphan then returned to the king with a report that his orders were being carried out. In addition, he read to the king the book of the law (vv 8-10).

Its message disturbed the king. He rent his clothes and sent messengers to inquire from the Lord; Josiah could only conclude that God was very angry with the Israelites since neither he nor the people nor their ancestors had obeyed the words of the book of the law (vv 11-13). The king's messengers, including the high priest, sought out Huldah the prophetess. Huldah is identified by her husband, Shallum, who is further identified by his father, Tikvah, and his grandfather, Harhas. Huldah spoke to them the word of the Lord (vv 14-15).

The messengers were to report to the king that God would bring the evil which the book of the law threatened on Judah and on its inhabitants. They had forsaken God and burned incense to other gods and had provoked God's anger by their deeds. Because of this, God's wrath would not be quenched. Huldah, however, had a spe-

cial message for Josiah. Because Josiah took the words of the book
of the law seriously and rent his clothes and wept, he would die
before God's wrath would come upon Judah (vv 16–20).

Interpretation

Historical critics emphasize the exemplary character of Josiah,
who did not turn aside either to the right or to the left from following in the ways of his ancestor David. He and Hezekiah are together Judah's outstanding kings. Within this context 2 Kgs 22 is
an illustration of Josiah's character: he set about the restoration of
the temple, even to the point of trusting the integrity of the workmen. Historical-critical scholars also emphasize the relationship of
this book of the law found in the temple to the core of the Book of
Deuteronomy (chaps. 12—26). They hypothesize that it may even
have been at this time, approximately 621 B.C., that parts of Deut
were composed and some of its sources compiled.

Equal attention ought be given to the prophet of the Lord who
proclaims the word of the Lord and possesses the power of the Lord.
Huldah is not the only woman to whom the word "prophetess" is
applied; she is one of four (i.e., Miriam, Deborah, Noadiah; cf. Isa
8:3). Huldah may be the most important of the four, however. She
speaks the word of the Lord to announce the fall of Judah and to
announce that the fall will not take place until after Josiah's death.
She is among the prophets who speak and act to accomplish the
Lord's will. The king's messengers sought her, not because she was a
woman, but because she was a woman of God.

Summary

Why is it that the episodes recorded in 1 Kgs 17—2 Kgs 9 have
Elijah and Elisha as their major characters (the prophet Micaiah
is the critical character of 1 Kgs 22), and 2 Kgs 22 has Josiah as its
major character? In each of the chapters the king must reckon
with the prophet of the Lord who speaks the word of the Lord.
Just as Elijah and Elisha and Micaiah triumph over the evil king
Ahab, so Huldah informs Josiah of Judah's future and of his own.
The king has no power to change the word of the prophet. Should
we not then conclude that, just as 1 Kgs 17—2 Kgs 9 centers on

the prophets Elijah, Micaiah, and Elisha, 2 Kgs 22 centers on Huldah?

Huldah is as critical to Judah's future as the northern prophets are to Israel's. In fact, the word she speaks brings the monarchy and the dynasty—in fact, the history recorded in Josh through 2 Kgs—to an end. The patriarchal author may have confined Huldah's identity and her message to a mere seven verses, yet Huldah's significance for Judah's future, within the literature of the Deuteronomistic History, cannot be ignored.

CONCLUSION

The Deuteronomistic History consists of the Books of Joshua, Judges, 1–2 Samuel, and 1–2 Kings, all of which are governed by the covenant theology of the Book of Deuteronomy. Blessings will accrue to those who faithfully follow Yahweh; curses will come upon those who disobey. The women of the Deuteronomistic History are as diverse as women of every time and place. Some are faithful and some are unfaithful—to God, to their husbands, to themselves. For example, Deborah and Huldah emerge as prophetesses (Judg 4—5; 2 Kgs 22), Rahab as the courageous harlot of Jericho (Josh 2; 6), and Jezebel and Athaliah as power-hungry queens (1 Kgs 17—2 Kgs 9; 2 Kgs 11). Besides those who have an identity and a story, many are defined by the men who are their fathers, their husbands, or their sons, while others are never even named. The culture which produced the traditions behind the texts as well as the various redactions of the History was patriarchal, and all the women carry scars from that culture. A few, however, emerge from the culture as exceptions to it. The stories of these women are her-story and bear retelling.

RECOMMENDED READINGS
The Deuteronomistic History

Bal, Mieke. "The Rhetoric of Subjectivity." *Poetics Today* 5 (1984):337–76.
Berlin, Adele. "Characterization in Biblical Narrative: David's Wives." *JSOT* 23 (1982):69–85.

Camp, Claudia V. "The Wise Woman of 2 Samuel: A Role Model for Women in Early Israel." *CBQ* 43 (1981):14–29.

Craigie, P. C. "Deborah and Anat: A Study of Poetic Imagery (Judges 5)." *ZAW* 90 (1978):374–81.

Lasine, Stuart. "Guest and Host in Judges 19: Lot's Hospitality in an Inverted World." *JSOT* 29 (1984):37–59.

Levenson, Jon. "1 Samuel 25 as Literature and as History." *CBQ* 40 (1978):11–28.

Lindars, Barnabas. "Deborah's Song: Women in the Old Testament." *BJRL* 65 (1983):158–75.

Liptzin, Sol. "Rahab of Jericho." *DD* 9 (1981):111–19.

Mosca, Paul G. "Who Seduced Whom? A Note on Joshua 15:18//Judges 1:14." *CBQ* 46 (1984):18–22.

Niditch, Susan. "The 'Sodomite' Theme in Judges 19—20: Family, Community, and Social Disintegration." *CBQ* 44 (1982):365–78.

Poulssen, N. "An Hour with Rispah: Some Reflections of 2 Samuel 21:10." In *Von Kanaan bis Kerala. Festschrift für Prof. Mag. Dr. Dr. J. P. M. van der Ploeg O.P. zur Vollendung des siebzigsten Lebensjahres am 4. Juli 1979,* edited by W. C. Delsman et al. AOAT 211. Kelevaer: Butzon & Bercker, 1982.

Swidler, Arlene. "In Search of Huldah." *TBT* 98 (Nov. 1978):1780–85.

Taylor, J. Glen. "The Song of Deborah and Two Canaanite Goddesses." *JSOT* 23 (1982):99–108.

Trible, Phyllis. "A Meditation in Mourning: The Sacrifice of the Daughter of Jephthah." *USQR* 36 Supp (1981):59–73.

———. *Texts of Terror.* Philadelphia: Fortress Press, 1984.

Wilkinson, Elizabeth. "The *hapax legomenon* of Judges iv 18." *VT* 33 (1983):512–13.

✦ PART III ✦

THE MAJOR AND MINOR PROPHETS

INTRODUCTION

Whereas the Pentateuch and the Deuteronomistic History may each be studied as a literary unit, the Prophetic Writings comprise fifteen separate books. Each is associated with a certain century or a particular period—from the eighth century B.C. to the postexilic period—though they may also contain later additions. Although some of the contents of most of the books is thought to have been proclaimed by the prophets whose names they bear, all of the books contain additions by others and some reflect extensive editing.

Interpreters have traditionally spoken of three Major Prophets (excluding the Book of Daniel) and twelve Minor Prophets. The terms "major" and "minor" do not refer to the relative *importance* of the books but to their *length*. The Book of Isaiah is the longest, containing sixty-six chapters, Jeremiah is next with fifty-two chapters, and Ezekiel contains forty-eight chapters. Because of the length of each of these books, each was copied on its own scroll. The other extant prophetic books—Micah, Amos, Hosea, Nahum, Zephaniah, Habakkuk, Obadiah, Haggai, Zechariah, Joel, Jonah, and Malachi—are short and thus were copied together onto one scroll.

Historical Considerations

The Book of *Amos* is addressed to the Northern Kingdom of Israel in the eighth century B.C. The book accuses the Israelites of gross social injustice, of selling the righteous for silver and the needy for a pair of shoes. Set before Israel fell to Assyria (721 B.C.), the poems threaten doom. Unless the people will repent, seeking good and not evil, they will be destroyed. It is often suggested that the final verses of the final chapter of the book (9:11–15) are from the hand of a later author, one who had experienced the destruction and who therefore uttered words of hope and restoration to a fallen people.

The Book of *Hosea* is believed to have been composed for the Northern Kingdom of Israel in the eighth century B.C., before its fall to Assyria. The book condemns Israel's rampant practice of idolatry and threatens doom. Historical critics have tried to determine: (1) the relationship between chaps. 1—3 and the remainder of the book; (2) whether or not Hosea did, in fact, have a wife Gomer or whether she is "only" a literary construct; and (3) whether Hosea took a second harlot or whether the woman referred to in 3:1 is Gomer after her adultery. Scholars have also studied in detail the covenantal language of the book and its relationship to the Book of Deuteronomy.

Most historical critics believe that there were at least three authors of the Book of *Isaiah*. Basing their position on considerations of content and style, these scholars determine the bulk of chaps. 1—39 to be from an eighth-century B.C. poet directing his message to Judah. They relegate Isa 40—55, or "Second Isaiah," to later authorship. They believe the poems of these chapters to have been produced toward the end of the exile (mid-sixth century B.C.). Chapters 56—66 are attributed to "Third Isaiah," and are believed to have been composed a generation or so after those of Second Isaiah.

First Isaiah (chaps. 1—39) proclaims its message against the backdrop of the Syro-Ephraimite War and the Assyrian crisis of Hezekiah's reign. In the mid-eighth century B.C., Assyria was an obvious threat to Israel. Israel, to stave off the threat, joined an alliance with its former enemy, Syria. Even together, however, they were not strong enough to ward off Assyria. They therefore sought Judah's help. When Judah refused to join the alliance, they, in their desperation, contrived a plan to remove Judah's king and replace him with a more cooperative one. To prevent this from happening, Judah's king, despite Isaiah's warning, entered into an alliance with Assyria.

Judah had somehow come to believe that, with Yahweh as their God, nothing really bad could happen to them; they could never be totally destroyed. The text of First Isaiah warns otherwise. The people's very arrogance and pride would cause their downfall. Although the book consoles the people that a remnant will return, nevertheless, before that can happen, Judah will fall. The book warns the people of Judah, who were no longer turning to Yahweh in their time of need but were appealing for help to foreign powers, that the very nations whom they were seeking as allies would soon become their enemies.

The Book of *Micah* is thought to be the product of the eighth century B.C. in Judah. In contrast to the city setting of much of First Isaiah, the text of Micah contains rural imagery and has rural concerns. Whereas First Isaiah condemns Judah and warns of their downfall, the Book of Micah asserts that even Jerusalem will be destroyed. The book addresses its warnings and threats to Judah's leadership. The capitals, both Samaria and Jerusalem, have been centers of evildoing; the prophets lead God's people astray; the rulers abhor justice. With such attitudes and behavior by those who are meant to speak and do the word of the Lord and those who are meant to implement covenant fidelity, what can be expected from the people?

The poetry of the Book of *Nahum* gloats over the fall of Assyria. Whether it was produced shortly before or immediately after the nation's fall is uncertain and relatively unimportant. What is important is that the outcome was inevitable; Assyria was doomed. The nation which had conquered so many others would itself be conquered; the country which had treated its victims so cruelly deserved and would itself receive cruel treatment. Assyria had destroyed Israel; even Judah had been its victim. Now Assyria would be brought low. The Nahum poetry vividly portrays both the conquest of the nation and the humiliation of its people. The Lord's people are avenged.

The Book of *Zephaniah* claims to have been proclaimed during the reign of King Josiah. Because of the nature of its content, one is likely to conclude that it should be dated either to the years before Josiah's reform or to the years following his death. The text proclaims the day of the Lord as a day of doom. Whereas the Lord's coming might naively be awaited as a day for celebration, the Book of Zephaniah warns its hearers that the day of the Lord will be a day of wrath, of distress, of anguish, of ruin and devastation, of darkness and gloom, of clouds and thick darkness, of trumpet blast and battle cry. Because Judah shows no signs of repenting of their sins, their punishment is inevitable. The leadership is condemned—the officials, the judges, the prophets, the priests. The final verses of the book may be an exilic addition; they imply a reversal of circumstances—the Lord will again look with favor on the punished people. Yahweh will again take up the role of king—one which David and the monarchs had assumed until the exile—and the role of warrior, implying Yahweh's help in reentering the land.

The Book of *Habakkuk* is thought to have been produced when Babylonia was close to Judah's borders, that is, when Judah's doom was practically sealed. The book tests God—and deuteronomistic theology. How is it, the speaker wants to know, that evil people prosper, while good people suffer? In other words, why is it that Babylonia is allowed to oppress Judah even though the people of Judah, bad as they are, are better than the Babylonians? And why is it that the bad people of Judah are faring well while the righteous in Judah are brought low? The Book of Habakkuk answers the question with God's assurance that the faithful will live because of their faith. In other words, blessings will accrue—though maybe not in the immediate and foreseeable future—to those who remain faithful in spite of domestic difficulties and the Babylonian threat.

Historical critics have traditionally distinguished three major sources within the Book of *Jeremiah*. They refer to a Jeremian source, associated with the prophet himself, whom they believe to be responsible for the major portion of chaps. 1—25. They attribute a portion of the book (the bulk of chaps. 26—45) to Baruch, Jeremiah's scribe, who transcribed many of Jeremiah's prophecies, adding to them his own insights and interpretations. They acknowledge the contribution of the Deuteronomic editors, which included, among other things, the oracles against the nations (chaps. 46—51). Because of content and linguistic similarities to the Book of Deuteronomy, some scholars suggest interdependence and possibly even the same editor. Linguistic similarities to the Book of Hosea have also been noted.

The Book of *Ezekiel* spans both the preexilic and exilic periods. Scholars distinguish sections in the book: a preexilic segment (chaps. 1—24); oracles against the nations (chaps. 25—32); and writings of the exile (chaps. 33—48). The prophet Ezekiel himself is credited with producing the bulk of the material, minus several later additions. Because of the period in which much of the contents of the book was composed, its message is one both of doom and of hope. The Book of Ezekiel asserts a more individualistic attitude toward identity and responsibility than Judah's traditionally communal one.

The Book of *Obadiah* is the shortest book in the entire Old Testament, composed of only twenty-one verses. Its content is directed against the small kingdom of Edom which lay on the southeast border of Judah. Edom should have been an ally of Judah, so why had Edom not come to Judah's defense against Babylonia? The people of Judah resented their small, petty, powerless neighbor who took advantage of Judah's plight and looted their cities.

The prophetic text of *Haggai* is concerned with the rebuilding of the temple. In 539 B.C. Cyrus the Great conquered the Babylonian Empire once and for all and ushered in a period of Persian control. Although this did not mean that Judah was again an independent nation, nevertheless, the exiles were allowed to return to Judah.

The book explains the reason for the people's lack of success when they returned to the land. They had not made Yahweh and Yahweh's dwelling their top priority. They had been spending their time building their own homes, and planting their crops, and had not turned their attention to rebuilding Yahweh's temple. This they must do immediately. The new temple was completed in 515 B.C.

The Book of *Zechariah* is frequently divided into two parts, separated from each other by at least two centuries. Chapters 1—8 date to the same period as the Book of Haggai, while chaps. 9—14 are thought to have been composed under Greek rule. The book encourages the construction of a new temple; its message includes justice for Yahweh's enemies as well as hope for the restoration of Judah.

It is impossible to date the Book of *Joel* with any more precision than to say that it was probably produced sometime in the Persian period. One might be tempted to suggest from the book's message that the book is preexilic. It contains warnings about Judah's infidelity and threats of punishment and pleas for repentance. However, since the book contains no references to either the Assyrians or the Babylonians, since its poetry emphasizes priestly concerns, and since the book's language is late Hebrew, postexilic dating seems more likely. Because of its familiarity with the temple and worship, scholars have concluded that its author(s) derived from priestly circles.

The major image through the chapters is a plague of locusts. Whether the author(s) had a very vivid imagination, which is possible, or whether the author(s) actually witnessed such a natural disaster, which is more likely, the text brings to life Yahweh's threatening devastation of Judah for the people's sins.

Dating the Book of *Jonah* is almost impossible. It could have been composed before Assyria fell to Babylonia, in the hope that Assyria would repent and their disaster be averted. It is highly unlikely, however, that an Israelite prophecy would suggest such a scenario. Rather, it is more likely that the book was produced after the exile as a didactic story for Judah: let the people who have ears, hear.

The author(s) of the Book of *Malachi* probably lived in the fifth century B.C. Like other postexilic prophetic literature, the book shows a high regard for priest and temple. There is a major preoccupation with covenant fidelity.

Literary Considerations

Literary considerations are indispensable to any adequate study of the prophets. Poetry is the language of most of the literature. The messages were intended not to inform minds but to change hearts. It is therefore necessary to pay attention to the ways the poets spoke, the forms and techniques they used in their efforts to make their word as effective as possible.

Although most of the literature of the Major and Minor Prophets
is poetry, it does not possess the rhythm and rhyme to which we
are accustomed. Rather, its verses are usually composed of parallel
lines; the parallelisms are either synonymous (two lines saying the
same thing in different ways) or synthetic (the second line similar
to the first but building on it) or antithetic (the second line saying
the opposite thing from the first).

In addition, the poetry of the prophetic books is replete with the
literary techniques of personification (attributing to things the
characteristics of humans); formulaic expressions and oracular
statements; repetition; refrains; rhetorical questions; symbolic language; visions and plays on words; similes; metaphors; synecdoche
(allowing a part to stand for the whole); allegories and parables.
There is assonance (close repetition of vowel sounds) and alliteration (the repetition of initial sounds in adjacent words), though
these are not usually recognizable in translation.

Particular genre and literary techniques have come to be associated with certain of the prophetic books. For example, Hosea 1—3
uses a metaphor. Hosea's involvement in a bad marriage relationship is used to explain the infidelity of Israel toward Yahweh.
Yahweh creates and Yahweh loves creation; the people, however,
reject that love and seek other, lesser things to love. Yahweh will
punish their adultery, which is idolatry, but Yahweh's real longing
is for their return to the relationship. Contrary to Israel's marriage
laws, Yahweh will receive back the wayward lover. The symbolic
names of Gomer's children further emphasize the relationship.

Moreover, the verb yd^c, meaning "to know," helps to unify the
Book of Hosea. The verb carries with it overtones of great intimacy: when a man knows his wife, she conceives. The marriage
relationship which should exist between Yahweh and Israel is also
one of intimacy, but Israel does not "know" Yahweh. The relationship that should be life-giving is not, and can only become so if
Israel repents.

The *rib*, or law-case format, is a literary technique which appears
in the Book of Micah. God is the prosecutor, Judah is the de-
fendant, God is the judge. The prosecutor explains what Judah is

guilty of and proves its guilt; Judah has very little to call on in its own defense; the judge must determine sentence.

The Book of Malachi contains an extended question-answer format, while the Book of Zechariah incorporates the genre of apocalyptic. This latter book contains night visions of the last days; the visions are quite unusual, representing not a progression of history but a radical alteration of it.

The Book of Jonah is written as fiction—as allegory or parable. The function of the tale's major character, Jonah, is to provide a foil for the Assyrians. The entire narrative is woven around reversals. Jonah, the representative of God with the power of God to speak and do the word of God, disobeys. The Assyrians, that is, the people who are not the Lord's people, do what they should: they obey and repent! The prophet who should rejoice in repentance is angry; he prefers punishment. God, caring for people, even for the frustrated prophet, provides a tree to shade Jonah from the sun. When the tree dies, Jonah laments. Yahweh's conversation with Jonah assures Jonah that God cares more about thousands of living people than about a single dead tree!

More than any other section of Old Testament literature, the prophetic texts must be appreciated for their literary artistry as well as for the thoughts they contain. The message of Old Testament poetry, somewhat in contrast to its prose, cannot be understood apart from the language which expresses it.

THEMES FROM A FEMINIST PERSPECTIVE

Patriarchy and Hierarchy

The centuries which produced the prophetic poetry—the eighth through the fourth century B.C.—possessed basically the same culture which produced the Pentateuch and the Deuteronomistic History, that is, a patriarchal one. However, because, with few exceptions, the literature contained in the books of the prophets is poetry, the manner in which the patriarchal culture finds expression in the Prophetic Writings differs from its expressions in narrative. Because there are fewer characters and fewer plot complications in the prophets, expressions of patriarchy may seem more subtle and less extensive. They are no less objectionable, however.

Patriarchy finds expression when males become the norm for human activity. Whether males are the only sex intended for portrayal—they being history's only significant actors—or whether women are understood to be implied when men are named, not giving women their recognition as men's equals by one's choice of language spells patriarchy. The Prophetic Writings, like the Pentateuch and the Deuteronomistic History, are filled with references to men which exclude women, either deliberately or indeliberately but in fact. Choices such as "man" and "men," "father" and "fathers," "son" and "sons," "brother" and "brothers," the naming of the people and land after the patriarchs Israel and Judah are as prevalent among the prophets as they are in the historical narratives (e.g., Amos 1:9; Hos 1:10; Isa 9:6; Mic 1:5; Ezek 4:13; 8:12).

All cultures are based on unspoken but commonly agreed-upon assumptions. A patriarchal culture is, by its nature, hierarchical. The priest is superior to the people; the master to the slave; the mistress to her maid; the seller to the buyer; the lender to the borrower; the creditor to the debtor; the father to the son (e.g., Isa 24:2; cf. Mal 1:6). The presumption in a patriarchal-hierarchical culture is also that men are superior to other human beings, both women and children. One should not be surprised to learn that in such a culture men, especially priests, are the appropriate worshipers (e.g., Ezek 40:46; 43:19). Animals without blemish are the appropriate victims for sacrificial offerings—but not just animals without blemish, indeed only *male* animals without blemish (Ezek 43:22, 23, 25; 45:18, 23; Mal 1:14)! Conversely, virgins from Israel or the widows of priests are the appropriate wives for priests; other widows and divorcées may be appropriate for other men, but not for the superior men, the priests (Ezek 44:22).

When patriarchal hierarchy is assumed, it follows logically that the men rule. Obviously, any shift in this power relationship would be considered inappropriate. Isaiah 3:12 betrays patriarchal assumptions when the poet describes leaders who have misled the Lord's people as "women ruling." The presumption is: who can imagine anything worse? Even when the imagery is positive—Israel's first love for the Lord compared to that of "a bride" (Jer 2:2)—it implies the hierarchy which the patriarchal culture presupposes.

The first chapters of the Book of Hosea present the reader with a faithful husband and an unfaithful wife. This metaphor of Hosea's relationship with Gomer symbolizing Yahweh's relationship with Israel has been interpreted as an expression of Yahweh's intimate love for the people. Closer examination, however, reveals patriarchal prejudice. The man is the faithful one; the woman has gone astray. This eighth-century metaphor allows the woman, especially the harlot but also the adulteress, to symbolize the practice of idolatry (e.g., Hos 1:2; 2:8–13; cf. Mic 1:7; Jer 2:20, 33; 3:1–3; 11:15; Nah 3:4; Ezek 16; 43:7).

Micah describes an evil time in Judah when trust is no longer possible: guard the doors of your mouths from "her who lies in your bosom" (7:5). Second Isaiah's way of describing sinners in Judah is to accuse them of being "sons of the sorceress, and offspring of the adulterer and the harlot" (Isa 57:3). With either a sorceress or a harlot for a mother, no wonder the children behave so badly! One of Zechariah's visions is of a woman sitting on an ephah; she is a personification of Wickedness (Zech 5:7–8); the vision allows her to be removed by two women, each having the wings of a stork (affirmation of motherhood? v 9). These kinds of images continue to find expression in the Writings (see part IV below) and have permeated much of Judeo-Christian culture.

Because menstruation somehow made women unclean (Ezek 18:6; 22:10), men were not allowed to approach women who were menstruating. Ezekiel 36:17 even compares bad conduct to women who are made impure and unclean by their period. Not only a menstruating woman but any inappropriate sexual partner rendered a man unclean. For this reason the taking of inappropriate sexual partners became a fitting image of Jerusalem's sinfulness; Ezekiel accuses the men of uncovering their fathers' nakedness; of violating menstruating women; of violating their neighbors' wives; of defiling their daughters-in-law; and of defiling their own sisters (22:10–11; cf. 33:26).

Whereas female sexuality meant menstruation and uncleanness, male sexuality meant, for Israelites, circumcision. Women who belonged to Israelite men were subsumed under their men's circumcision. It is sadly ironic, however, that one way of speaking pejoratively of one's enemy was to call them uncircumcised, thus implying that they were outside Israel's covenant relationship with Yahweh (e.g., Ezek 31:18; 32:19, 21, 24–26, 28–30, 32; 44:7, 9). Women, like the enemy, were not themselves circumcised. Isaiah 52:1 parallels the uncircumcised and the unclean.

Although the prophetic literature condemns all false prophets (e.g., Jer 23:9–15), the Book of Ezekiel is particularly hard on false women prophets. Perhaps this type of woman and this behavior is relegated to a certain period; at any rate, at least some of the daughters of Judah were prophesying out of their own mouths, that is, speaking their own words and not the Word of God; Ezekiel was instructed to prophesy against them, to condemn these "women who sew magic bands upon all wrists and make veils for the heads of persons of every stature." These women lie for their own profit and lead the people of Judah astray. Ezekiel assures them that their visions and divinations are at an end (13:18–23).

Israel's History as Men's History

One way that men have dominated history is by the naming of houses and families after them. This is especially true of rulers, but it is not limited to them. The prophetic literature names houses belonging to

Hazael (Amos 1:4);
Jacob (e.g., Amos 3:13; 9:8; Isa 2:5, 6; 10:20; 46:3; Mic 2:7; Jer 2:4; 5:20; Ezek 20:5; Obad 17, 18);
Israel (e.g., Amos 5:3, 4, 25; 6:14; Hos 1:6; 5:1; Isa 5:7; 46:3; 63:7; Mic 3:1; Jer 2:4, 26; 3:18, 20; Ezek 3:1, 4; 4:3, 4; Zech 8:13);
Joseph (Amos 5:6; Zech 10:6; Obad 18);
Esau (Obad 18);
Jeroboam (Amos 7:9);
Isaac (Amos 7:16);

Judah (e.g., Hos 1:7; 5:12; Isa 22:21; 37:31; Jer 3:18, 20; 5:11;
  Ezek 4:6; 8:17; Zech 8:13; 10:3, 6);
David (Isa 7:2; 22:22; Jer 21:12; Zech 12:7–8; 13:1);
Ahab (Mic 6:16);
Levi (Zech 12:13);
Nathan (Zech 12:12); and
the king or kings (Hos 5:1; Jer 19:13).

It also makes reference to one's father's house in more general terms (e.g., Isa 3:6; 7:17; Jer 12:6).

Israel's primary religious experience, the exodus, is described by the prophets in typical patriarchal terms, that is, the Lord is understood to have brought "their fathers" out of Egypt (i.e., Jer 7:22, 25; 11:4, 7); it was with Israel's "fathers" that the Lord cut a covenant (e.g., Jer 11:10; 31:32; Mal 2:10); the land was promised and given to the "fathers" (e.g., Jer 3:18; 7:7; 11:15; Ezek 20:42; 36:28).

Men become Israel's models. For example, wisdom is associated with *Daniel* (Ezek 28:3); *Jacob* is the Lord's servant (Ezek 28:25; 37:25; cf. Isa 58:14; Mal 1:2); *Abraham,* God's friend, is associated with Yahweh's promise of the land to Israel (Ezek 33:24; Isa 41:8; cf. 63:16); the Lord made a covenant with *David,* the shepherd and king of God's people (Ezek 34:23–24; 37:24, 25; Isa 55:3); *Joseph* stands strong as the patriarch associated with the Northern Kingdom (Ezek 37:16, 19; cf. 47:13); *Noah* is associated with God's promise not to again destroy the world by water (Isa 54:9). In addition, *Moses* is celebrated for the exodus (Isa 63:11–12) and the law (Mal 4:4); *Israel* is acknowledged—with God and Abraham!—as one of the fathers of the land and of the people of Judah (Isa 63:16); the Lord made a covenant with *Levi* (Mal 2:4); and finally, the prophet *Elijah* will appear before the great and terrible day of the Lord (Mal 4:5).

A people's self-understanding is fashioned on their heroes and heroines, on the people who have made them who they are. In the memories of those who recorded Israel's history, all the people who really counted, the people from the past who were worth remembering, were men. There is only one female model cited: Sarah (Isa 51:2)!

Sometimes it is interpretation, not even the recorded history it-self, which possesses patriarchal bias. For example, whether Diblaim is the mother or the father of Gomer (Hos 1:3), whether Hilkiah is the mother or the father of Gemariah and whether Gemariah is male or female (Jer 29:3), whether Kolaiah is the mother or the father of Ahab and whether Ahab is male or female, whether Maaseiah is the mother or the father of Zedekiah and whether Zedekiah is male or female (Jer 29:22) is really unclear. There is so little information given about these characters that it is not possible to know. That the names Ahab, Zedekiah, Hilkiah, and Gemariah refer elsewhere in the Old Testament texts to males is not conclusive evidence that the persons spoken of here are males, since several Hebrew names are used for both males and females. Similarly, is the Gomer spoken of in Ezek 38:6 a woman or a city, or is the text deliberately ambiguous?

Admonitions and exhortations are usually addressed to men. Malachi challenges the men to be faithful to the wives of their youth (2:14–15). (There is probably no need to challenge the women to be faithful to the husbands of their youth since anything else would be unthinkable!)

Men make war (e.g., Amos 1:4, 13; Hos 9:13; Isa 3:2, 25; Mic 5:5–6; Jer 11:22; Ezek 9:2; Zech 10:5; Obad 9; Joel 3:9) and women are the spoils of war (Jer 38:22–23; Ezek 30:17–18). Women's per-sonal accomplishment in the patriarchal culture of ancient Israel was the bearing and rearing of sons. That is why both Amos (1:13) and Hosea (13:16) use the image of "ripping up pregnant women" to depict devastation, or "mothers being dashed in pieces with their children" (Hos 10:14). Not only the powerless but also the most vulnerable are the enemy's target, and the men are unable to defend them.

Language: Masculine by Preference
and God as Father

To further emphasize history as men's history, masculine nouns and masculine forms of personal pronouns are preferred (e.g., Amos 2:4, 11; Hos 1:2, 10; Isa 1:2, 4; Mic 2:2, 11; Jer 2:4; Zeph 1:8, 12; Hab 1:13; Ezek 2:3; Zech 9:13); the word "son," for example, becomes a synonym for the word "people" (e.g., Isa 1:4; 30:9).

The RSV chooses to perpetuate patriarchal bias when it translates literally "her" referring to a city or a people (e.g., Amos 1:7, 14; Hos 2:14–15) or "men" referring to people (e.g., Ezek 9:4; Isa 45:14); or "father" when "parent" might be just as appropriate (e.g., Isa 38:19); or "fathers" where "ancestors" would be equally appropriate (e.g., Jer 3:24–25); or "watchman" where "sentry" could be used (Hos 9:8); and the like.

Often the RSV will use the term "man" when the term "person" or "humans" would be much better, for example, when poetic parallelism juxtaposes "man" and God, or "man" and beasts (e.g., Amos 5:19; Hos 9:7; Isa 45:12; 47:3; Ezek 1:5). In the Book of Ezekiel, Yahweh addresses the prophet as "son of man" at least thirty-six times. The reference is really to Ezekiel as representative of humankind; surely a more inclusive designation could be found (e.g., "human one"). Scholars argue for keeping the term "son of man" because of its recurrence in the Book of Daniel and in the New Testament. Even there, however, the term refers to a human representative of God, one who may be male, but one for whom humanness is of more significance than maleness.

Israel's language attributes men's sex, men's activities, and men's honors to God. God is "he" (e.g., Amos 6:7; Hos 2:14–15; Isa 43:25). God is Hosea, while faithless Israel is his wife, Gomer (Hos 1–3). As men are warriors, God is warrior (e.g., Isa 13:4–5; 42:13; Jer 21:5; Ezek 21:5; Zeph 3:17; Zech 13:7–8; Joel 2:11). "He" is the Lord, the God of hosts (e.g., Amos 3:13; Hos 11:5; Isa 1:9; 44:6; Nah 2:13; Zeph 2:9; Zech 1:3; Mal 1:4). Just as Yahweh is defined by activity on behalf of the people—I brought you up out of Egypt—so God is also named by the patriarchs and by the people, named after the patriarchs, who are their ancestors. God is the Holy One of *Israel* (e.g., Isa 10:20; 41:16; Jer 50:29), the God of *Israel* (e.g., Isa 29:23; Jer 9:15; Zeph 2:9; Ezek 8:4), the Creator of *Israel* (Isa 43:15). God is the Holy One of *Jacob* (Isa 29:23), the Mighty One of *Jacob* (Isa 49:26; 60:16), the God of *Jacob* (Isa 2:3; Mic 4:2); Yahweh is the God of *David* (Isa 38:5) and the Lord who redeemed *Abraham* (Isa 29:22).

As men are masters, God is master (Mal 1:6). As men are fathers, so God is described as Father, as Everlasting Father (Isa 9:6;

63:16; cf. Jer 3:4, 19; Mal 1:6). As men are kings, so God is named King (Isa 41:21; Jer 10:10; 51:57; Zeph 3:15; Ezek 20:33). As men are bridegrooms, so God is a Bridegroom (Isa 62:5). As men are husbands, so God is named Husband (Isa 54:5; Jer 31:32). The metaphoric language used to name God is always predominantly masculine in a patriarchal culture. On the other hand, idols may be female. Some of the men and women of Judah are guilty of burning incense to the queen of heaven and of pouring libations to her (Jer 44:17–19, 25; cf. Jer 7:18; Mal 2:11). Jeremiah accuses the Israelites of crediting a stone with giving them birth (2:27).

Women as Men's Possessions

In a patriarchal culture a woman's identity derives from the man to whom she belongs. Men "take" wives and "give" daughters (Jer 29:6). It is no accident then that Gomer is identified as daughter of Diblaim, wife of Hosea (Hos 1:3; 2:16), mother of sons Jezreel and Not My People (Hos 1:4, 9; cf. v 10; 2:1, 23) and daughter Not Pitied (Hos 1:6; cf. 2:1, 23). Hamutal is the daughter of Jeremiah, the wife of Josiah and the mother of Zedekiah (Jer 52:1).

Women belonged to men—their fathers or their husbands (e.g., Jer 14:16). Jacob "bought" his wives—both Leah and Rachel—from his father-in-law, Laban, by shepherding Laban's sheep for fourteen years (Hos 12:12). Judgment means that men's houses and men's fields and men's wives will be taken away from them and given to others (e.g., Jer 6:12; 8:10; cf. Jer 38:23). Without a man, a woman had no identity. That is why Isaiah depicts Judah's time of suffering as one in which the supply of men is depleted, the ratio of men to women is one to seven, and the women are desperately seeking a man to claim them (Isa 4:1).

In contrast to the Deuteronomistic History which is replete with nameless women, the Prophetic Writings contain only a few: e.g., the woman of Hos 3 (if she is not Gomer); Isaiah's wife (Isa 8:3) who may or may not be the unnamed mother of Emmanuel (Isa 7–8); the weeping women of Tammuz (Ezek 8:4); and the nameless widow of Ezekiel (Ezek 24). Ezekiel uses his wife's life, or rather her death, as a symbol for the future of Judah. They too will die (v 18). Yahweh tells Ezekiel not to mourn his wife; Judah does not deserve to be mourned. Its fate is just punishment for its sin. And what of Ezekiel's wife? She is allowed to become a nameless expendable victim. Whereas Ezekiel does not mourn for his dead wife, Joel tells Judah to lament "like a virgin girded with sackcloth for the bridegroom of her youth" (Joel 1:8). Judah, the personified woman, needs to repent for her infidelity to Yahweh. A husband can afford to lose a wife and not mourn; no wife can so easily afford to lose her husband! These texts, products of patriarchal culture, are perfect metaphors for Yahweh's relationship with Judah.

The importance of motherhood is emphasized time and again in the Pentateuch and the Deuteronomistic History. The Prophetic Writings presume this importance when they transfer motherhood from the natural realm to the symbolic. What mothers experience, cities and countries and peoples will also experience (see "Woman as Metaphor for City, Country, and People" below).

There are a few exceptions, however, where the importance of a natural mother is at least implied. Children are "the fruit of the womb" (Isa 13:18). God formed Jeremiah "in the womb" (Jer 1:5; cf. 15:10; 20:14, 17–18). God called Israel/Isaiah from the womb, from the body of their mother (Isa 49:1, 5), and has borne them from their birth, carried them from the womb (Isa 46:3). It is unthinkable that a woman forget her sucking child and have no compassion on the child of her womb (Isa 49:15). Mothers are meant to be models for their daughters; unfortunately, however, those women who loathe their husbands may influence their daughters to do the same (Ezek 16:44–45).

Divorce is a man's prerogative. And if he divorces his wife and she leaves and is taken by another man, he will not take back the "damaged goods" (Jer 3:1; cf. Isa 50:1). When Yahweh is willing to take back the wayward wife (Hos 2:19–20), the forsaken wife (Isa 54:6), Yahweh is going far beyond the demands of patriarchal marriage. When Malachi exhorts against divorce, it is to the men that the poet speaks (2:14–16); women do not initiate divorce. When a man commits adultery, he sins by stealing the property of another man (e.g., Jer 7:9; Ezek 18:6, 11, 15), not explicitly by being unfaithful to his wife (wives).

Amos's condemnation of Israel includes the loss of a man's property, including his wife, his children, his land, and his country: "Your wife will be a harlot in the city; your sons and daughters will fall by the sword; your land will be parceled out by line; you shall die in exile" (Amos 7:17). Hosea describes Israel's unfaithfulness to Yahweh with the same imagery, the wife become harlot (Hos 1:2). The association of women with men's property may be the source of Israel's women being called "the cows of Bashan." Just as Bashan's cows were well fed and fat, healthy and sleek, Amos depicts Israel's women as lazy, and as seeking sensual gratification (4:1–3; cf. Isa 32:9–12).

Old Testament literature presents the reader with a patriarchal culture which allows a man to have more than one woman but allows a woman to belong to only one man. There are many examples of this form of discrimination in both the Pentateuch and the Deuteronomistic History. In condemning Israel's social sins, Amos names two men—a father and his son—going in to the same woman (2:6–8; cf. Ezek 22:10). A son steals if he violates a woman who belongs to his father.

Woman's inferiority translates into powerlessness within the culture and calls forth condemnations of those who would further oppress the already powerless (Mic 2:9; 3:5), especially the widow (e.g., Isa 1:17; 10:2; Jer 7:6; 22:3; Ezek 22:7; Zech 7:10; Mal 3:5).

Role Stereotyping and Sexual Discrimination

One way to legitimate a patriarchal culture is to define clearly appropriate ways of being and acting for each of the sexes, and to provide a seemingly logical rationale. Jeremiah does just that when the poetry distinguishes between punishments appropriate to the sexes: whereas the men will meet death by pestilence, the wives will become childless and widowed (Jer 18:21). The form that women's punishment takes suggests what behavior is appropriate to women in a patriarchal society and reinforces it. Whereas children gather wood and fathers kindle fire, the women knead dough (Jer 7:18). Whereas women are the professional mourners (Jer 9:17–18, 20; cf. Nah 2:7), men are messengers (Jer 20:15; Zech 7:2), farmers

(Zech 13:5), and traders (Ezek 27:15); they bury people (Ezek 39:14). Men are craftsmen and goldsmiths and blacksmiths (Isa 41:7). Women, in contrast, are expected to be conscious of their attire and ornaments, especially brides (Jer 2:32).

"Equal but separate" describes the mourning recommended in Zech 12:12–14. The family of the house of David is to mourn, and their wives by themselves are to mourn; the family of the house of Nathan is by itself to mourn, and their wives by themselves; the family of the house of Levi is to mourn by itself, and their wives by themselves; the family of the Shimeites is to mourn by itself, and their wives by themselves; and all the other families left are to do likewise, and their wives by themselves. Either the women are to participate in two services of mourning—with their families and with each other alone—or the men and women are to be separated for the mourning. The former may seem likely because women were generally associated with mourning rites. On the other hand, "separate but equal" is a common technique used by patriarchal cultures to obscure and therefore perpetuate sexual discrimination. Finally, male and female captives are valued differently. Whereas a boy is given in exchange for a harlot, a girl is sold for wine (Joel 3:3). The patriarchal culture in which the text was composed predisposes the reader to infer that the captor likes wine but prefers women!

Perhaps one can find the beginnings of the ever-contemporary presupposition that mothers-in-law will dislike daughters-in-law and that daughters-in-law will have problems with mothers-in-law in the comment to that effect in Mic 7:6. The fact that the poem omits synthetic parallelism—that there will be problems between fathers-in-law and sons-in-law—may be explained by the dictates of the poetry, but as the text stands there is present in it a devastating patriarchal bias which continues even today to have detrimental consequences for families.

Omission of the parallelism which would include women is a subtle way of making history men's history; it is an obvious expression of sexual discrimination. Malachi's first question to Judah (Mal 1:6) is an example of such discrimination. Malachi presumes that a son honors his father (with no mention of a daughter who honors her mother) and a servant, his master (with no mention of a maid who honors her mistress). Elsewhere old men are destined for destruction, but no mention is made of old women, of what will happen to them (Ezek 9:6; cf. Isa 65:20). Joel parallels the "old men" with the inhabitants of the land, the old men perhaps signifying the land's elders; if this is the case, the omission of any mention of old women is quite deliberate (1:2). The vision of Joel 2:28 parallels old men and young men, omitting the women entirely.

Woman as Metaphor for City, Country, and People

Although the Prophetic Writings have many expressions of patriarchal culture in common with the literature of the Pentateuch and the Deuteronomistic History, the books also betray their own biases. One such predisposition is the use of woman as a metaphor for a city or a country (e.g., Isa 1:21). A woman may be understood to have much in common with a city or a country: she may be more or less valuable, more or less beautiful, large or small, a greater or lesser source of nurture, faithful or unfaithful. It is a compliment to a city or a country to personify it; it is an insult to women that cities and countries are so personified!

At least fourteen cities are personified as women in the Prophetic Writings:

Gaza (Amos 1:7);
Rabbah (Amos 1:14) and her daughters (Jer 49:3);
Samaria (e.g., Amos 3:9; Hos 13:16; Ezek 16:46) and her daughters (Ezek 16:53, 55);
Zion (e.g., Isa 1:27) and her daughters (e.g., Isa 1:8; Zech 2:10);
Jerusalem (e.g., Isa 51:17; Ezek 16) and her daughters (e.g., Mic 4:8; Zeph 3:14; Zech 9:9);
the daughter of Gallim (Isa 10:30);
the daughter of Tarshish (Isa 23:10);
Sidon (Isa 23:4) and her daughter (Isa 23:12);
Tyre (Isa 23:15) and her daughters (Ezek 26:6, 8);
Bethlehem Ephrathah (Mic 5:2);
Sodom (Ezek 16:46, 48, 49) and her daughters (Ezek 16:53, 55, 56);

Rahab (Isa 51:9);
Gebal (Ezek 27:9); and
Tehaphnehes (Ezek 30:18).

A city's "daughters" are those villages outside the city walls but close enough to the city to be under its protection.

The countries that the Prophetic Writings personify as a woman include the following:

Moab (Isa 16:2);
Egypt (e.g., Isa 19:14; Jer 46:11, 24; Ezek 23:21);
Israel (e.g., Amos 5:2; Jer 18:13);
Judah (Jer 3:7-8, 10);
Babylonia (e.g., Isa 47:1; Jer 50:42; Ezek 23:17; Zech 2:7);
the land of the Philistines (Ezek 16:27, 57);
Edom (Ezek 16:57; 32:29); and
Elam (32:18).

The Books of Isaiah, Nahum, and Jeremiah condemn Israel's enemies by using the female imagery. The symbol carries with it connotations of inferiority, vulnerability, and powerlessness. The Egyptians, for example, will be like women (Isa 19:16); the Assyrian troops have become women (Nah 3:13); the heart of Moabite warriors will be like the heart of a woman in her pangs (Jer 48:41); the heart of the Edomite warriors will be like the heart of a woman in her pangs (Jer 49:22); and finally, the Babylonians will become women (Jer 50:37; cf. 51:30).

In a similar way, Jeremiah depicts unfaithful Zion as a woman "dressing in scarlet, decking herself with golden ornaments, enlarging her eyes with paint, beautifying herself for lovers" (4:30). Ezekiel uses the metaphor of two harlots, Oholah and Oholibah, to describe the evils of Jerusalem and Samaria (Ezek 23).

The suffering and pain of an oppressed people is often compared to the anguish experienced by a woman who is about to give birth to a child. She writhes in pain, she cries out when her time is near (e.g., Isa 13:8; Mic 4:10; cf. Isa 21:3; Jer 4:31). Isaiah 28:9 describes persons old enough to learn as "those who are weaned from the milk, those taken from the breast." Micah uses a pregnant woman's bringing forth as a metaphor for timing (5:3).

The Prophetic Writings describe punishment—sometimes for Israel, sometimes for Judah, sometimes for their enemies—with female imagery. They use symbols which portray women being deprived of their identity and their destiny as wives and mothers: no conception, no pregnancy, no birth (Hos 9:11; cf. Isa 23:4); a miscarrying womb and dry breasts (Hos 9:14); children coming to the birth but there being insufficient strength to bring them forth (Isa 37:3); the pangs of childbirth but the child not presenting itself at the mouth of the womb (Hos 13:13); the pregnant woman who does not deliver, who brings forth only wind (Isa 26:18); children brought forth only to die (Hos 9:16); conceiving chaff and bringing forth stubble (Isa 33:11); a forsaken wife (Isa 54:6); ravished women—wives and widows (Zech 14:2; Isa 13:16; Ezek 19:7); skirts lifted up (Jer 13:22, 26; Nah 3:5); mothers of young men destroyed (Jer 15:8); mothers of seven disgraced (Jer 15:9); your own mother shamed (Jer 50:12); exiled women—wives, mothers, and daughters (Jer 22:26; 38:22–23; 41:10); loss of children (Isa 47:9; Jer 18:21); an increase in the number of widows (e.g., Jer 15:8; Ezek 22:25); and a lack of compassion for widows (Isa 9:17). Rachel weeps because her children are no more (Jer 31:15).

The Prophetic Writings also describe Judah's restoration with female imagery. When Jeremiah prophesies restoration, it asks the men whether they can bear children; since they cannot, there is no reason for them to have their hands on their loins like women in labor (30:6; cf. 31:8). In other words, the people's oppression and anguish will soon end. When Zion's citizens return from exile, Zion will be like a bride putting on ornaments (Isa 49:18). Zion, which was bereaved and barren, will have children (Isa 49:21). The barren one who did not bear and who has never been in travail is to rejoice because she will have more children than the married woman (Isa 54:1). Restoration will also include "sucking the milk of nations and sucking the breast of kings" (Isa 60:16) and maidens rejoicing in the dance (Jer 31:13).

Third Isaiah expresses blessings with female fertility images: your land will be married (Isa 62:4); your children shall marry you

(Isa 62:5); the land shall be born in a day, the nation brought forth in a moment (Isa 66:8); birth shall take place before labor; without pain, a son (Isa 66:7); those who survive pregnancy will be born; the womb will open for them (Isa 66:9). Jerusalem as mother will provide breasts that her children may suck and be satisfied; she will carry them on her hip and dandle them on her knees (Isa 66:11–12). Jerusalem as mother will provide comfort (Isa 66:12).

Exceptions within a Patriarchal Culture: Prophetic Concern for the Powerless

Despite the fact that ancient Israel possessed a patriarchal culture, in certain situations men and women seem to be treated equally. Both, ironically enough, are victims of war (Amos 7:17; Jer 14:16); of thirst (Amos 8:13); of famine (e.g., Jer 11:22); both sin (Hos 4:14; Jer 44:9, 25). Adulterers stand beside harlots (Isa 57:3); female slaves beside male slaves (Isa 14:2; Jer 34:9; Joel 2:29); old women beside old men (Zech 8:4); women beside men (Jer 40:7; cf. 41:16); brides beside bridegrooms (e.g., Isa 61:10; Jer 7:34; 16:9); wives beside husbands (e.g., Jer 6:11); mothers beside fathers (e.g., Isa 8:4; Mic 7:6; Jer 16:3, 7; Ezek 16:3); daughters beside sons (e.g., Mic 7:6; Jer 3:24; Ezek 14:16); sisters beside brothers (Jer 22:18); girls beside boys (Zech 8:5; Joel 3:3); and maidens beside young men (Isa 23:4; Jer 51:22; Ezek 9:6; Zech 9:17). One biblical text even suggests a certain equality between the king and the queen mother (Jer 13:18).

Only three women from the literature of the Pentateuch reappear in the Prophetic Writings. They are Sarah, Rachel, and Miriam. Isaiah 51 parallels Abraham, Israel's father, with Sarah, who bore them (v 2), thus truly making Sarah a matriarch. When one thinks of all the men who are remembered and celebrated, one is justified in condemning the patriarchal bias and sexual discrimination which they represent. On the other hand, Sarah was remembered, and she is worth remembering.

Rachel appears in Jeremiah's poem of restoration (chap. 31). As the mother of the children of Jacob, she is portrayed as weeping from her grave at Judah's loss of land and exile. But Yahweh tells her to stop crying; her children live and will return to the land (vv 15-16). Though Rachel's claim to fame is quite traditional—motherhood—she nevertheless is here credited with being the mother of the children of Jacob, that is, she is the mother of the people of Israel. She, too, therefore, is matriarch.

Miriam is not, as far as we know, a mother. She is daughter of her father and sister of her brothers, but she is neither wife nor mother. Why then is she remembered? Miriam is prophetess and deliverer. Micah 6:4 gives her an equal role with Moses and Aaron in Israel's primary religious experience, the exodus. She complements the matriarchs—creation and salvation.

One expression of sexual equality which is worth noting is the image of old women sitting with old men "in the streets of Jerusalem, each with staff in hand for very age" (Zech 8:4). What is significant here is that the Hebrew word for "old women" is a *hapax legomenon,* that is, the word occurs only once in the entire Old Testament. The image is part of a larger image of Judah's restoration. Since the old men, the elders, were held in high esteem, were considered to be wise, and were sought after for judgment, the specification of old women with the men suggests greater sexual equality. In addition, the postexilic text of Mal 2:14-15 calls men to cease practicing adultery and to be faithful to the wives of their youth. When one considers these texts together—Zech 8:4 and Mal 2:14-15—one is tempted to conclude that the vision of restoration is one of greater justice and sexual equality (cf. Jer 31:22, 31-34 and Joel 2:28-30, pp. 174-77 below).

The prophets frequently use the Hebrew verb "to be compassionate" when they wish to describe God's posture toward the people Israel. Both the verb and its cognate adjective are derived from the Hebrew noun meaning "womb." Just as it was unthinkable that a mother forget the child of her womb, it was equally unthinkable that God would abandon the people. On the contrary, the people believed that God would always respond graciously to them, with mercy and compassion (e.g., Hos 14:4; Mic 7:19).

In addition to the above-named exceptions within the patriarchal culture, one must acknowledge the general prophetic thrust to condemn those within the society—the propertied, the prosperous, the leaders—who oppress the less powerful, especially the widows, the fatherless, and the aliens. Though the texts presume hierarchical relationships, they do not envision that such relationships should generate economic oppression. Quite the contrary. Those in positions of power and prestige within the society had a responsibility to provide for the weaker, the less powerful, the poor.

Contemporary feminists who read the prophetic texts today and believe them to be sacred identify women as victims not only of social oppression but of economic oppression as well. Moreover, they recognize the essentially interdependent nature of women's social and economic oppression. Consequently, they call both for just and equitable treatment from leadership and for the elimination of any hierarchical structures that legitimate and perpetuate oppression.

TEXTS FROM A FEMINIST
PERSPECTIVE

Victims of Symbolism:
Gomer, Hosea's Harlotrous Wife:
the Wife Whom Jeremiah Never Had:
Ezekiel's Unnamed Widow
(Hosea 1—3: Jeremiah 16: Ezekiel 24)

The Story

The Lord told Hosea to take a wife of harlotry and have children of harlotry (Hos 1:2). Yahweh's unusual command is quickly explained: the land of Israel was committing harlotry by forsaking the Lord. Hosea's marriage was to symbolize Yahweh's relationship with Israel. Whether Gomer was a harlot before Hosea married her or whether at that time she only possessed the propensity for becoming a harlot is uncertain. Hosea obeyed, taking Gomer who conceived and bore him a son. The text seems to indicate that Hosea was the father of at least her first son, Jezreel (v 3). The Lord told Hosea to name the daughter Gomer bore "Not Pitied," to symbolize the fact that Yahweh would no longer forgive Israel's unfaithfulness (v 6). After weaning Not Pitied Gomer conceived a son whom the Lord said should be named "Not My People," to signify that Israel was no longer Yahweh's.

Hosea is desperate to win back his wife and the children. He wishes the male child to be renamed "My People" and the daughter "She Has Obtained Pity" (2:1). He wishes Gomer to put away her adulterous harlotry, threatening her with painful consequences which will affect both her and the children if she refuses (vv 2-13). Hosea longs for a future which will return to the good old days, that time of first love and faithfulness when their relationship was one of lovers, when harmony and prosperity prevailed (vv 14-20). Clearly at that time the children will symbolize the compassion of Yahweh toward the people and covenantal bonding (vv 21-23).

Hosea's musings about what had been and what he wished would be were interrupted by the Lord's word to go again, to love the paramour and the adulteress. Whether the reference here is to Gomer or to another woman is uncertain. Hosea is to love the woman just as God loves idolatrous Israel (3:1). Hosea bought the woman. Then he told her that for many days she would have to be faithful to him; for his part, he would also, during that time, be faithful to her. This relationship was to represent the exile—Israel without king or religious ritual (vv 2-4).

Interpretation

Interpretation is built into the text. The poet explains not only what is happening but why. The poet uses marriage as a metaphor for Israel's relationship with Yahweh. Yet the explanation is also unclear and leaves the reader, from both a historical perspective and a literary one, with many unanswered questions. Did Hosea really have a wife who was unfaithful or is Gomer a literary fiction? And what about the children? Were the three children Hosea's or only the first? Was Gomer a harlot before marriage? Did Gomer return to Hosea? Was she then again unfaithful? Did Hosea give Gomer a bill of divorce? Was the paramour and adulteress referred to in chap. 3 another woman, keeping in mind that men could have more than one woman, especially if a husband had issued a bill of divorce to his wife? Because the Hebrew of the text is damaged and difficult, these questions remain the subject of interesting hypotheses but they cannot be answered conclusively.

From a feminist perspective, one thing is certain: the women and the children—the possessions and the powerless—are *used*. The relationship is hierarchical: just as God is superior to humans, men are superior to women. Men are godlike; women are sexually promiscuous and faithless. This symbolism has been one of the most damaging to women in the entire Old Testament. More perhaps than any other, it has served to legitimate sexual discrimination. Its implications continue to permeate much Christian theology.

The Story

In contrast to Hosea and Ezekiel, the prophet Jeremiah has no wife. Yet this is no accident. Jeremiah's marital status serves a symbolic function (chap. 16). The word of the Lord regarding the exile predicts that Judah's people will die: by disease, by sword, and by famine. The people will neither be mourned (cf. Ezek 24) nor buried. Jeremiah is saved the suffering of marrying a wife and begetting children only to witness their deaths (vv 1-7).

Interpretation

Within the patriarchal culture of ancient Israel, a woman's self-understanding lay in the roles of wife and mother. To save Jeremiah from the pain of losing his wife and children, the Lord commands him not to take a wife. Jeremiah, deprived of wife and progeny, represents the land, itself to be deprived soon of fertility and prosperity. Who can deny that for Jeremiah not to beget sons would be a tragedy?—there would be no one to carry on his name. Yet, Jeremiah's not having his own name carried on would be relatively unimportant beside the death of his nation. What is never focused on is that Jeremiah's bachelorhood denies to some woman the opportunity to become wife and mother; it deprives some woman of the most common identity and credibility available to women within the patriarchal culture of ancient Israel.

The Story

Ezekiel 24:15-18 records a word of the Lord to Ezekiel. He is told that his wife will die suddenly and that when she does, Ezekiel is not, in any public way, to mourn her death. In the morning Ezekiel preaches to the people; in the evening his wife dies; Ezekiel obeys the Lord.

Interpretation

To understand this text one must know the context as well as the text's symbolic intent. Judah was guilty of heinous crimes of violence. The Lord had acted to mollify them, but in vain. Judah was not interested in change and repentance (24:1–14). Judah would die; they would be taken into exile; Judah's death was well deserved; there was no reason to mourn. The people of Judah should follow Ezekiel's example. When the time comes for their demise, mourning will not be appropriate (vv 19–24). (A few scholars suggest that mourning will not be appropriate because Judah's death will, in time, lead to restoration.)

From a feminist perspective, Ezekiel's wife is another victim of patriarchy. She is nameless, a mere functionary. The only identity she has is to be found in her death. Similar to Hos 1—3, patriarchy and hierarchy are assumptions behind the metaphors. Though nothing is said of her personal sinfulness, she, nevertheless, is made to stand for Judah, the sinner. In contrast, Ezekiel, the prophet of God with the power of God who speaks the Word of God, is male and godlike.

Summary

Most introductory courses to the Old Testament study these texts but few study them together. When one looks, however, at Gomer, Jeremiah's would-be wife, and Ezekiel's unnamed wife as one way that women were used as symbols by Israel's culture, one is less likely to miss the patriarchal prejudices hidden within the texts.

God's Womb-derived Compassion
(Hosea 1—3)

The Story

Gomer's three children are given symbolic names, "Jezreel," "Not Pitied," and "Not My People." Jezreel is the son whose name represents both the valley where Israel will be defeated (Hos 1:5), and then, later, Yahweh's sowing of Judah and Israel (1:11; the noun is, in Hebrew, a verb meaning "Yahweh will sow"). Not Pitied is the daughter whose name symbolizes Yahweh's no longer having compassion on Israel or forgiving their sins (v 6), and then, later, the name is transformed into "She Has Obtained Pity" (2:1). In other words, the Lord will again have compassion. Not My People is the son whose name symbolizes that Israel is no longer the people of Yahweh and Yahweh no longer Israel's God, and later, whose name is reversed to mean "My People" (2:1), sons of the living God (2:10).

Interpretation

Whereas Gomer's son Not My People renamed My People represents Israel's covenant bond with Yahweh, Gomer's daughter Not Pitied renamed She Has Obtained Pity represents God's attitude toward the people of Israel. (According to Hosea, God had not stopped having compassion for Judah.) That a daughter serves as this symbol is no accident; the verb meaning "to be compassionate" derives from the Hebrew noun meaning "womb." She Has Obtained Pity represents God's loving compassion toward Judah and God's reestablished rapport with Israel. Wherever God is described as being compassionate, as acting with compassion (and the texts are not infrequent; e.g., Isa 49:10; 54:10; Jer 31:20), the reader should hear echoes of God's maternal concern.

An Unnamed Woman Bears Immanuel
(Isaiah 7—8)

The Story

Isaiah tries to convince King Ahaz of Judah that he should not become involved in an alliance with Assyria. Ahaz feels pressured into forming such an alliance because of advances against him by Israel and Syria. Isaiah tries to convince Ahaz that both Syria's and Israel's days are numbered, that he has nothing to fear from those nations. When Isaiah tells Ahaz to ask a sign from God, some indication to prove that Isaiah is telling the truth, Ahaz refuses. As a consequence, the Lord provides Ahaz with the sign for which he has not asked: a young maiden will conceive and bear a son and his name will be "Immanuel," that is, "God with us." The prophet then assures Ahaz that it will not be too long—before the child is even old enough to choose between evil and good—before the very countries which Ahaz fears, because of which he is entering into an alliance with Assyria, will be destroyed. Furthermore, Assyria, that country with which he is now allied, will soon—before the child can know good from evil—be at Judah's borders. In other words, over the long haul, the alliance will be in vain.

Interpretation

Historical-critical scholars have concentrated on two aspects of this narrative. First, who is Immanuel? Does the prophet have in mind his own son? Is the reference to the future king Hezekiah? Is it to another historical figure who remains anonymous? The other consideration concerns the timing of the sign. Whereas the sign Isaiah asked Ahaz to request was meant to convince Ahaz not to form an alliance with Assyria, this sign serves, only after the fact, to say, "I told you so!"

Feminist interpreters point to the nameless mother-victim. If she is meant to represent Isaiah's wife, she is done an injustice; she is another example of the nameless wife of a named husband and named son. If, on the other hand, the referent intended is the mother of Hezekiah, then not even her derived prestige—the wife of a king and the mother of a king—has saved her in this text from anonymity. And if she is intended to be neither Isaiah's wife nor Hezekiah's mother, she is nevertheless the nameless and uncredited instrument of men's history.

God as Mother
(Isaiah 42:14; 45:10; 49:15; 66:13)

The Contexts

The context of Isa 42:14 is an exhortation to praise the Lord for what God is about to do on behalf of the people. Within the patriarchal culture which produced the verses, a warrior's victory was life-giving. Often Yahweh is depicted as acting like a mighty man, like a man of war who stirs up his fury and shows himself mighty against the enemy (Isa 42:13), but rarely is God described as acting like a woman about to bring forth new life. Yet God does proclaim, "I will cry out like a woman in travail, I will gasp and pant" (Isa 42:14). The two verses thus complement one another. God acts like a woman about to become a mother.

Isaiah 45:8–12 seeks to establish what should be obvious: God is not human. People arguing with their Creator are just about as foolish as a pot talking back to the potter. It does not make sense for clay to demand an accounting from its fashioner; certainly it is not appropriate—it is even ludicrous—for a fetus to ask its father for an accounting or to ask the woman who bears it what she is bearing. Equally ludicrous is asking God to render an accounting of divine behavior. Hierarchy is here presumed but not a hierarchy of the sexes. Rather God and woman stand together on the ladder. Just as God is superior to humans, so potters are superior to both their clay and their pots; so a father is to his future offspring and so a pregnant woman is to the fetus in her womb. In that sense, a pregnant woman, about to bring forth life, is like God.

A few chapters later Second Isaiah again likens God to a mother. When Zion laments that God has forsaken and forgotten it, the Lord replies, "Can a woman forget her sucking child, that she should have no compassion on the child of her womb? Even these may forget, yet I will not forget you" (Isa 49:15). The presumption here is that a woman does not forget her child, so Zion can be quite confident that Yahweh will not forget it; just as a child can count on its mother, so Zion can count on God.

Isaiah 66:13 lies in a context of hope and a promise of prosperity. Using a simile, the poem compares the Lord to a mother. The Lord promises to comfort Jerusalem just as a mother comforts her child.

Summary

Three times in Second Isaiah and once in Third Isaiah God is compared to a woman. The Lord is like a woman in travail (Isa

42:14; 45:10), like a woman very conscious of her sucking child (49:15), and like a mother comforting her child (66:13). Though texts which describe God as being like or acting like a woman are rare in the Old Testament, the very existence and survival of any such texts is quite remarkable. Despite the patriarchal culture which produced the texts, their authors seem to have understood that God could be more adequately described if the predominantly male imagery were complemented by its female counterpart.

A New Thing on the Earth: A Woman "Protects" a Man (Jeremiah 31:22)

The Story

This verse appears in a chapter which describes restoration and consolation for God's people. Imagery of life replaces imagery of death. The poetry proclaims that the Lord loves with an everlasting love and continues to be faithful; consequently, the Lord will again bring prosperity to the people. The Lord's people shall, with much rejoicing, return from exile. The poetry promises hope for the future; life will be like a watered garden; sorrow will be turned to joy. In this context the poetry calls virgin Israel to return to their cities, the faithless daughter to stop wavering. It asserts that "the Lord has created a new thing on the earth: a woman 'protects' a man."

Interpretation

Much conjecture and debate have gone into finding an appropriate translation for the final phrase of Jer 31:22, an image used to describe the reversals which will take place at Judah's restoration. The text's precise meaning is unclear. Is it meant to be taken literally, that a woman will "surround" a man and become a man's protector? Does it mean that the hierarchy of patriarchy will be reversed? Will there no longer be a need for protection? Will the "weaker sex" be able to provide more than adequate security for men? Jeremiah's vision of a restored land includes everything which appears too difficult even to imagine—and what could be more difficult to imagine than the role-reversal implied?

Summary

This text alone might well be judged a poetic aberration if it were not for the texts of Jer 31:31–34 and Joel 2:28–30. See the following explanations.

**Behold the Days Are Coming:
Hierarchy Gives Way to
Equality of Participation
(Jeremiah 31; Joel 2)**

The Story

Jeremiah 31:31–34 has been singled out for much exegesis for this passage contains the promise of a new covenant. In some distant but definite future the Lord will make a new covenant with Judah and Israel. God will be their God, and they will be God's people. Yet it will not be like the covenant which God made with their ancestors at the exodus. They broke that covenant in spite of the fact that Yahweh was their husband/master. The new covenant will be different: the Lord will put the law *within* the people, write it *on their hearts.* They will no longer have to teach each other to know the Lord, because everyone will know the Lord, from the least to the greatest.

Interpretation

Christians have seen in this text a promise of the new covenant which is made in Jesus' blood (e.g., Mark 14:24; Matt 26:28). The particular aspects of how the covenant differs from the Sinai covenant have, however, often been overlooked. This text destroys the master-disciple/teacher-learner relationship. If the law is within, written on hearts, then everybody—the least every bit as much as the greatest—knows, and nobody has to depend on somebody else who possesses a superior knowledge of God to dispense it. The egalitarian thrust this text represents is rarely highlighted in the text's explication. The future promised will be radically different from the present.

When feminists—Jews and Christians alike—read this text with a heightened awareness of their own experiences and their own context, they wonder how its contents could have been so successfully skewed. The life-giving future which the verses promise is not a hierarchical one!

The Story

The second part of Joel 2 exhorts the Lord's people to repent and describes their restoration to well-being. The Lord will send them grain and wine and oil—every manner of fecundity and prosperity—and will remove their enemies and their reproach. At some future appointed time the Lord will pour out God's spirit on all flesh—even on maidservants and menservants. Daughters and sons will prophesy; old men will dream dreams and young men see visions.

Interpretation

This depiction of future restoration is mathematically patriarchal in its explicit articulation. Menservants, sons, old men, and young men—four male groups—are the recipients of God's spirit while only maidservants and daughters—two female groups—are mentioned. The text, however, is quite remarkable in its mention of these women's groups. The women spoken of are not the wives of kings or the mothers of Israel's leaders. They are the powerless women—the maidservants and the still husbandless and childless daughters. The text looks forward to a time when the privilege of possessing Yahweh's spirit is not limited to male leadership or to extraordinary females, but to the very lowly. The text challenges the legitimacy of hierarchy.

Summary

Jeremiah 31:31–34 and Joel 2:28–29 are both directed toward a distant but certain future for the Lord's people. Jeremiah 31:31–34 promises that the Lord will give a new covenant; Joel 2:28–29 promises the outpouring of the Lord's spirit. These themes have not gone unnoticed nor should their importance be minimized. On the other hand, the egalitarian aspect of these texts has rarely been sufficiently highlighted. The new covenant will abolish the hierarchy that is implied in "the haves and the have-nots," that is, in those who know the Lord and the others who depend on these to teach them; it will make knowledge of the Lord a possession of the least just as it is a possession of the greatest. Moreover, the Lord's spirit will be poured out on everyone, including the least, that is, the female servants. The least, that is, the daughters as well as the sons, will also prophesy. Contemporary feminists derive great hope from these promises.

Oholah and Oholibah:
Jerusalem and Samaria
(Ezekiel 23)

The Story

Two women, sisters, practiced harlotry in Egypt from their youth (Ezek 23:2–3). The older sister's name was Oholah and the younger's, Oholibah. The Lord came to possess both the women, that is, Samaria, the elder, and Jerusalem, the younger. Oholah, while belonging to Yahweh, played the harlot with Assyria, with their men and their idols (vv 4–7). The woman who had played harlot in Egypt kept to her old ways. Yahweh's response was to hand her over to her lover, to the Assyrians. The Assyrians cruelly abused both her and her children (vv 8–10).

Oholibah followed in her sister's footsteps. She practiced harlotry with the Assyrians also, but then she took her infidelity one step further, and played the harlot with the Babylonians (vv 11–18). After being saturated with Babylonia she became disgusted with them. Yahweh's response to her behavior was also disgust; in fact, Yahweh rejected Oholibah. She just got worse, however, true to her early harlotry in Egypt.

Yahweh then turned Oholibah's lovers against her. She who had become disgusted with the Babylonians now became their victim. They treated her very cruelly, raping and killing her, humiliating her in every way. Oholibah was to be punished just as Oholah had been.

The Lord proclaimed to the two sisters—the two capitals—the reasons for their punishment: they had committed adultery, violence, idolatry, child sacrifice; they had profaned the Lord's altars.

Interpretation

Ezekiel 23 presents another metaphor of woman as city, two women in fact. Again, just like Gomer in Hosea, who represents unfaithful Israel, harlot and adulteress, here Oholah represents unfaithful Samaria, and by synecdoche, faithless Israel, harlot and adulteress. The other woman, Oholibah, represents the even more unfaithful city Jerusalem, and by synecdoche, the faithless Southern Kingdom of Judah, harlot and adulteress. (Whereas when Hosea was being written the Southern Kingdom of Judah was understood to still be acting in accord with its covenant obligations, by the time Ezekiel's prophecy was composed, Judah was judged equally faithless.) Ezekiel portrays these women as harlots from the beginning. The Israelites were faithless in Egypt and, in spite of the exodus and the covenant at Sinai, the people continued to reject Yahweh. As in Hosea, the woman represents the unfaithful wife, the sinner, the sexual offender, harlot, and adulteress. The extended metaphor of Israel and Judah as faithless women accurately typifies the prejudice of Israel's patriarchal culture.

CONCLUSION

The prophetic literature stands in contrast to the Pentateuch and the Deuteronomistic History. Most obviously, the bulk of it is poetry. Little is narrative, per se. Moreover, whereas the Pentateuch and the Deuteronomistic History are thought to be, in their present form, the product of priestly and deuteronomistic redaction respectively, each of the prophetic books is thought to have had its own author(s) and editors.

The fifteen books of Prophetic Writings share Israel's patriarchal culture with the literature of the Pentateuch and the Deuteronomistic History. For example, they presume hierarchies. Women are understood to be men's possessions. Society is to protect its powerless, and who lacks power in a patriarchal society more than the widows and the fatherless? Moreover, history is men's history; they have been, and continue to be, remembered as the chief actors, the key models. They are the heads of houses. God is like them; they are like God. Most often the texts use masculine forms of personal pronouns "by preference." The unfaithful woman continues to be associated with idolatry.

In addition, the Prophetic Writings use the feminine in different ways from the historical literature. The most obvious is the metaphor of a woman to signify a country, a city, or a people. Then, Israel and Judah's experiences are frequently compared to experiences peculiar to women: anguish at childbirth, birthing, and nurturing. Finally, faithless Israel and still more faithless Judah are portrayed in female terms. They become women who have strayed from the law and from cultural constraints, that is, adulteresses and harlots—for example, Gomer, Oholah, and Oholibah. In the patriarchal culture of ancient Israel, there could be nothing worse. They were the lowest of the low. No one could better symbolize the sin of Yahweh's people. And yet, to portray Yahweh as male while portraying faithless Israel and faithless Judah as females was unjustly to relegate the female sex to an inferior status from which it has not yet recovered.

In fact, the Pentateuch and the Deuteronomistic History allow more women to emerge from the patriarchal culture as exceptions to it than do the Prophetic Writings. Only three women emerge from Israel's past—Sarah, Rachel, and Miriam. Two are matriarchs. The other ranks with Moses and Aaron as leader of the exodus.

All of the above notwithstanding, a few passages do emerge within the Prophetic Writings which give women hope. In addition to the general commitment of all of the prophetic texts to the safeguarding of the powerless, a few passages suggest a nonhierarchical future of equality. Moreover, Second and Third Isaiah suggest female imagery with which to name God.

RECOMMENDED READINGS
The Major and Minor Prophets

Bronner, Leila Leah. "Gynomorphic Imagery in Exilic Isaiah (40—66)." *DD* 12 (1983/84): 71–83.

Brueggemann, Walter. "Theodicy in a Social Dimension." *JSOT* 33 (1985): 3–25.

Clark, David J. "Sex-related Imagery in the Prophets." *BT* 33 (1982): 409–13.

Delcor, M. "The Cult of the 'Queen of Heaven' according to Jeremiah 7:18; 44:17–19, 25 and Later Developments." In *Von Kanaan bis Kerala. Festschrift für Prof. Mag. Dr. Dr. J. P. M. van der Ploeg O. P. zur Vollendung des siebzigsten Lebensjahres am 4. Juli 1979,* edited by W. C. Delsman et al. AOAT 211. Kevelaer: Butzon & Bercker, 1982.

Gruber, M. I. "The Motherhood of God in Second Isaiah." *RB* 90 (1983): 351–59.

Hall, Gary. "Origin of the Marriage Metaphor." *HS* 23 (1982): 169–71.

Holbert, John C. "Deliverance Belongs to Yahweh: Satire in the Book of Jonah." *JSOT* 21 (1981): 59–81.

Hunt, Harry B., Jr. "Attitudes Toward Divorce in Post-Exilic Judaism." *BibIll* 12 (Summer 1986): 62–65.

Kruger, P. A. "Israel, the Harlot (Hos 2:4–9)." *JNSL* 11 (1983): 107–16.

Lemke, Werner E. "Jeremiah 31:31–34." *Int* 37 (1983): 183–87.

Mollenkott, Virginia. *The Divine Feminine: The Biblical Imagery of God as Female.* New York: Crossroads, 1983.

Potter, H. D. "The New Covenant in Jeremiah xxxi 31–34." *VT* 33 (1983): 347–57.

Rice, Gene. "A Neglected Interpretation of the Emmanuel Prophecy." *ZAW* 90 (1978): 220–27.

Schmitt, John J. "The Motherhood of God and Zion as Mother." *RB* 92 (1985): 557–69.

Thompson, Michael E. W. "Isaiah's Sign of Immanuel." *ExpTim* 95 (1983): 67–71.

Trible, Phyllis. "The Gift of a Poem: A Rhetorical Study of Jeremiah 31:15–22." *ANQ* 17 (1977): 271–80.

———. *God and the Rhetoric of Sexuality.* OBT. Philadelphia: Fortress Press, 1978.

✦ PART IV ✦

THE WRITINGS

INTRODUCTION

Historical Considerations

The books which fall under the heading "Writings" are diverse in authorship, in period of composition, and in content. Some would credit Jeremiah with authoring the Book of Lamentations, but this position is not universally accepted. Partially because of the books' contents (ritual emphases, including extensive descriptions of the temple and temple accoutrements and personnel), 1–2 Chronicles and Ezra-Nehemiah are usually attributed to priestly authorship. David may have written some of the psalms, but certainly not all of them. Despite the assertions made in Prov 1:1 and Song 1:1, Solomon is not the author of either book. Scholars are at a loss when it comes to identifying the precise authors of books which compose the Writings.

Dating the books presents the same sort of problem. For most of the Writings dating is approximate; for some, it is impossible to determine with a relative degree of certainty even an approximate date of composition. From its content one can surmise that *Lamentations* was probably written during the exile—whether or not Jeremiah was its primary author.

The *Psalms* are a compilation of liturgical and private prayers from the monarchial, exilic, and postexilic periods of Israel's history. Some psalms may even predate the monarchy. Some are, for all practical purposes, ahistoric—that is, they cannot be dated, even approximately, by their content or by their poetic language and style.

The *Song of Solomon,* also called the Canticle of Solomon or the Song of Songs, is usually considered, principally because of its language, to be postexilic; it is often dated to the fourth or third century B.C. Just as the date of the book's composition or compilation is uncertain, so also are various other aspects of the text. It is unclear whether the content of the poems originally possessed any inherent unity; the author(s)'s original purpose in composing the poems is likewise unknown. Perhaps they were meant as wedding songs. Because of its erotic suggestiveness, Jews and early Christians debated the appropriateness of including the book within the canon. The decision to include it is based on an allegorical reading.

Most scholars believe *1-2 Chronicles* to be the product of the postexilic period in Judah. The content of the books is the monarchy—the history of King Saul only insofar as he prepared the stage for David, an expanded and idealized version of the reign of David, an extensive description of Jerusalem's temple and the roles of those who served it, and a history of David's dynasty.

The content of Chronicles was dictated by the date and the author. At a time when the people of Judah had nothing, they needed to be reminded of their glorious past if they were to retain hope that a future better than their present was possible. Though they had returned to the land, the land was poor and they were poor; though they had rebuilt the temple, the new temple possessed nothing of the grandeur of the original. They desperately needed the good old days as an inspiration for the possibility of good days to come. The postexilic leadership provided it with their selective rewriting of Israel's history.

The Books of *Ezra* and *Nehemiah* are relegated to the fifth century B.C. since one of their concerns is the rebuilding of Jerusalem's walls. Many scholars consider these books to have originally been one single book, and to have been written as a supplement to the Books of Chronicles by the same author(s). The books are concerned with events in Judah some seventy-five or more years after the first exiles had returned to their homeland. By this time the temple had been rebuilt. The walls of the city needed to be rebuilt, however, if Jerusalem's safety was to be secured. Also of major concern was the rebuilding of the people's lost identity. The leadership of Nehemiah who served as Judah's governor during this period made possible the rebuilding of the walls. The leadership of the scribe Ezra, with his emphasis on Mosaic observance, did much to strengthen Judah's identity.

Because of the placement of the Book of *Ruth* in the Christian Old Testament, it was originally presupposed that the book was a product of the monarchy and that it was, more or less, historically accurate. The purpose of the book—to introduce the reader to the ancestors of David—seemed to corroborate this early dating. More recent studies have challenged this thesis, however. One theory is that the book is a product of the postexilic period, and that it was composed as a statement of protest against those who would exclude non-Jews from membership in the people of Yahweh. After all, how could the Jews dare to exclude non-Israelites if the great-grandmother of King David was a Moabite? Some scholars combine positions and assert that the book had a long history, that parts of it were transmitted orally even before the monarchy, but that the book did not achieve its final form until late in the postexilic period.

The Book of *Proverbs* is a compilation of several sections, and each of these dates to a different period. Some of the book may be ancient while the remainder is dated to the late third century B.C. The setting for this literature was very likely a teaching situation, more or less formal. The older members of the family or tribe would share the wisdom they had gleaned from their own lives and experiences, and from observing the lives of others, as bits of sound advice for the young. It is young males to whom the message is consistently directed.

The Book of *Ecclesiastes* or Qoheleth ("the preacher") is dated to the late postexilic period. Because of its emphasis on reason rather than faith, it contains striking similarities to Greek philosophy. The philosopher reflects on life and experience and comes to challenge the wisdom tradition. Whereas the Jews took for granted that reward follows obedience while punishment follows disobedience,

Qoheleth reflects that all the living die. And since there is no life after death, ultimately the fate of the good is the same as the fate of the evil. Therefore, the fidelity-reward/infidelity-punishment thesis is relative or even meaningless. No matter what the reward and no matter what the punishment, they are only temporary. In the last analysis, there is no real difference between them.

Qoheleth's analysis of the human condition did not, however, lead the author to despair. The preacher concluded that being is better than nonbeing, that it is better to have lived for a time than never to have lived at all. While living, one has the possibility of enjoying the good things life has to offer—the opportunity to work, to eat and to drink, to enjoy one's spouse. The book's conclusion, that one should fear and obey God who judges good and evil, may very well be an addition, intended to make the book conform to more traditional thinking.

Dating the Book of *Job* is problematic. There are scholars who believe that an oral version of the story circulated in premonarchial days and was refined with additions during the monarchy. Others believe that the challenge to deuteronomic theology presented in the poetic parts of the book is postexilic; among those who hold this latter thesis, there are those who believe that the prose sections (the prologue and epilogue) predate the poetry and there are others who believe that biblical poetry is always older than its corresponding prose and that this case is no exception.

If one accepts that the poetic portion of the story was at one time independent of the prose, then one places the story in the context of a period when deuteronomic theology was being questioned and a new way of articulating the covenant relationship with Yahweh was being sought. One may then understand the prose to be an addition, an attempt to conform the story to what had been, and what in some circles still was, the mainstream theological perspective.

Some historical critics believe the Book of *Esther* to be a product of the Persian period (late sixth through mid-fourth century B.C.) while others date it into the Maccabean period (second century B.C.). The purpose of the book is to celebrate the Jews' victory over their enemies. Jewish ritual has come to celebrate their victory on the feast of Purim. The Hebrew version of the book (there are Greek additions) contains no explicit allusions to God, for which reason the book was accepted into the Jewish canon only with great difficulty.

The Book of *Daniel* used to be taken at face value and was therefore believed to be a product of the Babylonian exile, the mid-sixth century B.C. More recently, however, historical critics concur that the book is a product of the Maccabean period. Scholars believe the purpose of the book was to motivate Jews to be faithful to Yahweh despite the Antiochean persecutions. Antiochus IV demanded from the Jews not only political submission and economic dependence, but also religious observance, worship of himself as God's manifestation on earth. The book stresses that Yahweh protects those who are faithful and trusting. Using Babylonian domination as a decoy for Antiochus's oppression enables the author to communicate the message without its threatening either the proclaimer's or the hearers' safety. Despite the fact that the Book of Daniel is placed in English Bibles among the Prophetic Writings, from a historical perspective, it is more appropriately included among the Writings.

Literary Considerations

The genres of these books also differ. The Book of Lamentations is a vivid poetic lament over the loss of Zion suffered at the exile; its poems are interspersed with desperate hopeful cries that the Lord's steadfast love is never-ending. In its present form the book is comprised of five closely related acrostic poems. In the first four poems, the first letter of each stanza of each of the poems begins with a consecutive letter of the alphabet (i.e., the Hebrew equivalents of "a," "b," "c" through to "z"). The fifth poem has only twenty-two verses, the number of letters in the Hebrew alphabet. In this final poem, each verse begins with a consecutive letter. The entire Book of Lamentations is a metaphor: Zion is a widow.

All of the poetic techniques which make the prophetic literature so rich are also found in the Writings: for example, parallelism, both synonymous and synthetic; alliteration; assonance; rhetorical questions; personification; and similes.

The Song of Solomon is a collection of love poems which are

filled with passion and vivid imagery. The book overflows with appeals to each and all the senses: one inhales the perfumes; one savors the taste; one trembles at the touch; one listens longingly; one devours with the eyes.

The Psalms have been organized, since the end of the nineteenth century, into categories according to their subject matter. Thus there are psalms of praise, thanksgiving, petition, and lament. There are royal psalms and wisdom psalms and torah psalms. There are psalms intended for communal worship and psalms suggestive of an individual's prayer. Scholars have further refined these categories to suggest that many psalms are a combination of contents. Some, for example, begin with a lament, then move to a petition, and finally, end with thanksgiving, certain that God will hear and answer their prayer.

Most contemporary scholars believe the Book of Ruth to be fiction, a novella, although it may contain a historical kernel. They point to character development, complication of plot, climax, and denouement. They distinguish between scenes and study the role of the narrator and the quality of the dialogue. The story has two heroines—Ruth and Naomi—and a hero, Boaz. Ruth is one of only two books in the Old Testament named for a woman (cf. Esther)!

Most scholars believe the Book of Job to be fiction, either allegory or parable or drama. There are scenes and characters, dialogues, and conflicts. There is a climax and a resolution of the action. Job is not thought to be a historical personage but a typical person. He represents many people who have, in their own ways, shared his experience. He stands for all the people who cannot understand why, though they are innocent, they still must suffer. The answer Job receives to his query is a nonanswer but the only answer that can be given. That Archibald MacLeish has updated the classic in his drama *J. B.* testifies to the timelessness and continued relevance of the book's subject matter.

Although there may be some basis in historical fact for some aspects of the Book of Esther, it is not history; it is legend. The story reveals how a beautiful Jewish girl, Esther, became the wife of a Persian king, and how she was able to save her people from destruction.

The Book of Daniel is usually associated with apocalyptic literature. It predicts an end time when God will be manifest; God will usher in a new age, not as a continuation of the present time but as one radically different from it, one in which God's overarching rule over human destiny will prevail. The book uses marvelous visions to articulate a radical break with the known and the inauguration of a new age.

THEMES FROM A FEMINIST
PERSPECTIVE

Patriarchy and Hierarchy

The Writings are no less patriarchal than the historical and prophetic literature, though some of the books included under this heading are more so than others. This may be a function of content rather than a consequence of the period in which the books were produced. For example, 1–2 Chronicles is a priestly rewriting of parts of the Books of 2 Samuel and 1–2 Kings, and consequently, its patriarchal presuppositions find expression in much the same manner as the counterpart literature of the Deuteronomistic History. In contrast, two of the books included as Writings, Ruth and Esther, are named after women and these woman play significant roles in the literature which bears their names. The Books of Ruth and Esther also contain patriarchal prejudice, but the expressions of that bias differ.

One means of preserving the memory of men is by the creation of genealogies. The Books of Chronicles use genealogies to bridge time; history moves from man to man, from father to son. These books include additional genealogies to those contained in the Deuteronomistic History (cf. Ezra 8:1–14; Neh 7:5–65; Ruth 4:18–22). Moreover, it was men—the fathers—to whom the land was given (Neh 9:23, 36) and it is men whose burials are recorded (e.g. 2 Chr 21:20; Neh 2:3).

The Books of Ezra, Nehemiah, Proverbs, and Daniel are consistent with most of the Old Testament literature in denouncing foreign women. Intermarriage is condemned (e.g., Ezra 9:12, 14;

10:2–3, 10–11, 14, 17–19, 44; Neh 10:30; 13:3, 23, 25, 27). Just as iron and clay do not mix well, neither do foreigners mix with the people of Judah (Dan 2:43). Behind this text is the concern that foreign women are a major cause of idolatry (cf. Ezra 9:2; Neh 13:25–27; Prov 2:16–19). Idolatry was a principal cause of their demise in the first place and they must not allow themselves to be so taken in by women that such a thing could happen again. In a similar fashion, idolatry is equated with harlotry (Ps 106:39).

The Writings presume hierarchy among persons and classes. For example, the master is over the servant, the mistress over the maid (Ps 123:2); princes are over slaves (Prov 19:1); lender over borrower, rich over poor (Prov 22:7); Esther is over her maids and the eunuchs (Esth 4:4–5; cf. 4:16) as is the woman of Prov 31 (v 15; cf. Job 41:5). Whereas obedience to one's father is demanded at all times, Prov 23:22 implies that obedience to one's mother is restricted to her old age. Husbands were always over wives, fathers over daughters, and brothers over sisters. It is unusual, but still in keeping with Israel's patriarchal culture that Job 17:14 seems not to differentiate between a man's mother and his sister. Whereas the father is clearly superior to both, the women seem equal and almost indistinguishable. Radical reversal of the hierarchy is depicted by the vision of an unloved woman getting a husband, and a maid succeeding her mistress (Prov 30:23).

Not naming women is a way of denying them identity, the counterpart of which is the fact that they, like things, belong to men. In the Book of 1 Chronicles, Machir's daughter, the wife of Hezron and mother of Segub, is unnamed (2:21), as are Sheshan's unnamed daughters (v 34), Jabez's unnamed mother (4:9), Mered's unnamed wife and the mother of Jered, Heber, and Jekuthiel (4:18), Hodiah's unnamed wife and the sister of Naham (4:19), Manasseh's unnamed concubine and the mother of Asriel and Machir (7:14), the unnamed wives of Huppim and Shuppim (7:15), Ephraim's unnamed wife and the mother of Beriah and Sheerah (7:23–24), the unnamed daughters of Eleazar (23:22), and Heman's three unnamed daughters (25:5).

Several more unnamed women appear in 2 Chr: the daughters of Dan (2:14), Rehoboam's eighteen wives, his sixty concubines, and his sixty daughters (11:21), the many wives of Rehoboam's sons (11:23), thirteen of Abijah's wives and his sixteen daughters (13:21), Jehoram's wives (21:14–17), and Joash's wives (24:2). Moreover, Barzilai's daughter and wife are unnamed (Ezra 2:61), as are Meshullam's daughter, Tobiah's daughter-in-law, and Jehohanan's wife (Neh 6:18), Artaxerxes' queen (Neh 2:6), Shallum's daughters (Neh 3:12), Job's wife (Job 2:19), the woman of Prov 31, and Belshazzar's queen (Dan 5).

Another more subtle form of discrimination is the inclusion of both females and males but the inclusion of males in greater number. Psalm 148:12, for example, speaks of maidens, but they stand beside young men, old men, and boys. Lamentations 5:11–14 speaks of women and virgins but then specifies priests, elders, young men, boys, old men, and young men (cf. Prov 11:16). Both seven and three are numbers used symbolically in the Old Testament to signify completion. Seven is used more often than three but seven is not usually associated with any greater degree of completeness than three. The reference in Job to seven sons and three daughters, however, may be seen, in light of pervading patriarchal prejudice, to have this implication (2:10). This use of more masculine gender nouns than feminine ones also applies to animals in the same literature. Whereas the ostrich is female (Job 39:13–18), the mountain goats (vv 1–4), the wild ass (vv 5–8), the wild ox (vv 9–12), the horse (vv 19–25), the hawk (v 26), the eagle (vv 27–30), and even Behemoth (40:15–24) and Leviathan (41:1–34) are male.

In addition to the number of male and female forms, patriarchy is preserved by the ordering of the genders. Daughters, for example, were sold into slavery before sons (Neh 5:5).

Israel's History as Men's History

Many texts included among the Writings are addressed explicitly to men or else, by their content, indicate that men are the presumed recipients of the message (e.g., Pss 50:20; 69:8; Prov 30:19; Eccl 9:9). Other passages may be intended for both women and men but, if so, the women are subsumed into the masculine forms which are preferred. Examples of this occur in each and every one of the thirteen books here referred to as Writings. More-over, in certain books of this literature, as in the Pentateuch, the Deuteronomistic History, and the Prophetic Writings, men con-tinue to be warriors (e.g., Lam 2:12; Song 3:8; Ps 76:5; Neh 4:14–18; Prov 6:11; Dan 3:28; 11:10) and God continues to be associated with war (e.g., Ps 17:13).

One way of establishing and reinforcing patriarchy is to name Israel's history as men's history and the makers of that history as men. David's name, for example, appears at the beginning of at least sixty-nine of the psalms (e.g., Pss 5—9; 11—17; 21—32); in addition, he is named within the body of certain other psalms (e.g., Pss 72; 78; 89) and in other Writings (e.g., Ezra 3:10; Neh 3:16; Ruth 4:17; Prov 1:1; Eccl 1:1).

Moreover, the Writings are replete with the names of other men who, in one way or another, helped to shape Israel's history. Men whose names first appeared in the Pentateuch are recalled: Ham (e.g., Pss 78:51; 105:23); Cush (Ps 7:1); Abraham (e.g., Ps 47:9; Neh 9:7); Abimelech (Pss 34:1; 52:1); Melchizedech (Ps 110:4); Lot (Ps 83:8); Isaac (Ps 105:9); Korah (e.g., Pss 44:1; 45:1); Benjamin (e.g., Ps 68:27; Ezra 4:1; Neh 11:4); Manasseh (Ps 80:2); Zebulun (Ps 68:27); Naphtali (Ps 68:27); Joseph (e.g., Pss 77:15; 78:67); Ephraim and Judah (Ps 108:8); Levi (Ps 135:20); Moses (e.g., Ps 77:20; Ezra 3:2; Neh 1:7; Dan 9:11, 13); Aaron (e.g., Ps 99:6; Neh 10:38); Dathan and Abiram (Ps 106:17); and Sihon and Og (e.g., Ps 135:11; Neh 9:22).

In addition to David, other characters emerge from the Deuteronomistic History: Jabin and Sisera (Ps 83:9); Oreb, Zeeb, Zebah, and Zalmunna (Ps 83:11); Obed (Ruth 4:17, 22); Jesse (Ps 72:20; Ruth 4:17, 22); Samuel (Ps 99:6); Saul (e.g., Pss 18:1; 52:1); Phineas (Ps 106:30); Doeg (Ps 52:1); Nathan (Ps 51:1); Solomon (Song 1:15; Ps 72:1; Ezra 2:58; Neh 7:57; Prov 1:1); Ethan (Ps 89:1); Heman (Ps 88:1); Absalom (Ps 3:1); Joab (Ps 60:1); and Zedekiah (Neh 10:1; 12:39).

Moreover, men whose names are recorded in the prophetic liter-ature also appear in the Writings, for example, Zerubbabel and Jeshua (Ezra 2:2; Neh 12:1); Haggai and Zechariah (Ezra 6:1, 14). A few characters named only in the psalms or else named only there and elsewhere in the Writings emerge: Jeduthun (e.g., Pss 39:1; 62:1); and Asaph (e.g., Ps 50:1; Ezra 3:10; Neh 7:44). The names of a few men known to us only through the Writings appear only in the books which bear their names or in other books of the wisdom literature: Nehemiah (e.g., Ezra 2:2; Neh 12:26); Ezra (e.g., Ezra 7:1, 6; Neh 8:1–2); Job (e.g., Job 1:1; 2:11); and Daniel (e.g., Dan 1:6, 11).

The people themselves and the land are named after a patriarch (e.g., Lam 1:3; Ps 105:10; Ezra 1:3; Neh 1:2; Ruth 1:1; Prov 1:1; Eccl 1:12; Esth 2:6; Dan 1:1). Houses are named after fathers (e.g., Ps 45:10; Ezra 1:5; Neh 1:6; Esth 4:14) or brothers (Job 1:4, 13, 18) in general, or after specific men: Israel (e.g., Ps 98:3; Ruth 4:11); Judah (Ezra 1:5; Neh 4:16); Benjamin (Ezra 1:5); Aaron (e.g., Ps 115:10); Levi (Ps 135:20); Perez (Ruth 4:12); and Jeshua (Neh 7:39). The presidents and the satraps were all men (Dan 6:5, 11, 15).

Language: Masculine by Preference and God as Father

In addition to the recording of history as almost exclusively men's history, patriarchy and hierarchy as cultural phenomena in ancient Israel find expressions in language. Children are "sons" (e.g., Lam 3:33; Song 1:6; Ps 2:7; Ezra 2:3; Neh 2:2; Ruth 4:15; Prov 1:8; Job 1:6; Eccl 1:1; Esth 5:11; Dan 2:25); persons and people, singular and plural in number, are "man" and "men" respectively (e.g., Lam 3:33; Song 8:7; Ps 12:2; Ezra 1:4; Neh 1:2; Prov 24:1; Job 4:13; Eccl 9:14; Esth 9:6; Dan 9:7); parents and ancestors are "fathers" (e.g., Lam 5:7; Ps 22:4; Ezra 4:15; Neh 2:3; Prov 1:8; Job 8:8; Dan 2:23); the orphan is the "fatherless" (e.g., Ps 9:14); siblings are "brothers" (e.g., Ps 22:22; Ezra 3:2; Neh 1:2; Ruth 4:10; Prov 6:19; Job 22:6; Eccl 4:8). In Neh 5:1 the Hebrew speaks of "the people" but both the translator and the reader can conclude that only males are being referred to, since the Hebrew adds "their wives."

The RSV perpetuates patriarchy when it translates "sentry" as "watchman" (Ps 130:6; Job 27:18) and by the addition of several masculine terms which are not present in the original Hebrew, added no doubt, "for clarity's sake": "man" or "men" (e.g., Neh 13:15; Prov 1:2; Job 15:28; Eccl 3:14; Esth 1:14), and "father" (Eccl 5:14). An even more serious translation error is the rendering of "raping a woman" by the phrase "committing adultery" (Prov 6:32). The translation transfers the focus of the action from the female victim to the male oppressor.

Sometimes the reader becomes so accustomed to the results of patriarchy that a male is presumed when, in fact, the person desig- nated may be female. Such is the case with Ephrathah (1 Chr 2:24). Is the name meant to signify the otherwise-unnamed daughter of Machir spoken of in v 21? Need the reader presume patriarchy and conclude that Miriam named in 1 Chr 4:17 is a male, even if the Miriam of the exodus is undoubtedly female? Is the Beraiah re- ferred to in 1 Chr 8:21 a mother or a father, that is, male or female? Or is the name Maacah referred to in 1 Chr 11:43 a mother or a father, that is, male or female? Who can know since the name occurs only here in the entire Old Testament (cf. 1 Chr 8:29; 9:35). Only patriarchal bias can assume that the person so designated is male.

The same kind of query may be made of the Micah referred to in 1 Chr 8:34–35 and 9:40–41. Does the name's designation of a male elsewhere demand that this reference is also to a man? Such a determination cannot be made conclusively from the evidence since other Old Testament names apply to both men and women. Was Azriel the mother or the father of Jeremoth (1 Chr 27:19)? Was Adriel the mother or the father of Azmaveth (2 Chr 27:25)? Is the Athaliah of Ezra 8:7 a woman (cf. 2 Kgs 11), and if so, what about the others named in the genealogy, that is, Shecaniah, Zer- ahiah, Johaziel, Jonathan, Michael, Jehiel, Josiphiah, Bebai, Hak- katan (vv 2–12)?

When patriarchy pervades the culture, is it any wonder that a people's God is named in male terms? God is the God of men, that is, of the fathers (e.g., Ezra 7:7; Dan 2:23); of Abraham (Ps 47:9); of Jacob (e.g., Ps 20:1); of Israel (e.g., Ps 41:13; Ezra 1:3; Ruth 2:12); of Daniel (Dan 6:26); of Shadrach, Meshach, and Abednego (Dan 3:28–29). God is king (e.g., Ps 5:2; Dan 4:37); and father (e.g., Ps 68:5; cf. 103:13; Prov 10:1); shepherd (Ps 80:1); and protector of widows (Ps 68:5). Men are superior to other humans; and God, who is superior to men, is certainly more like men than like any lesser beings. It follows quite logically therefore that God is a "he" (e.g., Ps 2:7; Prov 2:7; Eccl 3:14). Men are Israel's warriors and the patriarchal culture of ancient Israel transferred this quality of Israel's men to their God. God is behind the destruction of Judah (Lam 1:15; cf. Neh 4:20); Yahweh is Lord God of hosts (e.g., Ps 24:10), like a mighty man (Ps 78:65).

Women as Men's Possessions

In the Old Testament Writings, as in the Pentateuch and the Deuteronomistic History, women continue to be identified by the men to whom they belong—their fathers, their husbands, their brothers, their sons (e.g., Ruth 2:5, 10; Job 31:10; Esth 1:15, 20, 22; 2:8-9). The Books of Chronicles provide an especially good example of this phenomenon. The women are named, but their own accomplishments, except of course for the bearing of sons, go unrecorded. Azubah is the wife of Caleb; Jerioth is the woman by whom Caleb had three named sons (1 Chr 2:18-19). Ephrath, besides being one of Caleb's wives, is also the mother of Hur (2:19, 50). Ephrathah, the wife of Hezron, became a sexual partner to Caleb (by Levirate marriage?) and the mother of Ashhur (2:24; cf. 4:4). Ephah, one of Caleb's concubines, became the mother of Haran, Moza, and Gazez (2:46). Maacah, another of Caleb's concubines, became the mother of Sheber, Tirhanah, Shaaph, and Sheva (2:48). Caleb, then, had at least six women!

A daughter of Machir became another of Hezron's wives and the mother of Segub, but whether her name was Ephrathah is unclear (2:21, 24). Atarah, one of the wives of Jerahmeel, became the mother of Onam (2:26). Abihail, the wife of Abishur, became the mother of Ahban and Molid (2:29). Helah, the wife of Ashur, became the mother of Zereth, Izhar, and Ethnan (4:7). Naarah, another of Ashur's wives, became the mother of Ahuzzam, Hepher, Temeni, and Haahashtari (4:5-6). Since Serah is listed as Ashur's daughter, by neither Helah or Naarah, and sister to four named brothers, there must have been at least a third woman in his life (7:30)!

Bithiah is the daughter of Pharaoh, the wife of Mered, the mother of Miriam, Shammai, and Ishbah (4:17). Maacah is identified as the sister of Machir but she may also have been his wife who bore Peresh (7:15–16). Hammolecheth is the sister of Gilead, and the mother of Ishhod, Ahiezer, and Mahlah (7:18). Sheerah is the daughter of Ephraim (7:23). Shua is the daughter of Heber and the sister of three named brothers (7:32). Baara is the wife of Shaharaim (8:8). Hushim, another of Shaharaim's wives, bore two named sons (8:11). Hodesh, a third wife of Shaharaim, became the mother of seven named sons (8:9). Maacah is the wife of Jeiel and the mother of Gibeon (8:29; 9:35). Abihail is the daughter of Eliab, a woman to Jerimoth, and a mother to Mahalath (2 Chr 11:18). Mahalath, the daughter of Jerimoth, became the wife of Jeroboam and the mother of three named children (2 Chr 11:18–19). Maacah, the daughter of Absalom, became a wife to Rehoboam and the mother of four named children (2 Chr 11:20–21). Maacah is also identified as the mother of King Asa (2 Chr 15:16).

Shelomith is the daughter of Zerubbabel and the sister of Meshullam and Hananiah (1 Chr 3:19). Hazzalelponi is the daughter of Etam, and the sister of Jezreel, Ishma, and Idbash (1 Chr 4:3). One notes that a man can have more than one woman (cf. Dan 5:2, 3, 23), but a woman can only very rarely have more than one man, and then only in cases of Levirate marriage (Ruth 4:5, 12–13) or of adultery (e.g., Prov 30:20).

Men wish to possess not just women but *beautiful women*. This characteristic of patriarchal culture is more obvious in the Writings than in the other Old Testament literature. Sometimes the comment is made that women are beautiful (e.g., Job 42:15; Ps 45:11; Song 1:8, 15); at other times a woman's beauty determines her fate (esp. Esth 2).

Moreover, a patriarchal society supports motherhood as well as naming women through the sons they bear (Song 6:9). The woman's womb is the place where these sons originate (e.g., Pss 86:16; 116:16; Job 14:1; 15:14; 25:4). A person comes naked from its mother's womb (Job 1:21; Eccl 5:15; cf. Ps 31:18). To specify sin from the beginning, the psalmist speaks of being conceived in sin and brought forth in iniquity (Ps 51:5); one may also go astray from the womb, and err from birth (58:3). More positive images include God knitting a person in the womb of its mother (139:13) and one's leaning on God who claimed that person from its mother's womb, from birth (71:6).

Bones grow in the womb of a woman with child (Eccl 11:5). A mother's breast quiets a child (Ps 131:2). Sons are a heritage from the Lord, the fruit of the womb a reward (Ps 127:3). To bless a man is to assure him that his wife will be a fruitful vine and his children like olive shoots (Ps 128:4).

When Job laments his dilemma, he uses imagery signifying birth problems: coming forth from the womb and expiring (Job 3:11); a hidden untimely birth like infants that never see the light (3:16). The woman who has borne no sons is, within the patriarchal culture, truly an object of pity (e.g., 24:21). That is why Yahweh gives the barren woman a home, making her the joyful mother of children (Ps 113:9).

Birthing imagery is frequently used in the Writings as a metaphor. Because of the intense pain involved in childbirth, it is an appropriate symbol for any kind of anguish (Ps 48:6; Song 8:5). Moreover, Job speaks of the womb of the sea (38:8), the womb of the ice (38:29), and giving birth to the hoarfrost (38:29). Elsewhere Sheol is a barren womb (Prov 30:16). Because of the importance of fertility and fecundity to the survival and well-being of Israelite society, one should not be surprised to find an abundance of references to both the womb and the act of giving birth. The terms themselves become, in Israel's literature, especially in the poetry, "pregnant symbols" of life and death, of beginning and end, of joy and pain.

Adultery was conceived of, not as an offense against a female victim, but as a sin against the man whose woman the victim was, that is, her father or her husband. Men sinned against men by taking and damaging property which belonged to another; the woman was simply the property taken, the thing defiled (Prov 6:29; Job 31:9–10). To avoid this sin, a man was encouraged to rejoice in the wife of his youth (Prov 5:18–19; cf. 18:22; 19:14). The proverb compares her to a lovely hind, a graceful doe. Such similes of praise, common in the Song, were not originally meant pejoratively, though women in today's culture would resist a comparison with animals! There were two kinds of women: a good wife and she who brings shame (Prov 12:4).

Women were transferred from their fathers to their husbands at marriage. For this reason, when a married woman's husband died, she was left powerless. She belonged to no adult male who would provide for her and her children. For that reason God would provide for the have-nots within society, including the widows. God would protect (Ps 68:5) and uphold (Ps 146:9) them. It was therefore evil to send a widow away empty (Job 22:9), to take her ox for a pledge (24:3), or to cause her eyes to fail (31:16). But widows were easily victimized, in language and in fact. For example, one way of a man's saying that he wished another man's death was to hope that the latter's wife would become a widow (Ps 109:9), condemnation that was intended for the man but that would punish the innocent woman. Evildoers have no qualms: they would do no good to the powerless; they would even slay widows (Ps 94:6; cf. Job 24:21).

Wives in the patriarchal culture of ancient Israel could not divorce their husbands, but husbands could divorce their wives. Though incidents of divorce are mentioned less frequently in the Writings than in the historical literature, two of Shaharaim's wives, Baara and Hushim, were cast off (1 Chr 8:8).

An orphan, in the patriarchal culture of ancient Israel, was not a child having neither mother nor father. Rather, the term was equated with a child who was fatherless, since even if the child's mother was living, she could provide no access. This aspect of Israelite society explains Job's condemnation of the evil person who would snatch the orphan from the breast (Job 24:9).

Because women were men's possessions, they could be given and taken for the mutual well-being of the men to whom they belonged. It is for this reason that Jehoshaphat, king of Judah, made a marriage alliance with Ahab, king of Israel (2 Chr 18:1). It is for this reason also that women were used for men's amusement. The term "diversions," in Dan 6:18, is a euphemism for women (cf. Esth 2:3–4)!

Role Stereotyping and Sexual Discrimination

One method used by patriarchal culture to secure the superior position of men in society is the stereotyping of roles. Women in such a society perform certain tasks and occupations deemed appropriate for them while men perform other work, which is reserved exclusively for them. One function which women, especially widows, seem to have performed in ancient Israel (if not exclusively at least considerably more than men) was mourning and lament (e.g., Lam 2:10; Ps 78:64; Job 27:15). Women were also more commonly associated with playing musical instruments (Ps 68:25). Maidens made marriage songs (Ps 78:63; cf. Eccl 12:4). Women spun wool and flax; they made clothing both for themselves and for sale. Women were allowed (or expected) to provide food for their household and tasks for their maids; they even bought fields (Prov 31:13-19, 22, 24). Whereas men did the fighting, women remained at home, and in the case of a military victory, the women divided the spoils (Ps 68:12).

Men, in contrast to women, were involved in building—cities, and gates, and the temple (Ezra 4:21; Neh 3:2-3; 11:10-12, 22); men did the reaping and bound the sheaves (Ps 129:7; Prov 10:5). Men owned vineyards and served as their keepers (Song 8:11); they also were the scribes (Prov 25:1). These so-called complementary roles guaranteed that women would never surpass men in the work they did. Since they rarely did the same kinds of work, no comparisons were possible. Thus, the myth of male superiority and the consequent discrimination against women could be maintained.

Woman as Metaphor for City and Country

Using the metaphor of a woman to portray a city or a country is particularly common in the prophetic books. The phenomenon is not confined to that literature, however. Three books included in the Writings do likewise. The entire Book of Lamentations, for example, portrays exiled Judah as a bereft woman, a widow. References are made within the book to the (virgin) daughter of Zion (e.g., 1:6; 2:1; 4:22); to the (virgin) daughter of Judah (1:15; 2:2, 5); to the daughter of Jerusalem (2:13, 15), and to the daughter of my people (2:11; 3:48; 4:3, 6, 10).

The daughters of Jerusalem reappear in the Song (e.g., 1:5; 2:7) as do the daughters of Zion (3:11; cf. Ps 9:14). The Book of Psalms also uses the metaphor, in the form of the daughter of Tyre (45:12), the daughters of Judah (48:11; 97:8), and even the daughter of Babylon (137:8). The "daughters" referred to in these passages may well have been, in the case of the major cities, their surrounding villages, those outside the city walls but within the radius of their protection. The "daughter" or "daughters" of countries may be their cities.

Exceptions within a Patriarchal Culture:
Toward a More Universal Perspective

For every rule there is an exception, and within the Writings of the Old Testament there are expressions which seem to signify exceptions to the pervading patriarchal culture of ancient Israel. Some of these exceptions take the form of women standing beside men (e.g., Ezra 10:1; Neh 8:2-3; Esth 4:11); of young men beside maidens (Lam 1:18; Ps 148:12); of mothers beside fathers (e.g., Ps 109:14; Ruth 2:11; Prov 1:8); of daughters beside sons (e.g., Ps 106:37-38; Neh 4:14; Job 1:13); of sisters beside brothers (e.g., Job 42:11); of queen beside king (Esth 7:6); of maidservants beside menservants (Ezra 2:65; Neh 7:67; Job 31:15); of female slaves beside male slaves (Eccl 2:7); and of female singers beside male singers (Ezra 2:65; Neh 7:67; Eccl 2:8). The woman of the Song proclaims: "My beloved is mine and I am his" (2:16).

Although this literature parallels the sexes, these parallels are clearly insufficient evidence to prove sexual equality—especially in light of historical evidence to the contrary. Nevertheless, the texts point to at least a certain reciprocity or complementarity. God is spoken of as having a "bosom" (Ps 74:11), but men also have bosoms, better rendered in English as "chests." From the context—power, might, king—"chest" might seem to be a better rendering, yet the use of a term common to both men and women—and more frequently referred to in women—is poetically pregnant!

Both women (Prov 31:16) and men (Song 8:11) own and plant vineyards. One might therefore conclude that there is no role stereotyping, no distinguishing between men's and women's work. The context of Prov 31, however, indicates that the woman referred to is clearly exceptional. Men usually own vineyards and men usually serve as their keepers. This exceptional woman, however, bought fields and planted vineyards. A similar exception is the case of Sheerah (1 Chr 7:24). Whereas men are generally the builders, Ephraim's daughter Sheerah built both the Lower and Upper Bethhoron and Uzzensheerah.

A more radical exception to the prevailing patriarchal culture is the fact that Job's daughters as well as his sons receive an inheritance (42:15). More exceptional still is the fact that Job's daughters receive names—Jerimah, Keziah, and Kerenhappuch—whereas his sons do not (42:14). Another exception to patriarchal bias appears in a proverb. Whereas the consistent custom is to render the generic by a masculine noun or to subsume females—wives, daughters, sisters, and so on—under males, Proverbs 29:15 uses the Hebrew word for "mother" when a more generic "parent" is implied. This is the only example of "female by preference" in the texts.

Just as we have looked at history as men's history, men as the subjects and actors of those aspects of history which other men deemed significant enough to be repeated or recorded, men are also more commonly the recipients of blessings. In fact, Ruth is the only exception to the custom. She is explicitly blessed, and by an allusion to her husband's foremothers: May she be like Rachel and Leah (Ruth 4:11).

In addition to the isolated instances cited above, the Writings present the reader with the Song, in which two lovers, a woman and a man, seem equally paired, and then two other books, both of which are named after women who are the major characters in the books, that is, Ruth and Esther. The Books of Ruth and Esther present the reader with additional female characters of significance: Naomi, Orpah, and Vashti. Because of the roles these women play, their stories will be taken up in this section in greater detail. Though these women are products of patriarchal culture, they are also striking exceptions to it.

Finally, the Writings include two books—Ruth and Jonah—which seem to build on the more inclusive theology of Second Isaiah. Isaiah's God was Creator and Redeemer, God of *all* the nations. Ruth was not a Jew; she was a Moabite foreigner, yet she became a faithful Yahwist and the great-grandmother of David.

The text of Jonah describes how the Assyrians, traditionally the enemies of God's people, heard the Word of God proclaimed by Jonah and repented. Although only one of these stories deals explicitly with a woman, both push toward greater openness and inclusivity. The hierarchy which presumed the Israelites' religious superiority over the nations—both the Moabites and the Assyrians—is here shattered. Not unchangeable national origin but faithfulness to God is what counts. Reflection on these texts has helped women to realize that just as national origin does not determine superiority and inferiority neither does unchangeable sexual identity. A feminist agenda is an inclusive one.

TEXTS FROM A FEMINIST PERSPECTIVE

Zion, the Widow (Lamentations)

The Story

Whereas other Old Testament books use metaphors, and Hos 1—3 is an extended metaphor, the entire Book of Lamentations is built on one. The setting is Judah, shortly after the fall of its capital city, Jerusalem, and the destruction of Yahweh's temple on Mount Zion. By synecdoche, the poetry of Lamentations allows both Jerusalem and Zion to stand for fallen Judah; Zion also represents the temple. The poet plays by paralleling and making synonyms of the country, the city, the temple, and the mountain on which the temple had rested.

All are depicted as a woman, a woman once pregnant and filled with children. Judah, like the woman, had once been prosperous and overflowing with loyal citizens; Jerusalem, like the woman, had once been the source and center of Israelite life; Mount Zion, on which Yahweh's temple had once stood, was the dwelling place of Yahweh's Name, the religious center of the covenant people.

Now the woman has become a widow (cf. 5:3). She is barren and withered; she is bereft of husband and offspring; she is alone. Judah is that woman. Many of its inhabitants have been taken into exile (4:16; 5:2, 8); those remaining are hungry (1:11, 19; 2:11–12, 19–20; 4:4–5, 9–10; 5:4, 6, 9–10, 13); the land has been devastated and looted (2:11). Jerusalem is that woman. Its walls have been destroyed (2:8–9); its majesty, departed (1:6; 2:1, 15; 4:7–8; 5:16). Zion is that woman. The temple is no longer the focus of Yahweh's Name for it has been burned (1:10; 2:6–7; 4:1–2; 5:18). Women stereotypically are associated with mourning and laments. How appropriate here! The woman laments (e.g., 1:2, 4, 16, 21–22; 2:5, 10–11, 18; 3:48, 51; 5:15) but there is no one left to comfort her (e.g., 1:2, 9, 16–17, 21).

Yet the woman is not without responsibility for her fate. She, like Hosea's unfaithful wife Gomer, chose other lovers (e.g., 1:2, 9, 19); her transgressions were many (1:5, 14, 18–20, 22; 3:42; 4:13–14; 5:7, 16) and grievous (1:8). Now her grandeur has been removed (1:6). Nor have the women of Jerusalem gone without punishment for what has happened to the city; they have been captured as spoils of war (1:4, 18; 3:51); they have become victims of rape (5:11).

The woman, however, still has hope in her God (2:13, 18–19; 3:19, 21–41, 55–66; 4:22; 5:2, 19–22). She prays that, just as her enemies have brought Judah low, they may have happen to them what happened to Judah (1:21–22; 4:21–22). Though others are instruments, Yahweh is the ultimate cause of Judah's punishment and that punishment she deserved. Yahweh also can deliver. The basis of Judah's confidence is Yahweh's steadfast love (3:22, 32; 5:19).

Interpretation

Part of the story's interpretation is provided by the story itself, most especially by the metaphor of woman for country, city, hill, and temple. Traditional interpretation has involved hypotheses regarding the book's author, date of composition, delineation of literary units, and its additions and redactions.

A feminist interpretation recognizes that, in a patriarchal culture which legitimates sexual discrimination with the rhetoric of complementarity, woman is an appropriate metaphor for Judah, Jerusalem, and Zion. Men are the makers of history; they interact in relation to "it." Since the Hebrew language has no neuter gender, however, their interaction with "the other"—the country, the city, the site of the temple—must be conceived in sexual terms, that is, in relation to females. When one pursues the metaphor, one begins to understand just how well it can work in this context. The men of Judah had possessed their temple, their city, their country; all were fecund and prospering. Now there was devastation. Since patriarchy identifies women by the men who possess them and values women by the number and quality of their sons, they become the perfect metaphor to express the people's experience of exile. Just as the woman bereft of husband and sons was in a sorry state, so were the men of Judah, deprived of their temple, their city, and their country—all, like the women, valued possessions.

The Woman of Beauty
(The Song of Solomon)

The Story

The Song in its present form is a love poem in five movements. The two lovers are united (chaps. 1—2), they are then separated, though perhaps only in a painful dream (chap. 3), they are then reunited (4:1—5:1), then again separated (5:2—6:3), and finally, they are again reunited (6:4—8:14). Their separation leads to longing; their union, to ecstasy. In addition to the dialogue between the lovers, there is an audience to whom each of the lovers describes the beloved, and to whom questions are directed. These daughters of Jerusalem are the only other speaking characters in the book. They function in a fashion similar to a Greek chorus.

Interpretation

Depending on which translation of the Bible is being used, one may or may not find editorial aids as one reads through this book. The RSV prints the text as closely as possible to the original Hebrew, for which reason it does not indicate who the speaker is for particular verses (though this can be determined by reading the verses). In contrast, the NAB as well as the New English Bible

(NEB) and the New International Version (NIV) do indicate who is speaking. The editors of these Bibles, however, use different significations which are themselves significant. The NAB and the NEB refer to a "bride" and a "bridegroom" while the NIV speaks of a "lover" and a "beloved." The reason for the choice may be dependent on what the editors believe to be the original setting of the poems. It is common among scholars to locate them at weddings. Some scholarship, however, has challenged this presumption—if not for the original setting of the individual poems at least for the book in its present form. The literature itself gives no indication that the male-female relationship described in the book is marital.

The next problem to be acknowledged is the difficulty of the text itself. Several of the forms appearing in it are *hapax legomena,* that is, they appear only here and nowhere else in the Old Testament literature. Other words occur only very rarely. Those facts make unachievable certainty regarding the accuracy of the rendering. And finally, there is the problem of the ordering of the verses. Again, the approach of the RSV is conservative; as little change as possible is made in the Hebrew text. The NIV does not reorder verses either. In contrast, however, the NAB and the NEB do make a few verse rearrangements in order to facilitate, at least from the editors' perspective, clarity of content.

From a feminist perspective, this story has been understood to reverse traditional patriarchal bias about women. The woman is not here portrayed as subservient to the man; in fact, she is portrayed neither as wife nor mother, and therefore outside the traditional hierarchical relationship presupposed by patriarchal marriage. The only hints of the patriarchal culture which produced the story are the references to David and Solomon and the fact that *she* does the longing when *he* is absent! She is not viewed as a sexual object, however, but rather as an attractive sexual person. Her physical attributes are a source of his celebration (1:8–10, 15; 2:2, 14; 4:1–12; 5:1; 6:4–12; 7:1–9; 8:13), no more or no less than his physical attributes are a source of her delight (1:2–4; 2:3–6, 8–9, 17; 4:13–14, 16; 5:10–16; 8:14).

There are scholars who would interpret the Song as a deliberate reversal of the relationship established as a curse in Gen 3:16. No longer should the relationship between men and women be one of superior to inferior. No longer should texts legitimate portrayals of women like those to be found in Hos 1—3; Ezek 16; 23; and so on. Just as the exile had produced a widow (Lamentations, see pp. 200–202 above), the exile was meant also to produce a woman equal to a man; the exile was to call forth a radically new beginning, one in which there would be no more unfaithfulness, no more harlotry, no more adultery, no more female victims of subservience. Would only, for the sake of women, that Judah had taken this message seriously!

Noadiah: Prophetess with an Evil Spirit
(Nehemiah 6:14)

The Story

The setting is Judah in the mid-fifth century B.C. Nehemiah, the governor of Judah, has set about rebuilding the walls of Jerusalem. This has been allowed by Persia but is resented by lesser people, by Judah's enemies who wish to continue to gloat over Judah's humiliation and who fear the day when Judah will regain power. Among the enemies are Sanballat, Tobiah, and Geshem (6:1). Nehemiah refuses to succumb to his enemies' tactics. He will not go to them for this would delay the work on the walls; he will not flee into the temple, for this would misrepresent him to the people. Sanballat, Tobiah, and Geshem use intermediaries, including Shemaiah and the prophetess Noadiah, to try to persuade Nehemiah; he, however, resists.

Interpretation

Noadiah never speaks. She is mentioned only in a phrase, and one adverse to Judah's cause at that. Nevertheless, for several reasons she is worthy of note. The text explicitly identifies her as a woman. This is important because the name Noadiah occurs only once elsewhere in the Old Testament, and that reference is to a male, a Levite (Ezra 8:33). The same name occurs twice, therefore, once for a male and once for a female. Like many other Old Testament names, one cannot determine from it the sex of the person being designated. The *āh* ending is feminine and suggests a female, but as the Levite indicates, such is not always the case. Noadiah may be legion, that is, there may be many names in the Writings and throughout the Old Testament which seem, from their presence in genealogies or from the reader's patriarchal bias, to designate men but which do, in fact, name women.

Second, Noadiah is a prophetess. The entire Old Testament has presented the reader with only three other named female prophets: Miriam, Deborah, and Huldah. Third, Noadiah is a postexilic prophetess. Whereas Miriam and Deborah precede the monarchy and Huldah prophesies its downfall, Noadiah suggests that not only prophecy but prophecy by women survived the exile. Finally, Noadiah represents an evil prophetess. The role of prophecy apparently did not discriminate between sexes. There were good men prophets and good women prophets; there were also evil men prophets and, as Noadiah testifies, evil women prophets.

Women's Story: Ruth, Naomi, and Orpah (Ruth)

The Story

This drama contains four scenes, the first of which takes place in Moab. An Israelite family—husband Elimelech, wife Naomi, and two sons Chilion and Mahlon—had fled there to avoid the famine in Israel. And there in Moab Naomi's two sons had married. Unfortunately, Naomi's husband died, and in time her sons died also. She was left a childless widow with two Moabite daughters-in-law, also childless widows. The story begins with Naomi's desire to return home. The famine in Israel had ended so there was no reason to remain in a foreign land. Having lost husband and sons, she did not have to continue to suffer also the loss of her homeland (1:1–6).

Naomi's daughters-in-law had begun the journey to Israel with Naomi. Naomi realized, however, that if Orpah and Ruth accompanied her, while she would gain her homeland, they would be deprived of theirs. Naomi is the first to speak. She tells these women to go back, each to her mother's house. She wishes them well, that is, she wishes for each a new husband. When Orpah and Ruth protest, Naomi lays out their situation. Their returning with Naomi to Israel means a dead-end to their own futures. Naomi has no other sons for them to marry, and even if she were not too old to remarry, even if she were to conceive sons this very day, too much time would elapse before they would be old enough to marry. It would be too late for Orpah and Ruth. Orpah conceded to Naomi's reasoning. Ruth persisted in her determination to accompany her mother-in-law (vv 7–14).

The next dialogue, still in Moab, takes place between Naomi and Ruth. Naomi continues with her effort to convince Ruth to remain in her own land among her own people. Ruth is obstinate. She will not abandon Naomi, her mother-in-law, an old, alone, and power-less woman. Where Naomi goes, that is where Ruth will go; Naomi's God will be Ruth's God; where Naomi dies, Ruth will die. Naomi realizes that Ruth is beyond convincing. The women go together to Israel (vv 15–19a).

The second scene takes place in Bethlehem, in the city and in its fields. When Naomi and Ruth arrive, a few of the women recognize Naomi. She has changed a bit, however; aged perhaps. They ask if she is the same Naomi they used to know; she replies that she is no longer "Naomi." The name "Mara" ("bitter" in Hebrew) is a more appropriate designation because of the bitter turn her life has taken. The narrator makes a transition to the next movement in the story by announcing that the women returned at the beginning of the barley harvest and by introducing a new character, Boaz, a kinsman of Elimelech's, a man of wealth (vv 19b–22).

Ruth asks Naomi to allow her to go and glean in the fields wherever someone will permit her. Naomi consents. Ruth then goes out; she is working on Boaz's land when he comes out from the city to check on things. He inquires of his workers who she is, and his servant explains that she is the woman who came back with Naomi from Moab. The servant makes a complimentary comment to Boaz about Ruth's industry (2:1–7).

The next conversation takes place between Boaz and Ruth. Boaz offers Ruth his fields for gleaning, his water for drinking, and protection from the young men who might otherwise take advantage of her. She praises his generosity, especially to a stranger. Boaz confesses that her reputation precedes her; he has heard about her solicitude for Naomi. Ruth again expresses gratitude (vv 8–13).

A little later, when it is time to eat, Boaz invites Ruth to join his reapers. She does. He then instructs them to look after her, to make sure she has enough to glean. The narrator reports that Ruth's labor produced about an ephah of barley. She brings this, and the leftovers from her meal, back to Naomi (vv 14–18).

Naomi asks Ruth where she worked, and Ruth reports that it was in Boaz's fields. Naomi's whole comportment then changes. The God who had given her affliction has again begun to show her favor. Boaz is one of their relatives. Ruth comments that Boaz's generosity extends to the future, through the harvest. Naomi replies to Ruth that this turn of events is fortunate; she will not be molested. The narrator notes that Ruth continued to live with her mother-in-law and work in Boaz's fields through both the barley and the wheat harvests (vv 19–23).

Naomi begins to plot how to bring Boaz, Elimelech's kinsman, and Ruth together. She tells Ruth what to do. Ruth is to enhance her appearance, then she is to proceed to the threshing floor at night, to where Boaz has lain. She is to uncover his feet (here used as a euphemism for genitals?) and lie down. Boaz will then tell Ruth what to do. Ruth obeys Naomi and everything happens as she said it would (3:1–8).

Boaz, when he realizes that a woman is lying at his "feet," asks who she is. Ruth identifies herself and then tells Boaz to spread his skirt over her, explaining to him that he is her next of kin. Boaz is very impressed by Ruth's request. She could have made age a priority, even before wealth, but instead she chose, in keeping with Israelite custom, to seek out the next of kin. Boaz then explains to Ruth that he is not really her closest relative but that there is a man closer. He assures her, however, that if that man is unwilling to act as next of kin to her, he will. He tells her to stay where she is until morning, and she obeys. Boaz then orders that her presence that night at the threshing floor be kept secret. He gives her barley which she takes back to Naomi (vv 9–15).

When Ruth returns to Naomi, Naomi wants a report. Ruth complies, and explains that the barley is for Naomi. Naomi expresses confidence that Boaz will get Ruth's situation settled that very day (vv 16–17).

The next scene takes place at the city gates between Boaz, ten of the city's elders, and Ruth's closest of kin. Boaz explains the situation to the next of kin. Naomi is selling Elimelech's property and the next of kin has the first option to buy. The next of kin accepts, until he discovers that with the land comes Ruth, and it will be his role to restore her dead husband's name. The kinsman changes his mind and declines the offer; he does not wish to threaten his own inheritance (4:1–6).

The contract was ratified; Boaz was to purchase the belongings of Naomi, including Ruth. Further, he was to see to it that Ruth's dead husband's name would be perpetuated. The kinsman, the ten elders, and the other people present at the city gates were all witnesses to Boaz's testimony. They blessed him, wishing for him a very fertile wife (vv 7–12).

The narrator concludes the story. Ruth bore a son. Naomi who was once bereft was given new hope and a new life. The women of the city assured Naomi that Ruth was of more value to her than seven sons! The son whom Ruth bore would be grandfather to the great king David (vv 13–17). A genealogy concludes the story, tracing Obed's line from Perez, Tamar's son, through Obed to David (vv 18–22).

Interpretation

Some scholars suggest that the story is about God's empowering the powerless. Since there was no one more powerless in Israel than a childless widow, and since Naomi, Ruth, and Orpah all belong to that category, the story is about how God vindicates them. Naomi generously allows Orpah to return to her own people, to, interestingly enough, "her mother's house," so that she may remarry and bear children. The reader has no reason to doubt Orpah's success.

Naomi is vindicated through Ruth, who, in addition to being a childless widow, is also a foreigner. Ruth, though a Moabitess, acts like a faithful Israelite. She provides for a powerless widow, and she keeps her dead husband's name alive by marrying his next of kin. Ruth chooses to embrace her mother-in-law's God also. The God she chooses blesses her. Ruth is given a husband and a son. Naomi is also blessed. The child whom Ruth bears is her son, her dead son's son, her grandson.

Some feminist interpreters highlight the characters of the women. Despite the patriarchal setting of the story, the women's courage is outstanding. Orpah was willing to leave her homeland to be with her mother-in-law; Ruth insisted on doing so. Naomi wanted to leave her daughters-in-law in Moab, even though that would mean going back alone to Israel and a future alone.

Other feminist interpreters believe that one should not highlight the women's courage without also denouncing the culture which the details of the story bring to light. They would argue that one should denounce the phenomenon that a woman not attached to a man is powerless, denounce the law which provides for a widow's marrying her husband's next of kin, denounce women's lack of choice and lack of opportunity for self-direction.

The climax of the story includes the elders' words of well-wishing to Boaz about Ruth. They wish for Boaz a wife who will be like Rachel and Leah (4:11). On the one hand, the blessing is typically patriarchal; the woman is to assume the traditional role which is the source of her value to her husband: she is to bear him children. Rachel and Leah, together with their maidservants, bore twelve sons (and one daughter) to Jacob.

On the other hand, women here function as models, and since women rarely function as models in the Old Testament, the verse is worth noting. Verse 12 follows with another female model, Tamar. For Ruth to be like Rachel and Leah, she must also be like Tamar. Tamar contracted a Levirate marriage with Judah in order to raise up Perez for her dead husband; Ruth would marry Boaz and bear Obed. But more than that, Tamar's courage proved to be outstanding; by Judah's own testimony, she was "more righteous than he." Ruth's courage was equally outstanding.

Even more noteworthy is the passage which follows three verses later. This time the women are speaking to Naomi about Ruth. They assert that Ruth is more to Naomi than seven children, seven "sons"! Within the patriarchal culture, what could mean more to Naomi than men—husband and sons? The number and quality of a mother's sons did much to determine her prestige within the society. But Ruth did more for Naomi than sons, no matter how many. (Seven is a symbolic number for totality.) On the lips of the women is an altered consciousness, a challenge to the presuppositions of the patriarchal culture. It is grounded in the women's experience.

Dame Wisdom and Dame Folly
(Proverbs 1:20–33; 8:22—9:12; 9:13–18)

The Story

Within the Writings, Wisdom is often personified as a woman, a woman contrasted with Folly. She is first described almost as a herald: she cries aloud in the streets and the markets, on the walls and at the city gates. She tries to persuade the simple, the scoffers, and the fools to change. If they do not heed her message, then she will not hear them in the day of their distress. On the other hand, those who take her words to heart will be protected.

Proverbs 8—9 describes Wisdom in greater detail. The Lord created her at the beginning, before anything else (8:22–26). She was beside God at creation, delighting God (vv 27–31). Wisdom is understanding; she possesses counsel, and insight, and strength, as well as riches and honor. She believes that the instruction she gives is better than silver, and the knowledge she has, better than gold. In fact, she is convinced that she herself is worth more than anything a human being could desire. She exhorts people to learn prudence from her; she utters noble truth. She teaches that pride and arrogance are the opposite of fear of the Lord. She enables rulers to govern, and takes care of those who love her. On the other hand, Wisdom hates perverted speech and wickedness, and those who hate Wisdom love death.

In chap. 9 the narrator continues the description of Wisdom. She is a woman with a seven-pillared house—surely one which is secure; she has slaughtered beasts and mixed wine, and prepared a table. She sends out her maidens to try to entice the foolish men of the town to come to her banquet; she wants them to leave behind their foolishness and to learn from her. Wisdom offers practical insights for their instruction: for example, that one can tell a lot about a person by how the person responds to correction. A wise person will be grateful; a scoffer will not. Instruction has the effect of making a wise person wiser, and a righteous person more learned.

Wisdom is not the only one who is seeking out foolish persons, however. Dame Folly is doing likewise (vv 13–18). Folly also tries to entice passers-by by her words and gestures. Unfortunately, the passers-by do not always realize that the way of Dame Folly leads to death.

Interpretation

Historical critics date these texts to the postexilic period, to the fourth or third century B.C., and suggest also the possibility of Greek influence. They cannot ignore the personification of Wisdom as a woman. Many, recognizing that Israel practiced monotheism among surrounding peoples who practiced polytheism, view Wisdom as Yahwism's version of a female consort. Wisdom is not God, the One, the Only, who in Israel is depicted as male, but Wisdom is the female who was created before all else and was with God at creation. She is the companion of God.

Intertestamental scholars show how the character of Wisdom is developed in apocryphal literature, including the Wisdom of Solomon and the Wisdom of Ben Sirach. New Testament scholars suggest the relationship between the Wisdom of God in the Old Testament and the Word of God made flesh in the person of Jesus Christ (cf. John 1:1–14).

Feminist scholars believe that the female personification of one so close to God—closer to God than any other—has been deliberately ignored in exegetical and theological studies, partly because of patriarchal bias. Though woman as symbol of temptress (Dame

Folly), and female harlotry and adultery as symbols of idolatry appear frequently enough in Old Testament literature, woman as symbol of the Wisdom of God is comparatively rare. Nevertheless the importance of Dame Wisdom cannot be overestimated.

That many Christians and Jews—even among those who are fairly familiar with the Bible—are unaware of the role played by Wisdom is surely a lamentable state of affairs. Feminist interpreters seek to eradicate such ignorance; they wish to make known and to celebrate Dame Wisdom.

An Unnamed Female Model
(Proverbs 31)

The Story

Verses 10–31 of Proverbs 31 comprise an acrostic poem. There are no Hebrew words for "wife" and "husband." Rather, the words "man" and "woman" are transformed into "husband" and "wife" either by the context in which they occur, or by the addition of prepositions indicating possession or possessive suffixes. Sometimes the Hebrew word for "master" can be translated "husband" as is the case here. A husband was, indeed, master over his wife.

Just as Wisdom is better than jewels (Prov 8:11, see pp. 210–12 above), so a woman of strength is also worth more than jewelry (31:10). She always does good and not evil for her husband (v 12). She is a hard and willing worker (vv 13, 17, 19, 25, 27); she rises early and retires late (vv 15, 18); she provides food and warm clothing and efficiently administers her household (vv 15, 21, 27); she makes good investments which produce handsome profits (vv 16–18, 24); she plans for the future (v 25).

But that is not all. This woman of strength does what a good Israelite should; she shares generously with the poor and the needy (v 20). She speaks both wisely and kindly (v 26); she fears the Lord (v 30). Because of this woman's behavior, she has won the praise not only of her husband and children (v 28), but also of the city's elders (v 31).

Interpretation

In many ways this text is typically patriarchal. The husband is master of the woman. Her sphere of control and influence is predominantly domestic. On the other hand, this is a woman of intelligence, of strength, of prudence and good judgment, a woman with sound business sense, a woman who earns the respect not only of her family but of the city officials. (The situation suggests affluence.) One might even suggest that it is only due to the demands of poetic form that no explicit causal relationship is drawn between her accomplishments and the fact that her husband is recognized at the city gates (v 23)!

Women's Story: Vashti, Esther, and Zeresh (Esther)

The Story

The Book of Esther 1:1—2:4 presents the reader with the character of Vashti. She is a queen, the wife of King Ahasuerus of Persia. The story opens with the notice that Ahasuerus hosted two banquets in the third year of his reign. The first, which lasted 180 days, was for all his princes, nobles, and servants (1:1–4). The second banquet, which was quite lavish and which lasted for the following 7 days, was for all the people of his capital city, Susa (vv 5–8). The narrator reports that Vashti also hosted a banquet; hers was for the women.

On the final day of all the partying when the king was "merry with wine," he sent for Vashti. He wanted to show her off to all his guests. The queen, however, refused to obey the king's order; she refused to come before the men. Her behavior made the king angry (vv 10–12). He inquired of his advisors what he should do about his disobedient queen (vv 13–15). One of them, Memucan, convinced the king of the extent as well as the gravity of the queen's offense. He feared that when other women heard how Vashti had acted toward her husband, they too would revolt. Memucan recommended that Vashti be permanently banished from the presence of the king and replaced with a "better" person. The severity of that punishment would send out signals to the other women who would then docilely honor their husbands (vv 16–19).

Ahasuerus likes Memucan's advice and follows it. He issues a decree reaffirming that each man be master in his own house. The narrator continues, however, that with the lapse of time, Ahasuerus's anger diminished and he thought of Vashti. Whether Ahasuerus's thoughts contained desire or remorse is somewhat ambiguous, though the former explanation seems more likely. The king's servants suggest that all the most beautiful virgins in the kingdom should be brought to Susa so that the king can have his pick of them, so that he can find a fitting replacement for Vashti. The king likes his servants' suggestion and agrees to it (1:20—2:4).

Interpretation

Whereas most literary critics consider this first chapter merely an introduction to the story (an explanation of how it happened that Esther, a Jewess, became the Persian queen), feminists point not to Vashti's disobedience but to her courage. The patriarchal culture had provided for separate banquets, one for the men and one for the women. The men had been drinking, some for 187 days, others for a mere 7 days. The reader's imagination can surely supply what condition they were in. It was at precisely this time that Ahasuerus wanted the queen brought in; he wished to show off his precious property. His opulence had been manifest. Now the queen would appear as the crown of his possessions, herself wearing a crown. Vashti never speaks yet her actions speak loud and clear: NO! She will not become the sexual object of drunken men! Vashti resists patriarchal expectations. The author does not explain why, but feminists suggest that, though she may comply with the demands of patriarchy up to a point, she will not tolerate the kind of abuse the setting would lead her to expect. She has the courage to risk unknown consequences because the unknown could not be any worse than the known!

Feminists wish to emphasize that Vashti's banishment is not because of her disobedience but because of the potential effects of her disobedience. If Vashti were not punished, her decision could be the start of a major revolution. Other women might look to her as their model; her example would then empower them to rebel against the domination of their husbands. She was cast off because she was an enormous threat to the patriarchal status quo.

While some historical critics dismiss these details of the story, others suggest that the society which produced them could have been involved in great social turmoil. Women—perhaps only those Israelite women of wealth, leisure, and prestige—perhaps influenced by the women of surrounding cultures, may have been in the process of challenging the traditional roles. If this hypothesis is true, then the details of this "fiction" are meant to be didactic: do not mess with the system, or you too will be rejected. The fiction then presents the model to which it would have women aspire.

The Story

The king's servants set about effecting their proposal. They would see to it that the beautiful virgins of the kingdom were made available for the king. Esther, a Jewish girl who had been orphaned and then adopted by her uncle Mordecai, was one of the women brought to Susa. She impressed Hegai, the eunuch in charge of the women, who forwarded her cause (2:5-11).

The narrator then explains to the reader the procedure which had been developed in order to give Ahasuerus the best possible opportunity to choose the right woman to become his queen. The women who had been judged sufficiently attractive to be considered were beautified for an entire year. Then each one in turn would leave the custodial care of Hegai to spend a night with the king. The next morning, since they were no longer virgins, they would go into the custodial care of Shaashgaz, who was in charge of the concubines. Unless the king were to send again for a particular woman, she would never again appear before him (vv 12-14). The narrator reports that when it was Esther's turn to appear before the king, she was a brilliant success. Ahasuerus crowned her queen (vv 15-17). The story then continues with how Esther delivered her people from persecution.

Interpretation

Most scholars recognize that the story is fiction but note that it functions to explain the reason for the Jewish feast of Purim. When this is considered the story's purpose, it makes sense to name Esther the heroine. Her courage and her cleverness convince Ahasuerus of Haman's wickedness. Esther, a powerless Jewish orphan girl, saves the Jewish people.

More recently, however, feminist interpreters have begun to see that buried in Esther's character is also full compliance with patriarchy. In contrast to Vashti, who refused to be men's sexual object and her husband's toy, Esther is the stereotypical woman in a man's world. She wins favor by the physical beauty of her appearance, and then by her ability to satisfy sexually. She concentrates on pleasing those in power, that is, men, both Hegai (2:15) and Ahasuerus (v 17). Her access to power is through these men. Rather than defend Vashti's decision and protest the injustice of her banishment, Esther uses Vashti's rejection for her own benefit. When feminists compare the two women, they extol Vashti, though they are not at all surprised that the literature, produced as it was in a patriarchal culture, honors Esther and relegates Vashti to oblivion. Their concern, however, is to reclaim Vashti.

The Story

Most interpreters give Zeresh little attention, if they notice her at all. She is merely the wife of Haman (5:14), the woman who, along with his friends, suggests to her husband that he have a gallows built for Mordecai (5:14), and the woman who, again along with others, this time the wise men, predicts the Jews' well-being and her husband's downfall (6:13).

Interpretation

A closer look at the character of Zeresh, however, likens her to at least two other Old Testament wives, Jezebel and Abigail. Jezebel, the wife of King Ahab, plots evil action on her husband's behalf, in that case the stealing of Naboth's vineyard (1 Kgs 21); Abigail, the wife of King David, predicts his future (cf. 1 Sam 25:28). In

Abigail's case, however, the future predicted is good tidings for
David. The future Zeresh predicted is bad news.

Summary

The three women of the story do not interact (in contrast to the
three female characters in the Book of Ruth). Each one is a
product of a patriarchal culture, that is, each one functions in
relationship to the men in her world. Yet the contrast between
them is striking. Vashti "wins" by losing. She triumphs over patriarchal domination and control. Esther "wins" by playing the man's
game which puts her in a position to effect good for her people.
Zeresh "wins" only insofar as she confronts her egotistical husband
with painful truth. That she has initiative, intelligence, and wisdom will, unfortunately, have little effect on her own future.
Haman's downfall will be hers also. Most certainly there are elements of these three portraits that strike chords of resonance with
contemporary experience.

CONCLUSION

Included in that section of the Old Testament called the Writings are thirteen books, by at least ten different authors, some with
extensive editing, others with at least a few additions. Some of the
books may have begun as oral tradition in the premonarchial period; in their final form, however, they are all products of the exilic
and postexilic years. The books represent a widening of theological perspective, even theological contradictions. The Books of
Chronicles selectively rewrite material in Samuel and Kings and
betray their postexilic perspective. Ezra and Nehemiah are both
intensely nationalistic and seem to clash with the more inclusive
theology of the Book of Ruth. Three of the books are fiction—Job,
Ruth, and Esther. Three hardly mention God—the Song, Ecclesiastes, and Esther.

From a feminist perspective also these books are diverse.
Whereas Lamentations, the Song, Ruth, and Esther, one way or
another, emphasize women, 1–2 Chronicles, Nehemiah, and Ezra
merely allot the traditional roles to them. At least three women are

important in the Book of Proverbs—Dame Wisdom, Dame Folly, and the unnamed female model of chap. 31—though the contents of the book are addressed to men. Only nameless wives appear in Ecclesiastes and Job, though Job's wife does speak once and the book mentions his daughters. Women are also peripheral to the Book of Daniel.

RECOMMENDED READINGS
The Writings

Brenner, Athalya. "Naomi and Ruth." *VT* 33 (1983): 385–97.

Carmichael, Calum M. "A Ceremonial Crux: Removing a Man's Sandal as a Female Gesture of Contempt." *JBL* 96 (1977): 321–36.

Carr, G. Lloyd, and D. J. Wiseman. *The Song of Solomon.* TOTC. Downers Grove, Ill.: Inter-Varsity, 1984.

Carroll, Michael P. "Myth, Methodology and Transformation in the Old Testament: The Stories of Esther, Judith, and Susanna." *SR* 12 (1983): 301–12.

Craghan, John F. "Esther: A Fully Liberated Woman." *TBT* 24 (1986): 6–11.

———. "Esther, Judith, and Ruth: Paradigms for Human Liberation." *BTB* 12 (1982): 11–19.

Davies, Eryl W. "Ruth iv 5 and the Duties of the *Gō'ēl.*" *VT* 33 (1983): 231–34.

Exum, Cheryl. "Assertive *'ăl* in Canticles 1, 6?" *Bib* 62 (1981): 416–19.

Fischer, James A. "Everyone a King: A Study of the Psalms." *TBT* 97 (Oct. 1978): 1683–89.

Fox, Michael V. "Love, Passion, and Perception in Israelite and Egyptian Love Poetry." *JBL* 102 (1983): 219–28.

Goulder, Michael D. *The Song of Fourteen Songs.* JSOTSup 36. Sheffield: JSOT Press, 1986.

Hongisto, Leif. "Literary Structure and Theology in the Book of Ruth." *AUSS* 23 (1985): 19–28.

Lang, Bernard. *Wisdom and the Book of Proverbs.* New York: Pilgrim Press, 1986.

McCreesh, T. P., O.P. "Wisdom as Wife: Proverbs 31:10–31." *RB* 92 (1985): 25–46.

Mintz, Alan. "The Rhetoric of Lamentations and the Representation of Catastrophe." *Proof* 2 (1982): 1–17.

Murphy, Roland E., O.Carm. "Proverbs and Theological Exegesis." In *The Hermeneutical Quest: Essays in Honor of James Luther Mays,* edited by D. G. Miller. Princeton Theological Monographs 4. Allison Park, Pa.: Pickwick Press, 1986.

_____. "Wisdom and Creation." *JBL* 104 (1985): 3–11.

_____. "Wisdom's Song: Proverbs 1:20–33." *CBQ* 48 (1986): 456–60.

Nickelsburg, George W., and Michael E. Stone. "Lady Wisdom and Israel." In *Faith and Piety in Early Judaism: Texts and Documents*. Philadelphia: Fortress Press, 1983.

Scobie, Charles H. "The Place of Wisdom in Biblical Theology." *BTB* 14 (1984): 43–48.

Trible, Phyllis. *God and the Rhetoric of Sexuality*. OBT. Philadelphia: Fortress Press, 1978.

⟿ PART V ⟿

CONCLUSION:
THE TASKS OF FEMINIST
INTERPRETATION

This book has tried to examine the Old Testament from a feminist perspective. It has tried to do more than acknowledge—it has tried to bring to critical consciousness—the predominantly patriarchal and hierarchical character of the texts. It has not wanted to stop there, however. The book is also meant to cause its readers to reflect on those female characters who emerge as exceptions to patriarchal stereotypes as well as on those trajectories (e.g., concern for the powerless within the society and a more inclusive cultural posture) that open the way to a more egalitarian future.

A feminist literary approach such as the one attempted here serves to make its reader more aware of how the biblical texts—any text for that matter—can be both read and interpreted selectively. The fact that males have done most of the interpreting has made most female readers (as well as most male readers), until recently, unaware of the presence, the roles, and the importance of many female characters in the Old Testament.

A feminist methodology, such as the one used here, however, could run the risk of absolutizing certain kinds of behavior as always feminist and others as always patriarchal unless some attention is paid to the social world that produced the behavior (and the texts). Reflecting our own time and our own culture, feminists readily admit that women can freely choose motherhood, that is, motherhood is not necessarily a role enforced on women by patriarchy. Likewise, the presence of women in the paid labor force and the availability of day care are not necessarily consequences of feminism and liberation. A woman may be driven to working outside the home by economic necessity—the consequence of being on the bottom rung of the hierarchical ladder—and not at all by choice and feminist concerns. Several European countries have more and better day care than that generally available in the United States, but that does not mean that European women are more "liberated" than their American counterparts. Many a black woman would willingly choose participation in a patriarchal family structure rather than her present role as head of a single-parent family. In other words, women's participation in the public domain in addition to their participation in the domestic sphere may or may not be liberating; it is directly related to particular political, economic, and social circumstances.

Consequently, it is not enough to say that woman's most important role in the literature of the Pentateuch was motherhood or that barrenness was her greatest curse. One must ask *why* those were major concerns at the time when the stories were produced. One conjectures that just as China finds itself with too many people and is trying to make what it considers to be an appropriate response, so ancient Israel found itself with too few people—too few to survive a high infant-mortality rate, multiple kinds of disease, famine, drought, and the like, surely too few to dominate others—and they too sought appropriate response. The texts reflect a historically grounded social situation in which nothing could be more important—politically as well as personally, for women as well as for men—than motherhood and the bearing of sons.

Likewise, it is not enough merely to praise Deborah who led the Israelites to a military victory or Jael who killed Sisera. One must ask *why* characters such as these could emerge when they did. I am reminded of Nicaragua's revolution, and the role played in it by women. The contribution of women as well as men was needed if Somoza was to be overcome. And was it not the World Wars which thrust American women into the public sphere? The women of ancient Israel who lie behind the Deborahs and the Jaels of the biblical texts undoubtedly lived at a time when their participation—even militarily—was crucial to Israel's survival and development. And *why* does Deut 5:21 alter the wording of Exod 20:17 giving women a status different from men's other property? The later literature seems to suggest, in different ways including the naming of more women, greater recognition of them.

Further probing such as this of the economic and social situations which lie behind the texts is crucial to our understanding of the texts themselves—*why* are women portrayed as they are in the Old Testament? The culture was undoubtedly patriarchal and the texts are undoubtedly patriarchal in origin. Their particular patriarchal expressions are, however, determined by specific social situations and historical circumstances. Women may have had more leadership roles and greater autonomy at some times than at others. An investigation of the social conditions affecting women, though beyond the scope of this present introduction, is the next stage in understanding and explaining both the patriarchy of the Old Testament and also the feminist impulses that the culture produced. These latter have already become, and will continue to be, important elements in theology's future; in them reside the faith and hope of many religious women and men.

RECOMMENDED READINGS
General

Albenda, Patricia. "Western Asiatic Women in the Iron Age: Their Image Revealed." *BA* 46 (1983): 82–88.

Anderson, Bernard W. "Biblical Theology and Sociological Interpretation." *TToday* 42 (1985): 292–306.

Bass, Dorothy C. "Women's Studies and Biblical Studies: An Historical Perspective." *JSOT* 22 (1982): 6–12.

Batto, B. F. *Studies on Women at Mari.* Baltimore: Johns Hopkins Press, 1974.

Bird, Phyllis. "Images of Women in the Old Testament." In *Religion and Sexism,* by Rosemary R. Ruether, 41–88. New York: Simon & Schuster, 1974.

Brenner, Athalya. *The Israelite Woman: Social Role and Literary Type in Biblical Narrative.* The Biblical Seminar. Sheffield: JSOT Press, 1985.

Brown, John Pairman. "The Role of Women and the Treaty in the Ancient World." *BZ* 25 (1981): 1–28.

Brown, Robert McAfee. *Unexpected News: Reading the Bible with Third World Eyes*. Philadelphia: Westminster Press, 1984.

Brueggemann, Walter. "Israel's Social Criticism and Yahweh's Sexuality." *JAAR* 45 (1977): 349.

———. "Trajectories in Old Testament Literature and the Sociology of Ancient Israel." *JBL* 98 (1979): 161–85.

Cazelles, H. "La maternité royale dans l'Ancien Testament." *MDB* 32 (Jan.–Feb. 1984): 3–4.

Collins, Adela Yarbro. *Feminist Perspectives on Biblical Scholarship*. Chico, Calif.: Scholars Press, 1985.

Collins, Raymond F. "The Bible and Sexuality." *BTB* 7 (1977): 149–67.

Gottwald, Norman K. "The Impact of Ancient Israel on Our Social World." *TD* 25 (1977): 335–46.

———. "Social Matrix and Canonical Shape." *TToday* 42 (1985): 307–21.

Greenberg, Blu. "Marriage in the Jewish Tradition." *JES* 22 (1985): 3–20.

Greenspahn, Frederick E. "A Typology of Biblical Women." *Judaism* 32 (1983): 43–50.

An Inclusive Language Lectionary. Prepared for the National Council of Churches in the U.S. Philadelphia: Westminster Press, 1983.

Janzen, Waldemar. *Still in the Image: Essays in Biblical Theology and Anthropology*. Newton, Kans.: Faith and Life Press, 1982.

Johnson, Elizabeth A. "The Incomprehensibility of God and the Image of God Male and Female." *TS* 45 (1984): 441–65.

Kottackel, Joseph. "Morality and Sex in the Old Testament." *BibBh* 7 (1981): 147–59.

Lang, Bernard. "Old Testament and Anthropology: A Preliminary Bibliography." *BN* 20 (1983): 37–46.

Limburg, James. *Old Stories for a New Time*. Atlanta: John Knox Press, 1983.

McDonough, Sheila. "The Qur'an and Patriarchal Religion." *SR* 6 (1976–77): 535–50.

McHatten, Mary T. "Biblical Roots of Women." *Emmanuel* 89 (1983): 392–95.

McKim, Donald K. "Scripture as Mother of Models." In *What Christians Believe about the Bible*. Nashville: Thomas Nelson & Sons, 1985.

Meijer, Alexander, and Amos Meijer. "Matriarchal Influence in the Bible." *DD* 13 (1984/85): 81–87, 97.

Meyers, Carol. "The Roots of Restriction: Women in Early Israel." *BA* 41 (1978): 91–103.

Nannally-Cox, Janice. *Foremothers: Women in the Bible*. New York: Seabury Press, 1981.

O'Day, Gail. "Singing Woman's Song: A Hermeneutic of Liberation." *CurTM* 12 (1985): 203–10.

Osiek, Carolyn. "Inspired Texts: The Dilemma of the Feminist Believers." *SpT* 32 (1980): 138–47.

————. "Jacob's Well: Feminist Hermeneutics." *TBT* 24 (1986): 18–19.

Otwell, J. H. *And Sarah Laughed: The Status of Women in the Old Testament.* Philadelphia: Westminster Press, 1977.

Patai, Raphael. *Sex and Family in the Bible and the Middle East.* Garden City, N.Y.: Doubleday & Co., 1959.

Porter, Jean. "The Feminization of God: Second Thoughts on the Ethical Implications of Process Theology." *SLTJ* 29 (1986): 251–60.

Ruether, Rosemary R. "Feminist and Patriarchal Religion: Principles of Ideological Critique of the Bible." *JSOT* 22 (1982): 54–66.

Russell, Letty M. *The Liberating Word: A Guide to Non-Sexist Interpretation of the Bible.* Philadelphia: Westminster Press, 1976.

————, ed. *Feminist Interpretation of the Bible.* Philadelphia: Westminster Press, 1985.

Sakenfield, Katherine Doob. "The Bible and Women: Bane or Blessing?" *TToday* 32 (1975): 222–26.

————. "Old Testament Perspectives: Methodological Issues." *JSOT* 22 (1982): 13–20.

Segal, J. B. "The Jewish Attitude Towards Women." *JJS* 30 (1979): 121–37.

Stendahl, Krister. *The Bible and the Role of Women.* Facet Books. Philadelphia: Fortress Press, 1966.

Swidler, Leonard. *Biblical Affirmations of Women.* Philadelphia: Westminster Press, 1984.

Tolbert, Mary Ann. "Defining the Problem: The Bible and Feminist Hermeneutics." *Semeia* 28 (1983): 113–26.

————, ed. *The Bible and Feminist Hermeneutics.* Chico, Calif.: Scholars Press, 1983.

Trible, Phyllis. "Depatriarchalizing in Biblical Interpretation." *JAAR* 41 (Mar. 1973): 35–42.

————. "The Effects of Women's Studies on Biblical Studies." *JSOT* 22 (1982): 3–5.

————. "Feminist Hermeneutics and Bible Study." *CCen* 99 (Feb. 3–10, 1982): 116–18.

————. "Good Tidings of Great Joy: Biblical Faith Without Sexism." *CaC* 34 (Feb. 4, 1974): 12–14.

————. "Women in the Old Testament." *IDBSup.* Nashville: Abingdon Press, 1976.

Vellanickal, Matthew. "Just Society: Biblical Perspective." *BibBh* 8 (1982): 81–93.

Weber, Hans-Ruedi. *Experiments with Bible Study.* Philadelphia: Westminster Press, 1981.

Williams, James G. *Women Recounted: Narrative Thinking and the God of Israel.* Bible and Literature Series 6. Sheffield: Almond Press, 1982.

Wilson, Robert R. *Sociological Approaches to the Old Testament.* GBS. Philadelphia: Fortress Press, 1984.

Zappone, Katherine E. "A Feminist Hermeneutics of Scripture: The Standpoint of the Interpreter." *Proceedings of the Irish Biblical Association* 8 (1984): 25–34.

ABBREVIATIONS FOR RECOMMENDED READINGS

ANQ	*Andover Newton Quarterly*
AOAT	Alter Orient und Altes Testament
AUSS	*Andrews University Seminary Studies*
BA	*Biblical Archaeologist*
Bib	*Biblica*
BibBh	*Biblebhashyam*
BibIll	*Biblical Illustrator*
BJRL	*Bulletin of the John Rylands Library*
BK	*Bibel und Kirche*
BN	*Biblische Notizen*
BRev	*Bible Review*
BT	*The Bible Translator*
BTB	*Biblical Theology Bulletin*
BZ	*Biblische Zeitschrift*
CaC	*Christianity and Crisis*
CBQ	*Catholic Biblical Quarterly*
CCen	*Christian Century*
CTJ	*Calvin Theological Journal*
CurTM	*Currents in Theology and Mission*
DD	*Dor le Dor*
EgT	*Eglise et Théologie*
ER	*Ecumenical Review*
ExpTim	*Expository Times*
GBS	Guides to Biblical Scholarship
HS	*Hebrew Studies*
HTR	*Harvard Theological Review*
IDBSup	Interpreter's Dictionary of the Bible, Supplementary Volume

Int	*Interpretation*
ITQ	*Irish Theological Quarterly*
JAAR	*Journal of the American Academy of Religion*
JANESCU	*Journal of the Ancient Near Eastern Society of Columbia University*
JBL	*Journal of Biblical Literature*
JES	*Journal of Ecumenical Studies*
JJS	*Journal of Jewish Studies*
JLA	*Jewish Law Annual*
JNSL	*Journal of Northwest Semitic Languages*
JSOT	*Journal for the Study of the Old Testament*
JSOTSup	Journal for the Study of the Old Testament—Supplement Series
JTSoA	*Journal of Theology for Southern Africa*
LTQ	*Lutheran Theological Journal*
MDB	*Le Monde de la Bible*
OBT	Overtures to Biblical Theology
Proof	*Prooftexts: A Journal of Jewish Literary History*
RB	*Revue biblique*
RR	*Review for Religious*
SLTJ	*Saint Luke's Journal of Theology*
SpT	*Spirituality Today*
SR	*Studies in Religion*
TBT	*The Bible Today*
TD	*Theology Digest*
TNB	*The New Blackfriars*
TOTC	Tyndale Old Testament Commentaries
TS	*Theological Studies*
TToday	*Theology Today*
USQR	*Union Seminary Quarterly Review*
VT	*Vetus Testamentum*
ZAW	*Zeitschrift für die alttestamentliche Wissenschaft*

INDEX OF
NAMES AND SUBJECTS

228

INDEX OF
BIBLICAL REFERENCES

235